What Your Colleagues A

"I only wish that this book had been available during my service in public schools—as a principal, assistant superintendent, and superintendent. I would recommend that all leaders and educators who are interested in creating an environment of true understanding and equity use this text as the foundation for intentional professional learning, reflection, and committed action. For a leadership coach, this book will be an invaluable resource. Principal Leadership for Racial Equity *is a gift to both adults and, more importantly, students!"*

Lynn Macan
Leadership Coach
Learner Centered Initiatives, NY

"Lights! Camera! Action! Inequities in education for students of color are now in focus, and Principal Leadership for Racial Equity *addresses the actions to be taken to make sure all students are successful."*

Laura Schaffer Metcalfe, Ed.D.
Director, Early College Programs
Mesa Community College, AZ

"The timing for Principal Leadership for Racial Equity *is perfect, and the structure of this book will best support leaders addressing issues we all face in the field."*

Cathy Sosnowski
Assistant Professor
Central Connecticut State University, CT

"Leading for equity requires deep personal reflection, courage, and skill. This book provides tools and resources to tap into all three. Reading and completing the exercises within this book provide a platform for knowing yourself and developing that knowledge into a set of behaviors and actions that create equitable conditions within your school or organization. Leaders who are continually growing in their confidence to do what is just and their ability to guide whole communities of practice in this work will want to learn from the experience and expertise of these authors. It will make a positive difference in the lives of the students and families in their schools."

Shannon Hobbs-Beckley
Director of Teaching & Learning
Graded—The American School of Sao Paulo, Brazil

"Principal Leadership for Racial Equity *prompts deep personal reflection and goes beyond the surface-level work to get to the focus of this work. This topic can be a courageous undertaking, and this book provides the tools and personal reflection needed to truly engage in order to interrupt the cycle of practices that do not work for all students. It is not good enough to focus on success for most students—we need to focus on equity for all students!"*

Lena Marie Rockwood, Ed.D.
Assistant Principal
Revere Public Schools, MA

Principal Leadership for Racial Equity

To all educators who are courageously and intentionally leading to advance schooling for students of color.

"If you as a school know that you have a problem in terms of race . . . you need to look internally and see what you can fix, and you need to address it thoroughly and not quickly. . . . Really take your time and try and fix it, because you owe it to your students every single day."

—Onome Grell, 17, John D. O'Bryant School of
Mathematics and Science, Roxbury, Massachusetts

Principal Leadership for Racial Equity

A Field Guide for Developing Race Consciousness

Candace Raskin

Melissa Krull

Antonia Felix

Foreword by Glenn E. Singleton

FOR INFORMATION:

Corwin
A SAGE Company
2455 Teller Road
Thousand Oaks, California 91320
(800) 233-9936
www.corwin.com

SAGE Publications Ltd.
1 Oliver's Yard
55 City Road
London EC1Y 1SP
United Kingdom

SAGE Publications India Pvt. Ltd.
B 1/I 1 Mohan Cooperative Industrial Area
Mathura Road, New Delhi 110 044
India

SAGE Publications Asia-Pacific Pte. Ltd.
18 Cross Street #10-10/11/12
China Square Central
Singapore 048423

Program Director and Publisher: Dan Alpert
Senior Content
   Development Editor: Lucas Schleicher
Associate Content
   Development Editor: Mia Rodriguez
Production Editor: Astha Jaiswal
Copy Editor: Mark Bast
Typesetter: C&M Digitals (P) Ltd.
Proofreader: Ellen Brink
Indexer: Integra
Cover Designer: Gail Buschman
Marketing Manager: Maura Sullivan

Printed in the United States of America

Library of Congress Cataloging-in-Publication Data

ISBN: 9781071803820

This book is printed on acid-free paper.

21 22 23 24 25 10 9 8 7 6 5 4 3 2

Contents

Visit the companion website at
racialequityleadership.com
for downloadable resources and videos.

List of Figures

Foreword

by Glenn E. Singleton

"True teaching is not an accumulation of knowledge; it is an awakening of consciousness which goes through successive stages. . . . Growth in consciousness does not depend on the will of the intellect or its possibilities but on the intensity of the inner urge."

—Ancient Nile Valley Wisdom

As I sit to offer these prefatory comments on a deeply meaningful, uncompromising call to action that follows, the beginnings of the Pacific Educational Group, Inc. (PEG), do not escape me. Its founding, and this now 29-year walk, have and continue to bring me to relationships with so many brilliant, accomplished, and courageous leaders around the world who are moved to eradicate systemic racism in all its manifestations. And the future, opportunity, and efficacy of this journey to forge racial equity across the broad sectors of our social structures rests upon such relationships, both ongoing and yet to be established. It is indeed through such alliance that I am witness to the continued amazing leadership of a now longtime colleague and friend. I count among the bounty of blessings for which I am a most humble and grateful recipient, to be asked by Dr. Melissa Krull and her coauthors, Candace Raskin and Antonia Felix, to share my thoughts to open their significant addition to the growing canon on principal leadership for racial equity in education.

The decade ensuing that inauspicious beginning, characterized by an eerily quiet academy and deafening silence from board rooms, central offices, and school sites on the intersection of race, education, and devastating racial disparities became a driving force in the development and publication of the first edition of *Courageous Conversations About Race: A Field Guide to Achieving Equity in Schools (2006)*. In its call to break the silence, *The Protocol* was introduced, and our research and fieldwork defined three critical factors necessary to close intractable racial "achievement gaps." In addition to engaging, sustaining, and deepening interracial dialogues about race, *Passion, Practice and Persistence* were identified as absolutely necessary to an intentional desire to change how students are taught and supported in their learning.

The encore, *MORE Courageous Conversations About Race* (2013), highlighted that seven years afterwards, in the oft-repeated words of my closest and most important ancestor: "The more things change, the more they stay the same!" The elections of the nation's first African American president had significantly changed the conversations about race and racism that were and were not taking place. The community of leaders for racial equity had grown much larger and more intricately connected via technology. And so had the army of resisters trained to maintain and intensify social norms that exclude, segregate, and relegate children of color to inferior, poorly resourced schools. All along, school and government officials continuing to offer economic excuses for the failure to confront the crushing inequities facing our educational systems were remarkably similar. As the late Barbara Sizemore, an embattled and visionary urban school superintendent, would refer to as the denial and reluctance to identify, name, and address the cause of racial disparities as systemic racism, we were "walking in circles."

The imperative for school leaders to accelerate their knowledge, skill, will, and capacity to talk about race and transform schooling was and still is compelling. Their passion, practice, and persistence in the critical domains of the *Courageous Conversation Framework, especially in that of Leadership*, had to be fortified more deeply to move racial equity from theory to practice. It required purpose—an unfailing, unapologetic determination that is personal, local, and immediate. I called it a Personal Racial Equity Purpose (PREP) that must be mined, embraced, and embodied. The PREP, as the Kemetic maxims above inscribed on the walls of "the most select of places" teaches, is deeply personal, not merely an acquisition of knowledge but also a tiered emergence of consciousness driven by the intensity of its source and pursuit.

During this span of my walk, I had the pleasure to meet and partner with Melissa Krull, then the superintendent of Eden Prairie Schools (EPS), located in suburban Minneapolis, Minnesota. Dr. Krull led her district with courage and conviction. And when her passion, practice, and persistence were insufficient to withstand mounting resistance from the community and internal detractors, she discovered her PREP and pushed on, holding site and central office leadership accountable to her vision. Melissa sought adaptive solutions to the unanswered national racial equity challenges of shrinking fiscal resources, protection of white neighborhood schools, all-white school boards and executive leadership teams, and rapidly declining results for children of color in secondary education. She and other key district leaders at all levels stared down fundamentalists' attacks, launched from within their community as well as from around the nation, often having to choose what works for all children over what would earn them public admiration and keep them employed.

And Dr. Krull and her leadership team made remarkable progress. Working with their board of education, schools, parents, and community, EPS designed, developed, and successfully implemented a systemwide plan to eliminate racial and income isolation in its schools and dramatically closed racial and income disparities in student achievement. These laudable accomplishments, unsurprisingly, came at a price. Melissa, after surviving the bruising and contentious campaign to integrate her district's schools by race and socio-economic status, announced that after some 25-plus years serving EPS, the final 10 as superintendent, she would resign at the end of the 2011–12 school year. Melissa graciously documented fully this successful path in Chapter 11 of *MORE Courageous Conversations About Race*.

Eden Prairie's loss proved to be the state's and nation's gain. Shortly after her departure, Dr. Krull joined the faculty of Minnesota State University at Mankato as assistant professor in educational leadership. And in 2013, along with her university colleague and coauthor, Dr. Candace Raskin launched the Institute for Courageous Principal Leadership (ICPL) at the College of Education there.

Based on the well-established research and literature of school leadership, the mission of the ICPL is to develop racial consciousness in principals to help them maximize their impact on achievement in their schools. The institute transfers theory to practice, guides principals to understand their own racial identities as well as those of their students, deeply understand their school's culture and data, ground their practices in their beliefs, confidently act to ensure every child achieves, and know which practices actually impact student achievement. Its work is the subject of this new offering to administrators currently in service, and those aspiring to lead schools that nurture the spirit and infinite potential of all students, especially Black and Indigenous students and students of color.

Principal Leadership for Racial Equity: A Field Guide for Developing Race Consciousness amplifies the mission of the ICPL to empower principals to lead with fearlessness, skill, self-knowledge, and racial competence so that under their leadership every child fully achieves. I find its organization particularly intriguing as it aligns with the wisdom of my most ancient ancestors from the Nile Valley: to Know Thyself, Distinguish Knowledge from Foolishness, and Build for Eternity. Concurrently, it guides leaders, as does *Courageous Conversation*™, to pursue its mission through a "lens of racial equity" first and most importantly at the personal level, before seeking to transform professional and organizational environments. Raskin, Krull, and Felix also without coincidence or apology, eschew the nomenclature of shortening, broadening, and avoiding intentional engagement with race with less than courageous terms like equity, diversity and inclusion.

In *Principal Leadership for Racial Equity: A Field Guide for Developing Race Consciousness*, Chapters 1–3, the reader is guided first and foremost to examine self, for racial consciousness is cast from within. Leadership for racial equity requires an exploration and knowledge of a principal's why, as it is indispensable in discovering the PREP. Critical race theory provides a vital prism through which to view and understand self and race. Chapters 4–6 invite leaders to indulge a serious review of the myriad forces and constructs at work in rendering the color, culture, and consciousness of learning environments and processes as homogenous, exclusive, and inequitable. While the debate of whether beliefs drive practice, or vice versa, to render results, leaders for racial equity must be clear that knowledge must precede either. And in the culminating Chapters 7–9, the user is guided and supported to apply and integrate their knowledge and new understandings with school and context-specific strategies, tools, and activities aimed to transform school culture, climate, and outcomes.

The extraordinary events of 2020 have posed many unprecedented challenges to the need for schools to ensure that every child fully achieves. And these new dilemmas come as an overlay to systems of education already seriously compromised by racial inequity in that mission. As public education seeks to bounce back better, on what we hope are the heels of a global pandemic and persistent national negligence of our racial realities, *Principal Leadership for Racial Equity: A Field Guide for Developing Race Consciousness* sounds a much-needed call to action for those charged with leading our schools. While systemic transformation for racial equity is not a commodity that can be purchased but a process that must be engaged, sustained, accelerated, deepened, and scaled, this guide is a welcome and must-have addition to the repertoire for *Courageous Leadership.*

Glenn E. Singleton is the founder and president of Pacific Educational Group, Inc., established in 1992. He is the creator of *Courageous Conversation*™, and the author of *Courageous Conversations About Race: A Field Guide to Achieving Equity in Schools* (2006); *MORE Courageous Conversations About Race* (2013); and *Courageous Conversations About Race: A Field Guide to Achieving Equity in Schools, Second Edition* (2015). A third edition of Courageous Conversation is in development and due out in mid-2021.

Acknowledgments

Since this book is the outgrowth of our work in the Institute for Courageous Principal Leadership, our first thanks go to all the leaders who have participated in the institute over the past 9 years. Your authenticity, honesty, courage, willingness to be vulnerable, openness to personal transformation, and dedication to improving education for all children have not only changed your schools and communities but also made us better educators and people.

We are also deeply grateful to the school leaders who contributed to this book with their insights and stories of leadership: Chris Bellmont, Josh Fraser, Kirk Morris, Eduardo Navidad, Lee Vang, Tyrone Brookins, Angeline McGaster-Woods, Tami Reynolds, Chris Hester, Carla Hines, Todd Goggleye, Nan Yurecko, Michael Elston, Astein Osei, Rhoda Mhiripiri-Reed, Halee Vang, Shelley Nielsen, Nasreen Fynewever, Maria Graver, Silvy Un Lafayette, Jessica Busse, Michael Walker, Gene Ward, Marcus Freeman, Valeria Silva, Aldo Sicoli, Mike Favor, and Isabel Rodriguez.

Sharing our work in book form has been a long-awaited dream, and working with our editor, Dan Alpert, and the entire team at Corwin Press has been a heartfelt and rewarding experience. Dan's expertise in the field of equity in education and endless encouragement are a powerful combination for any writer who has the good fortune to work with him, and we are grateful to have made this journey under his guidance.

We also acknowledge school leaders across the country as they go above and beyond to meet the unprecedented collective challenges of a pandemic, economic crisis, and civil unrest. Your service to your students and families at this time is a lifeline to them and inspiration to us.

Publisher's Acknowledgments

Corwin gratefully acknowledges the contributions of the following reviewers:

Cathy Sosnowski
Assistant Professor
Central Connecticut
 State University
New Britain, CT

Debra Paradowski
Associate Principal /
 Administrator
Arrowhead Union High School
Hartland, WI

Dr. Jill Gildea
Superintendent
Park City School District
Park City, UT

Elizabeth Alvarez
Chief of Schools
Chicago Public Schools
Chicago, IL

Ellen S. Perconti
Superintendent
Goldendale School District
Goldendale, WA

Karen L. Tichy, Ed.D.
Assistant Professor of
   Educational Leadership
Saint Louis University
St. Louis, MO

Laura Schaffer Metcalfe, Ed.D.
Director, Early College
   Programs
Mesa Community College
Mesa, AZ

Lena Marie Rockwood, Ed.D.
Assistant Principal
Revere Public Schools
Revere, MA

Lynn Macan
Leadership Coach
Learner Centered Initiatives
Hilton Head Island, SC

Maryam Hasan
Vice Principal
Toronto District School Board
Toronto, Canada

Patricia Long Tucker
Retired Regional Superintendent
District of Columbia Public
   Schools
Washington, DC

Shannon Hobbs-Beckley
Director of Teaching & Learning
Graded—The American
   School of Sao Paulo
Sao Paulo, Brazil

Shelley Joan Weiss
District Director, Consultant,
   Commissioner
WI Department of Public
   Instruction, Wisconsin
   Association for Middle Level
   Education, Wisconsin Parent
   Teacher Association, Sun
   Prairie Area School District
Sun Prairie, WI

About the Authors

Candace Raskin, Ed.D., served as an educational leader in Minnesota public schools for 18 years as a superintendent; director of curriculum, instruction, and assessment; middle school and elementary principal; and high-potential coordinator. Her research on developing racially conscious leadership has been recognized nationally and is published in numerous scholarly journals. She currently provides leadership and teaches in the administrative licensure graduate program at Minnesota State University, Mankato, Twin Cities location. She also teaches doctoral courses and advises doctoral students as a professor in the Department of Educational Leadership. She is the cofounder and facilitator of the Institute for Courageous Principal Leadership.

Jody Russell Photography

Melissa Krull, Ph.D., has an extensive background serving in leadership capacities at a 10,000-student school district for 20 years, 10 of which were spent as superintendent. Her recent work includes leadership teaching and research toward the elimination of racial achievement disparities. She has served as a keynote speaker, panelist, and presenter for various organizations and universities, including Georgetown Law Center and the White House. Dr. Krull is the coauthor of a chapter in *More Courageous Conversations: From Theory to Practice* (2012). She currently teaches graduate courses in the administrative licensure graduate program and advises doctoral students through the Department of Educational Leadership at Minnesota State University, Mankato, Twin Cities location. She is the cofounder and facilitator of the Institute for Courageous Principal Leadership.

Antonia Felix, Ed.D., MFA, is the author of 23 books, including biographies of Senator Elizabeth Warren, Supreme Court justices Sonia Sotomayor and Ruth Bader Ginsburg, NATO commander Wesley Clark, and Secretary of State Condoleezza Rice. She has taught literature, writing, and seminars on public intellectuals at the college level, and her academic research focuses on the use of expressive writing to develop racial consciousness and process race-related stress and trauma.

Introduction

Race Matters: From Theory to Action

The epigraph at the opening of this book represents the call we believe students of color are making throughout the country. If we see a problem in our schools in terms of race, they tell us, we should take action to fix it. This action should be serious and thoughtful, not just a matter of tacking up posters containing equity slogans, placing equity mission statements on our school websites, or using equity buzzwords to talk a good game. Students are challenging us to step up and be antiracists who take action to call out racist policies and practices and replace them with those based on the uncompromising belief that all children can learn and deserve an exceptional education.

We are answering that call at this point in our careers by leading the Institute for Courageous Principal Leadership at Minnesota State University, Mankato, where we (Raskin and Krull) are on the Educational Leadership faculty. Our 2-year program gives principals and other school leaders the tools to upend practices that have resulted in our state having the largest racial achievement disparities in the nation. In partnership with Antonia Felix, who earned her Ed.D. in our department and has enjoyed a dual career as an educator and author, we have translated a decade of institute work into this book. We expand on that work by bringing in the voices of dozens of white, Black, Latinx, Asian, and Native American school leaders we know and admire for their equity practices to share their boots-on-the-ground experiences. Like us, they each have stories about their commitment to educational equity, the resistance they have encountered along the way, and how they dealt with resistance to keep the focus on students rather than on adult comfort zones.

What brought us here? I, Melissa Krull, remember the day and hour of my wake-up call about the reality of systemic racism in education. As the superintendent of a suburban district near Minneapolis, I was attending a superintendents' meeting about Glenn E. Singleton's work, led by Singleton himself. I left that meeting thinking, *I now know the work I have to do as a superintendent for at least the next 5 years.* Little did I know this is the work of a lifetime. Glenn had a tremendous impact on my thinking about my leadership and my obligation as a white female superintendent. In that meeting, I became conscious of race as the centerpiece for my own leadership work. I hadn't seriously looked at the data disaggregated by race within my own system, and once I did all the patterns emerged, and I realized that these racially disparate results were happening on my watch. Along with my colleagues we began studying the racial achievement patterns. We began our own educational learning journey, too. We changed our practices, our policies, and our mind-sets. Eventually outcomes began to improve for all students—but specifically for students of color. When I saw those results, I realized that indeed systemic disparities can be overcome. Eventually I came to understand the moral imperative of my leadership, especially as a white woman with privilege. My responsibility and commitment is to carry out race work with other leaders.

Like Melissa, I, Candace Raskin, who am also white, was serving as a superintendent when I discovered the range and full force of systemic racism in education. As a principal, I had been able to use my position to make changes at the building level to improve the learning for students of color, but at the district level, other factors I had never anticipated came into play. As a superintendent, I witnessed how racism, so deeply entrenched in the system, tried to block any attempts to disrupt harmful policies and practices. For the first time, I experienced the community-wide and political levels of resistance. I saw how whiteness and privilege made white people feel their children were entitled to things that Black and Brown children were not.

When I left the superintendency, I specifically came to this university because it is a practitioners' university. I could see the role I could play in counteracting systemic racism in our schools was by developing strong, racially conscious leaders. When you're in a building, you can change things for students of color. You can support teachers in developing the skills needed to teach all children, especially our students of color. Melissa and I are aware that many white leaders don't know what they don't know, make decisions based on their socialization and implicit biases, and put harmful policies and practices in place as a result. We are also aware that white leaders and leaders of color need specific, evidence-based tools to get results and change the educational landscape for students of color.

Each of us believes that when principals have an opportunity to examine themselves, hear from multiple voices, and learn to make decisions based on their school data and knowledge of the instructional practices that work best, they can create real change. It is complex, adaptive work, but we have seen it happen. We wrote this book to give you the same opportunity to learn about yourself as a white, Black, Latinx, Asian, Native American, Pacific Islander, or multiracial leader and forge a realistic path for racial equity in your schools.

We were nearly finished writing this book when the Covid-19 pandemic arrived and the police killing of George Floyd in Minneapolis ignited a resurgence of the Black Lives Matter movement with waves of protest across the country. As principals and superintendents scrambled to reshape education during school shutdowns and the uncertain future, they witnessed how the virus and its related economic crisis disproportionately impacted students and families of color. The intersecting crises of a pandemic, economic downturn, and civic unrest were exacerbated by the U.S. president who openly supported white nationalism, labeled Black Lives Matter protesters as "thugs," and perpetuated a race-based "crescendo of hate" that further divided the country (Costa & Rucker, 2020). We felt compelled to write an additional chapter about the challenges these events brought to school leaders, and that chapter concludes this book.

During this crisis-ridden time, an assistant principal we interviewed took action that gave us a striking new example of what courageous leadership looks like. Maria Graver, a Latina working in an urban middle school, was the only person of color on a team that drew up a call to action to the white teaching community following the death of George Floyd. The team believed that as part of the institution of public education they were responsible for Floyd's death, since more than 84% of educators are white people, most of whom "are not aware of the reality of white supremacy and how it affects them and their students," she said (M. Graver, personal communication, August 16, 2020). Her team shared the document with a group of leaders of color before disseminating it to several teaching networks. Their bold letter, excerpted as follows, did not mince words:

Dear White Educators of the Minneapolis Public Schools:

Like many of you, we fellow white educators woke up on Tuesday, May 26, 2020, horrified to learn about the merciless public killing of George Floyd at the hands of the Minneapolis Police Department. A video taken by a Minneapolis Public Schools student—one of our own children—recorded this tragedy. . . . We feel disgust, anger, sadness and helplessness that this continues to happen in our nation, our cities, and throughout Black, Brown, and Indigenous communities. We also woke up Tuesday to the realization that *we have not done enough to stop it*, and our silence and inaction allowed this to keep happening. *We are responsible.* To do nothing and continue to do what we always do is to confirm that George Floyd's life was not more valuable than a potentially fraudulent twenty dollar bill.

As white educators and staff inside the Minneapolis Public School System, we *cannot*, and *will not*, continue to stand by and let this happen. We cannot allow a system that routinely causes harm to Black, Brown and Indigenous communities to continue to perpetuate violence. Intentions without action are empty and meaningless, and serve only to soothe white guilt. We must act, and we must act *now*. We must move from good intentions to solid actions.

The letter then defined white supremacy and how it works in society:

We exist within a culture of white supremacy, one that advantages white people at every turn. This privilege is implicit and designed to go unnoticed by you and me, but it is always present and it is powerful. As white people living in the United States, we have always had collective control and continue to control the narrative of how events are told, reported and perpetuated. Because of this control, we shape what is believable and maintain our own plausible deniability: we can intentionally avoid hard truths in order to protect ourselves from discomfort.

Later in the letter, readers were invited to sign their names to express their commitment to 15 action steps, beginning with these four:

As a collective, we commit to:

- Always keep race at the center of the conversation and acknowledge race plays a role in everything.

- Actively question why things are being done the way they are. Whom does this action, policy, statement, process, etc. benefit?

- Speak up, interrupt, and challenge, individually and collectively, when an action, policy, statement, or practice is only or mainly benefiting the status quo, i.e., the white power structure.

- Ensure that a full and representative story is told in our teaching, including in our books, curriculum, speakers and tools of evaluation.

More than 600 recipients signed their names to the document, Graver told us. The letter was read nightly during a music program on a local public radio station, and the team followed up with weekly e-mails containing action steps teachers can do to support school leaders. This public call to action, sparked by tragedy, may have launched new personal journeys toward racial awareness that will have a positive impact on classroom practices and the lives of children. As illustrated in our Theory of Action roadmap (introduced in Chapter 1), these journeys begin with self-reflection about our socialization. For principals, these "knowing myself" steps evolve into knowing your schools through your data, observations of students, and assessment of teachers' engagement in equity practices. When you learn which instructional methods have the greatest impact and help your teachers implement them, you change the system and your students' experiences. As positive change shows up in your data, you gain more confidence to keep introducing new policies and practices, and achievement continues to rise. This step-by-step cycle repeats itself as you constantly educate yourself and reflect on your evolving racial consciousness.

The first steps of this pathway are explored in the five chapters of Part I: Developing Racial Consciousness. We then turn to the tools for implementing change in Part II: Integrating Knowledge Into Practice, which continues our use of mentors' stories to bring real-world experiences to life and exercises to guide your work. Several of the exercises involve videos and materials found in the book's companion website at racialequityleadership.com.

As this time of crisis exposes the realities of systemic racism in education and other institutions as never before, principals may find more receptivity to plans for replacing old, ineffective practices that have perpetuated teaching gaps for decades. You may find members of your staff more open to learning about the school experiences of students of color, such as the situation Collins (2009) describes: "Disempowered learners must find a way simultaneously to survive within institutions that were not set up with them in mind and to synthesize the best of what the school teaches and what they know from their life experiences" (p. 10). Even so, the work will be challenging. Talking to staff about race, addressing biased behavior, calling for racially conscious instruction, and revamping discipline policies takes courage and resilience.

Our goal is that the research-based material and diverse voices from the field we share in this book will inspire that courage in you. The fact that you have chosen this book proves that you believe, as we do, and as research supports, that principals can be the force for change that closes teaching gaps. Principals are positioned to transform schools mired in outdated, biased practices into learning environments that glow with high expectations for every student, strong relationships between teachers and students, an embrace of student voices and cultures, and a student-centered commitment to high achievement for *every* learner.

References

Collins, Patricia Hill. (2009). *Another kind of public education*. Boston: Beacon Press.

Costa, R., & Rucker, P. (2020, July 4). Trump's push to amplify racism unnerves Republicans who have long enabled him. *Washington Post*. Retrieved from https://www.washingtonpost.com/politics/trump-racism-white-nationalism-republicans/2020/07/04/2b0aebe6-bbaf-11ea-80b9-40ece9a701dc_story.html

PART I
Developing Racial Consciousness

Not everything that is faced can be changed. But nothing can be changed until it is faced.

—James Baldwin (1962)

Developing Myself as a Racially Conscious Leader

Becoming racially literate . . . involves developing our critical thinking, increasing our awareness of how race permeates our lives, forming meaningful relationships across difference, and using our knowledge to organize for antiracist transformations. And it requires brutal honesty.

—Crystal L. Fleming (2018)

Chris Bellmont, a white male elementary school principal in a Minneapolis suburb, came to our Institute for Courageous Principal Leadership doubting he had anything more to learn about racial equity. When his administrator signed him up for our 2-year program, he took the news with an eye roll. Not only had he been raised with a social justice lens (albeit in an all-white, Minnesota community), but for the past 10 years he had been mentored by a Black woman principal who taught him to "see, manage, and honor difference" (C. Bellmont, personal communication, November 29, 2019). Chris was a history teacher and then assistant principal under the mentorship of that leader in an alternative high school that served many of the students of color in his district. With that experience, he walked into the institute thinking he had seen it all and therefore knew it all. A couple of weeks into the work, however, he realized that when it came to racial consciousness, he had no clue. "I grew up completely culturally unaware, like a lot of white educators in Minnesota today," he said. "My 10 years at a multicultural high school introduced me to new ways of thinking, but I only applied them in a hit-or-miss way. At the same time, I was routinely using destructive language and behaviors without even knowing it."

Chris began the institute at the same time he started his new position as principal of Gideon Pond Elementary, and his new school was in transition. Among his approximately 450 students, 140 were English Language Learners, many of them Somali immigrants who had family members who grew up in refugee camps as their families fled civil war. Another 12% identified as Latinx, and 5% were Asian American. The white staff and teachers, Chris said, were going through a "grieving process of sorts" over these changing demographics. "There was some confusion in the white world," he said. "We weren't the white suburban neighborhood school anymore. Some people were caught up in the myth that if families who are different than you come into the community, you're going to lose power and control. The feeling of loss was tangible." By engaging in deeper layers of equity work over the next 2 years, Chris began to address those fears by building a community that embraced equity.

Chris began his work at the institute by examining how he was socialized around race, just as you will do in this opening chapter. Throughout the program, he moved from an expanded awareness of himself to a solid understanding of the power dynamics of race in education and other institutions and then onward to research-backed best practices for teaching and learning and how to implement that knowledge into his leadership practice. As the months rolled on, he grew increasingly confident about integrating new policies and practices that empowered all of his students to achieve. He learned firsthand that people can change—people like himself and the other white adults and students in his school. These shifts in attitudes, beliefs, and behaviors created an environment in which students and families of color could thrive. "There's really nowhere else to put your energy if you're working within multicultural settings," he said. "My journey went from an eye roll to one of the greatest experiences I could ever ask for. Our school's dynamics changed because of the students, families, and teachers who have embraced equity."

Not every white principal who entered the institute with Chris was ready to leave their comfort zone. While all of the principals of color stayed on, some white principals dropped out. Chris understood why the process was hard for some to handle. "Using the Courageous Conversations protocol helped," he said, "however, you still might feel defensive. When challenges rise up, you have to commit to the process, find support, and do the deep learning." He recalled one challenge in particular that compelled him to examine and transform himself. That day, the institute's group discussion time was led by a Black woman administrator who expressed her frustration over her white colleagues in the program. Chris later came to understand that she spoke for many of the leaders of color in the room. She described how disengaged the white folks were and how frustrating that was to watch. "Here was a successful leader who had a deep appreciation for everyone with whom she worked, emotionally expressing her frustration over the white people who seemed to be doing nothing," Chris said. "I kept my laptop shut after that."

Confronted with his white privilege, Chris suddenly realized that as a white male he got to "skip out" of anything he wanted, whenever he wanted. "She was absolutely right; I disengaged all the time," he said.

"We have all kinds of white code that lets us avoid things, like 'challenges in the building,' which means we can abandon equity programs we've begun, or 'student behavior,' which means the adults aren't responsible for anything. As soon as something gets uncomfortable, we can turn our backs on it."

This insight helped Chris understand that the challenges in his school were only symptoms of the real issue—implicit bias and all the destructive behavior it brings, such as low expectations for students of color. As he continued in the program, he began to model the beliefs and behaviors that would transform his school culture and student achievement. "Everything that happens in a school can be traced to the hearts and minds of the adults who are working with the children," he said. He developed the use of the language and tools that would help his staff and teachers "engage in this work," and when they did, the atmosphere changed from grieving to celebrating. "Once you check your privilege at the door, it opens up a whole new world," he said. "Our family events would bring tears to your eyes."

That improved atmosphere, Chris explained, allowed him and his team to manage challenges such as student homelessness and a rapid increase of multilingual students while continuing to improve outcomes for those students and all others. "The story of diversity in our schools does not have to be one of deficit and decline," he said. As an example of his school's trending positive growth, he highlighted the progress of his multilingual learners who are becoming proficient in reading in a shorter time frame than the typical period identified in national studies. Chris's commitment to leading for racial equity ignited the changes that are producing a new achievement trend in his school while also shaping a more engaged community. Let's take a look at the data that describes where we've been, where we are, and why we need the kind of change that principals like Chris—and you—can make.

White children have outperformed African American and Hispanic children consistently since 1975. This reflects a 43-year trend, making the data predictable as well as consistent. National Assessment of Education Progress (NAEP) data from 2017 (National Center for Education Statistics, 2017) reveal this pattern for predictable racial disparity. In the last 5 years, in both math and reading, the data show a steady and unchanged racial discrepancy between the achievement levels of white and Black students, where white students show results approximately 26% higher than Black students'.

To be specific, NAEP data report no significant change in the width of the gap in achievement levels between students of color and white students. Figure 1.1 displays the disparities in the fourth-grade mathematics and reading scores of white, Black, and Hispanic children.

Figure 1.1　Trends in Fourth-Grade Mathematics and Reading Scores by Race

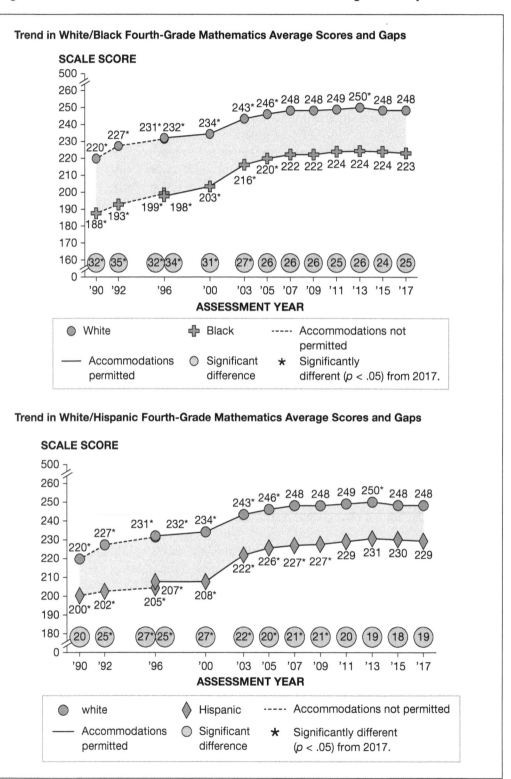

Trend in White/Black Fourth-Grade Reading Average Scores and Gaps

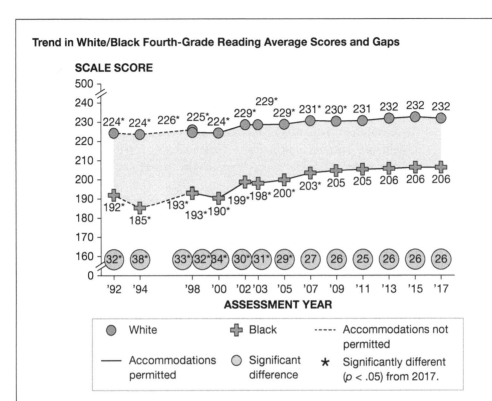

Trend in White/Hispanic Fourth-Grade Reading Average Scores and Gaps

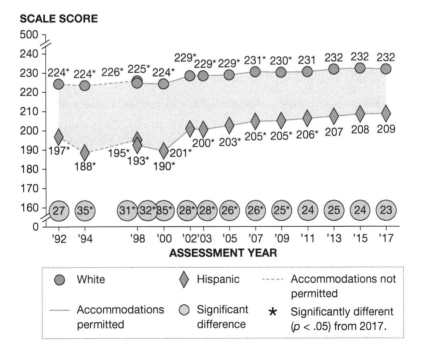

Source: National Assessment of Education Progress (NAEP), 2017.

How do the national data compare to your state or province? In Minnesota, our data reflect the worst gaps in the nation. During the 2016–2017 school year, we showed a 36% gap in reading and 40% gap in mathematics between white children and Black children (Minnesota Department of Education, 2017). We believe that leadership is the key place to address the change necessary in this era of unprecedented educational challenge. This book takes you through the stages to help you become a principal who leads with fearlessness, skill, self-knowledge, and racial competence so that under your leadership every child fully achieves.

We begin the journey by presenting our model for change, the Theory of Action that begins with knowing yourself. This pathway, as shown in Figure 1.2, is a continuous process that can guide your evolution throughout your career as a racially conscious leader. The exercises for the first step, Knowing Self (the top left square in Figure 1.2), are designed to engage you in examining your upbringing and socialization around race.

Theory of Action

Our Theory of Action framework traces our model of what happens as people move through a racially conscious journey in our program. We have witnessed that this is how it works for leaders. We have watched it

Figure 1.2 Theory of Action

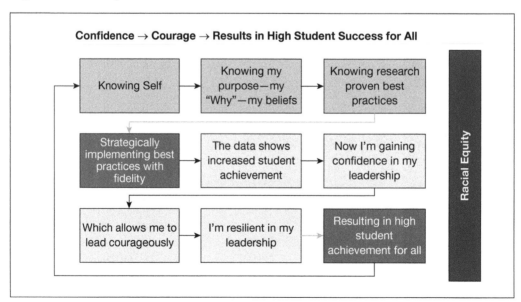

play out in our 8 years at the institute and seen the evidence in improved achievement in some of our participants' schools.

Each step we explore in the connected boxes is addressed through the lens of race. We start in the top row at the left: knowing myself, my socialization, knowing what has affected me. Who am I racially? Who impacted me? What institutions, media, music, or important people in my life sent me messaging that affected my ideas about race?

Next, I have to ask myself, what are my beliefs? What is my purpose, my why? Why am I in education? Do my beliefs align with my actions? If I'm a high school principal in a school where half of the students are children of color but everyone in my advanced placement classes is white, what I say and what I'm doing is disconnected. We will help you know yourself, why you're a school leader, and how to assess if what you believe is showing up in your actions.

The third step is understanding which best practices are research-proven effective and which are not. A lot of educational practices are in place that do not have high return for student achievement. They're there for political reasons, for parental and other non–fact-based influences. Good leaders need to know what research says about the best practices that impact student learning. For example, we spend lots of money reducing class size when we also know that lowering class size has a limited effect on improved achievement. So investing in that way does not give us the return on student achievement, yet we do it. Student homework, especially with elementary children, doesn't contribute to improved student achievement either, but when was the last time you saw a school website that didn't display a homework policy? As a leader, when you unearth the proven practices, begin to implement them, and see an increase in achievement, you will gain the confidence to say, "I now know what works, and we're going to stop using those practices that don't work."

Your new levels of confidence will inspire you to be much more courageous in your leadership. Courage allows you to be stronger in saying "this is what I believe, this is what I know." The idea that confidence leads to courage is the strongest pillar of our work. White leaders who don't have confidence in working with students of color simply don't know how, or their belief system blocks them. If we show them how, they gain confidence. The belief that disparities in achievement are based on deficits of students instead of deficits of the institution prevents leaders and teachers from confidently setting out to improve how all children learn. We know that kids come to us brilliant. And we know that leaders with more confidence will take more courageous action to lead. They are not afraid to fail, and their moral imperative will drive their actions.

The key piece we discovered in our research is that current principals are not aware of effective strategies for teaching students of color.

Our university programs are teaching them outdated practices. Principal preparation programs are not addressing race or strategies for equity, so leaders are not learning how to carry them out, model for others, or even assess for these approaches. Principals who participated in our institute reported that the path they undertook, which is outlined in this book, shifted their skill capacities, especially around understanding leadership strengths, race, and equity (Raskin, Krull, & Thatcher, 2015). They described their perceptions in language that revealed a change from staff-focused to student-focused thinking and an awareness of high-leverage leadership strategies, the importance of cultural competence, and engagement.

The best and most well-intentioned principals will get through the whole model, but when they encounter resistance from parents or the teachers' union, they slow down or back off. We created strategies for working through the fear of resistance, because once you do and see the data climb, you will gain confidence. Confidence wasn't on our radar when we designed our study, but when the principals talked about the elevation of their skill set and how it raised their confidence, we understood the crucial role confidence plays in developing successful, racially conscious leaders (Raskin, Krull, & Thatcher, 2015).

In the following stories from two of our institute graduates, the principals recount their experiences as they traversed the journey modeled in the Theory of Action.

Learning From Mentors

Living the Theory of Action

Josh Fraser

White male principal of a Minneapolis suburb middle and high school and current participant in the Institute for Courageous Principal Leadership

KNOWING MYSELF

I'm serving a community of people who didn't grow up like me and who don't represent me racially or culturally, so I was challenged to look in the mirror and uncover the foundations of my belief systems. This experience not only transformed my beliefs and ideas about the purpose of education but also provided strategies for making decisions with the backbone and integrity needed for leading for equity. Being able to say, "My job is to serve my community, which is mostly people of color, to create a school that is becoming antiracist" is much different than what I said when I was just starting out, such as "I'm here to serve you for your kids' education," or however it's printed in our mission statement.

I've learned that being transparent about my personal leadership beliefs and my team's leadership beliefs, and how they align with the district's beliefs, makes it easier to interrupt practices that aren't working for all students. It's also essential for me to be transparent about my learning alongside my colleagues on this journey. This creates an environment in which people must ask themselves if they want to change and be part of something bigger than any individual, to be part of what our community is demanding. If they don't want to change, this may not be the right place for them to work.

Strategically Implementing Best Practices With Fidelity

One of the first ways we put our new ideas into action was to change a T-shirt policy that reflected teacher expectations grounded in compliance instead of learning. The practice in our physical education department was to direct all students to purchase and wear our standard T-shirt with the school logo. As we sat down and analyzed this practice, we immediately recognized that it was completely inequitable, not just in terms of money but also in the broader sense of trying to teach "pride in school" through a uniform. We discussed how this created exclusion, forcing students who were not wearing the shirt to not participate and then get graded accordingly. Since this was just a procedure and not a district policy, it was easy to change. The dress procedures were refocused on safety and teaching the right way to dress for fitness with whatever you can access. We transformed the way we think about some of these traditional aspects of physical education that a lot of people assume are normal, and the change ruffled a lot of feathers in the community. Some people thought it would cause a lack of accountability, which to me is a word white people use for compliance. This example is a very technical interruption that leads to adaptive change and tension. Sitting in that urgency and in comfort as a staff is what led to the real conversations we weren't having, which led to more lasting change.

I'm Resilient in My Leadership: Dealing With Resistance

One of our priorities last year was to increase student voice and empowerment through the production of a series of videos in which students talked openly about their experiences in school and in their personal lives. The results were intensely moving. Every story revolved around race, culture, expectations, pride, what they wanted from our teachers and staff, and what they didn't receive from them. I planned on using the videos to discuss these issues with teachers and staff.

Some staff advised me to hold off on these discussions because we were about to transition to another school building site, saying that this could be a tough time in the middle of the year when people are stressed. I stayed with my plan and facilitated conversations with groups of 8 to 15 teachers after viewing the videos. They were the most intense discussions I've ever had with my colleagues. Their responses spanned the entire spectrum, from anger and resentment to relief and excitement over the opportunity to finally address these concerns. All of our

(Continued)

(Continued)

staff of color felt affirmed by the students' stories. They were in shock that people were mad.

Many white teachers were upset and decided to leave us at the end of the year. They couldn't come to grips with the fact that our students told them the real deal.

Some staff and teachers also pushed back on our new policy to stop using biased language that clearly singled out groups of students. Introducing this policy caused a ruckus and made several teachers leave, but a significant number of others were ready for it and just needed to hear that interruption from a leader in order to feel empowered to enforce it themselves.

A CONTINUOUS PROCESS

In this journey of leading for racial equity, you move from self-reflection to gaining confidence, then crafting your why and making sure it's part of your beliefs, and ultimately living those beliefs through your practice. This is how I live now. It's the way I talk, the way I behave, the way I believe. When what you learn at the institute advances beyond its walls and lives inside you, transformation happens.

ADVICE FOR PRINCIPALS WHO WANT TO LEAD FOR EQUITY

Stop looking for answers. What you're looking for is something inside of you that's challenging your belief system, so stay with that. Looking for answers somewhere else doesn't work because whatever answer you find is still part of this massive system of inequity. Also, understand that equity isn't a thing, it's the thing. It has to be grounded in your belief and your community's belief as to the purpose of school. If not, it becomes siloed and something done by a department, or a team, or a PLC, or on a mission statement. Lastly, individual interruptions of inequities are not leading for equity. There must be a shift in power. This has been a key learning for me (J. Fraser, personal communication, August 1, 2019).

* * *

Kirk Morris

> *Black male principal of a St. Paul elementary school and graduate of the Institute for Courageous Principal Leadership*

KNOWING MYSELF

Education changed my life, and I wanted to give that to others, so I knew I was in the right field as a classroom teacher and athletic coach. At one point I thought I was the only one who saw the mistreatment of our Black and Brown kids, yet I was okay with being a backseat-driver type of leader on the bus. Then I realized that I needed to be driving that bus. By understanding myself and my beliefs I've become comfortable enough to articulate them as part of my leadership. I'm now very comfortable in myself and my leadership, and I know without a doubt that all kids can grow and learn and achieve.

STRATEGICALLY IMPLEMENTING BEST PRACTICES WITH FIDELITY

In the institute, John Hattie's work [see Chapter 3] opened my eyes to how we spend our time as educators on things that don't necessarily impact achievement in a positive way. We continue to do things simply because it's what we have done in the past. I like to compare this to the definition of insanity, doing the same thing over and over and expecting a different result. This is what we do in public education, and we need to change our strategies to let go of the things that haven't worked in the past and raise our achievement.

Now, in my sixth year, I can see the impact of the changes we've made on not only the culture and climate of the school but also on the academic pieces. We are truly student centered, and evidence of this lies in the fact that adult learning is a priority for everyone in the building. We can't underestimate the power of professional development and talking about the data so we can achieve our academic excellence. We've changed our entire mind-set about adult learning. Everyone is expected to continue to learn and put our heads together so our kids can achieve. It's teamwork.

We have a lot of data that show that the professional climate has changed, but you can also feel it in the building. One example is our new literacy/reading learning lab, which we begin in a meeting and then practice in the classroom together with the kids. We coach each other side by side as we teach the lesson. We also have three dedicated coaches in the building, and all our teachers are required to receive coaching.

Our scores are low, but I'm convinced we'll see a spike this year and next year due to our changes in making sure we understand our standards and use resources to teach those standards. We're getting the right staff on board, and we know that three heads are better than one—we work together.

NAVIGATING RESISTANCE

As a Black man living in a predominantly white state and working in a multirace field, I've had to experience a lot of discomfort and have learned how to navigate the system through that discomfort. Discomfort helps people grow. I've had to grow a lot.

I've had people leave my staff by choice and others not by choice. I believe that one weakness in education is a lack of transparency and honesty. We like to fluff off too many things instead of being honest and transparent. In any major decision I make, I ask myself, *are you doing what's best for kids? Is this in the best interest of kids or adults?* As I've gained more confidence in myself and my practices, I've been preaching transparency and honesty in my evaluations of staff. At one point I had a group of staff that really didn't buy into this, and one was more vocal than the rest and had strong union ties as well. After each evaluation each person would leave my office and meet with this individual. The message got back to the new school board that I was marking too many teachers below standard. A school board member actually approached my supervisor and asked if they could meet with him and look at all the below-standards I had in evaluations for that school year. My response was that neither of them had been there for the evaluations, so looking for the below-standards was not going to help. I said that if they wanted to meet with me, that would not be appropriate either, because we don't discuss evaluations.

(Continued)

(Continued)

I stuck to my belief about doing the right thing. In the many instances in which I received pushback from a small group of staff I had to be transparent and honest with them. One was transferred to another school. Everyone knows I'm going to speak the truth to them and evaluate them honestly.

Another issue I constantly address and get pushback on is the point that "all means all." If you're having an all-class field trip or a school celebration, everyone gets to go, no matter what. It's tough to have to respond to those who think some students should be held back, but we take "all" literally in our school.

RESILIENCE

For me, developing resilience goes back to how I grew up in a small town in Mississippi, very poor, with everything separate: white and Black neighborhoods, parks, swimming pools. There were so many things I couldn't partake in because of the color of my skin, so I developed resilience early. But when I moved to Minnesota this changed because racism wasn't quite as in your face; it was more backhanded. I can see clearly how our Black and Brown kids have been discriminated against and mistreated here. The way we portray people who look like me needs to change. When I see mistreatment of any child, because most of the students in my school are Black and Brown, I'm going to address it. It's done with love, because our adults, no matter what race, need love too. I'm trying to help, not hinder. They tend to do better when they're treated that way.

LEADING COURAGEOUSLY

We adopted a new curriculum for guiding our literacy because I knew that what we were using wasn't adequate. Black and Brown kids with all-white material— we were not going to keep doing that. I explained the why of using better material, and it worked in our favor. I got support from the district to make that change.

Being an equity leader is an ongoing process. How I deal with something is based on which stage of development I'm in and which stage of the pathway I lean into at that time. As leaders, our beliefs have to be strong. As a racial equity leader, I have to be absolutely grounded in my beliefs or my actions are going to show something different. My actions are a result of what I believe. Our actions and beliefs have to align so we can do what's right in our decision-making process (K. Morris, personal communication, September 16, 2019).

The line at the end of the last box in the Theory of Action diagram goes back to the beginning, because the journey never ends. As facilitators of this work, we constantly follow this model ourselves. We always reflect on our beliefs and actions, examine new research on practices, and reposition ourselves, just as we challenge our principals to do. As a result, we are all disrupting the systemic nature of racism in public schools.

You will take the first three steps of this process—learning to know yourself, know your purpose, and know the *actual* high-return practices for student achievement—in this chapter and the following three.

Knowing Myself

"I Am From . . ." To delve into exploring your racial awareness, take a few moments to contemplate what defines you in an exercise called "I Am From." As seen in the two following examples, writing about yourself in this way creates a poetic statement about your perceptions of your identity around race, culture, and society. The first example is by this book's coauthor Candace Raskin, one of the creators of the Institute for Courageous Principal Leadership.

Candace Raskin: I Am From . . .

I am from sawdust

From Tab and homemade clothes

I am from white people

I am from "pull yourself up from your bootstraps" and knowing when it was payday

Which makes me feel sometimes proud and sometimes ashamed

I am from the France and Temple families

From Sunday dinners at Grandma's and an outhouse that I hated to use

I am a problem solver and too old to always follow the rules

I am the middle child and the responsible one

Even though I am white, I am female

From "you will flunk out of college" to doctorate in education

I am from Roberta and Ozzie

From walking to Sunday school with my siblings and wishing my parents attended

I am from white privilege and economic privilege

To strengthen my cultural competency, I must remain in racial discourse

In terms of social justice, I hope to help guide you through your own personal racial journey so you will lead for all children in our schools.

Elementary school principal Eduardo Navidad also shares his "I Am From" exercise written for one of our institute sessions.

After completing your "I Am From" poem (see Figure 1.3), reflect on the impact of this exercise. What surprised you as you called up snapshots

Eduardo Navidad: I Am From . . .

I am Eduardo Navidad, a leader from Laketown Elementary School

I am from arepas con queso blanco y croquetas de jamón serrano[1]

from el Caribe Venezolano and el reino de España[2]

I am from la clase alta de España y los Guaros de Barquisimeto in Venezuela[3]

from the fùtbol powerhouse of Madrid and the pottery and salsa/merengue capital of el Caribe

which makes me homesick and sad but proud to continue the legacy

I am from la familia Navidad with its proud Spanish history and family crest and Jiménez from Venezuela and the Canary Islands

from wine and formalities and fiestas until the morning

I am from respect and patriarchs to La Hacienda de Cafe[4]

Even though I am a Guaro Larense I'm a first-generation U.S. immigrant

From Maloso[5] and you can become anything you want if you put your mind and education first

I am from Abuelito Paco and y Abuelita Ligia[6]

From Catholics and New Age

I am from los barrios[7] de la Guaira and son of a doctor from the Spanish upper class

To strengthen my cultural competency, I must continue to learn my story in order to understand the story and experiences of other immigrants across the USA as I work to pave the way for new generations.

In terms of social justice in my school, I hope to become a racially conscious champion and a change agent for my staff as I work unapologetically to interrupt BIAS.

I am Eduardo, a leader.

---

[1] arepas with white cheese and serrano ham croquettes

[2] the Venezuelan Caribbean and the kingdom of Spain

[3] the Spanish upper class and people from the Lara State in Venezuela

[4] a coffee plantation

[5] nickname for energetic/hyperactive

[6] grandfather and grandmother

[7] the poor neighborhoods

Figure 1.3   Template for Writing "I am From . . ."

I Am From . . .

I am _____ , a leader from _____
(first name)   (school)

I am from _____
(a specific ordinary item from your family of origin)

from _____ and _____
(product name)   (product name)

I am from _____ people.
(the **race(s)** of your people)

from _____ and _____
(two examples of your **culture**: beliefs and traditions or practices, policies, and rules)

which make me _____
(elicit feelings or emotions or memories)

I am from from _____ and _____
(a family name)   (another family name)

from _____ and _____
(two examples of your **ethnicity**: religious practices, food choices, language/dialect, musical expressions)

I am from _____
(a family trait, habit, or tendency)

Even though I _____
(an example of your **diversity**: a way in which you are unique even within your same racial, ethnic, or cultural group)

From _____ and _____
(something you were told as a child)   (another)

I am from _____ and _____
(an ancestor)   (another ancestor)

From _____ and _____
(representation of religion or lack of)   (another)

I am from _____ and _____
(a **privilege**)   (another privilege)

To strengthen my **cultural competency**, I must _____
                                                        (area of growth)

In terms of **social justice** in my school, I hope to _____
                                                        (goal)

I am _____ , a leader.
(first name)

Source: Created by Dr. Natalie Rasmussen. Used with permission.

of your life? Did you struggle with certain statements? When is the last time you took the time to reflect about yourself in this way? How would you describe the value of this activity? Your "I Am From" writing is a warm-up to your racial autobiography, a longer reflection about your experiences with race. Developed by Glenn E. Singleton for his Beyond Diversity seminar, the racial autobiography invites you to fully explore your story.

Your Racial Autobiography. The following instructions from the Beyond Diversity seminar will guide you through the process of writing your racial autobiography. Feedback we've received from participants in our institute reveals the many ways this exercise can impact your leadership; for example, high school assistant principal Lee Vang shared, "Crafting my racial autobiography was reflective and metacognitive truth-telling about the formation and ongoing transformation of my spirit as a Hmong woman in America. As a test of my courage and an act of political resistance, publicly sharing my absent narrative—such personal and vulnerable information—was uncomfortable yet liberating and affirming. My racial autobiography remains a living, thriving testament of my journey and growth as an unapologetic woman of color, dedicated equity leader, and conscientious objector of systemic racism." Middle school principal Tyrone Brookins reflected that "developing my racial autobiography was empowering as it allowed me to reflect on the richness of my identity and all that encompasses me as a Black man. Sharing my racial autobiography with a captive audience allowed me the opportunity to share with others that brilliance is indeed in the room whether you recognize it or not."

Kirk Morris, a Black elementary school principal, stated, "While writing my racial autobiography, I experienced a wide range of emotions. I realize that I have grown through both my negative and positive experiences. Each time I've presented my racial autobiography, I've felt a sense of accomplishment and pride. I'm very proud of my journey and where it has led me." High school associate principal Angeline McGaster-Woods, another Black participant in the institute, said that "the racial autobiography assignment was a platform for me to be able to give my own personal narrative of my educational experience while isolating RACE. This assignment aligned with the absent narrative work my building has continued to promote to engage all learners." White administrator Tami Reynolds remarked that her racial autobiography is a continuous process: "I am learning and getting comfortable with the fact that writing my racial autobiography will never be 'complete' as our racial experiences change over and over again. Through listening to the stories of my colleagues in the cohort, I have deepened my own understanding and appreciation for race and the experiences of those who do not look like me. This experience has helped me become better as a whole person and the way I see my world."

Writing Your Racial Autobiography

Start with your Racial Autobiography Bookends. What can you recall about the earliest and most recent events and conversations about race, race relations, and/or racism that may have impacted your current perspectives and/or experiences?

- Earliest: What was your first personal experience in dealing with race or racism?

  Describe what happened.

- Most recent: Describe your most recent personal experience in dealing with race or racism. Describe what happened.

- To help you think about the time between your earliest and most recent racial experiences, jot down notes to answer the questions below. Let the questions guide but not limit your thinking. Note any other memories or ideas that seem relevant to you. When you have identified some of the landmarks on your racial journey, start writing your autobiography. Remember that it is a fluid document, one that you will reflect on and update many times as your racial consciousness evolves.

1. Family
   - Are your parents the same race? Same ethnic group? Are your brothers and sisters? What about your extended family—uncles, aunts, etc.?
   - Where did your parents grow up? What exposure did they have to racial groups other than their own? (Have you ever talked with them about this?)
   - What ideas did they grow up with regarding race relations? (Do you know? Have you ever talked with them about this? Why or why not?)
   - Do you think of yourself as white? As Black? As Asian? As Latino? As American Indian? Or just as "human"? Do you think of yourself as a member of an ethnic group? What is its importance to you?

2. Neighborhood
   - What is the racial makeup of the neighborhood you grew up in?
   - What was your first awareness of race—that there are different "races" and that you are a member of a racial group.
   - What was your first encounter with another race? Describe the situation.
   - When and where did you first hear the word *nigger* or other similar racial slurs?
   - What messages do you recall getting from your parents about race? From others when you were little?

(Continued)

(Continued)

3. Elementary and Middle School

- What was the racial makeup of your elementary school? Of its teachers?

- Think about the curriculum: What Black Americans did you hear about? How did you celebrate Martin Luther King Day? What about Asian Americans, or Latinos, or American Indians?

- Cultural influences: TV, advertisements, novels, music, movies, etc. What color God was presented to you? Angels? Santa Claus? The tooth fairy! Dolls!

- What was the racial makeup of organizations you were in? Girl Scouts, Soccer team? Band?

4. High School and Community

- What was the racial makeup of your high school? Of its teachers?

- Was there interracial dating? Racial slurs? Any conflict with members of another race?

- Have you ever been stigmatized because of your race or ethnic group membership?

- What else was important about your high school years, racially speaking—maybe something that didn't happen in high school but during that time?

- What is the racial makeup of your hometown? Of your metropolitan area? What about your experiences in summer camp, summer jobs, etc.?

5. Present and Future

- What is the racial makeup of the organization you currently work in? Of your circle(s) of friends? Does it meet your needs?

- Realistically, think about where you want to live (if different from where you are now). What is its racial makeup? Social class makeup? Where do you want to work in the next 10 years? What is its racial makeup? Social class makeup?

6. General

- What's the most important image, encounter—whatever—you've had regarding race? Have you felt threatened? In the minority? Have you felt privileged?

Debby Irving (2014), author *of Waking Up White and Finding Myself in the Story of Race*, contributed a racial autobiography-like essay to *The Guide for White Women Who Teach Black Boys* (Moore, Michael, & Penick-Parks, 2018) that evokes vital reflection for educational leaders. As a white woman confronting her beliefs, Irving's story is filled with the "brutal honesty" that Fleming (2018) said is required of equity work in the epigraph to this chapter. Our questions posed at the end of Irving's essay will guide your analysis of the racial messages you received from your teachers, giving you insight into this specific type of impact that may bring realizations beyond your racial autobiography.

"Ready to Make a Difference, the Old-Fashioned Way" by Debby Irving

From *The Guide for White Women Who Teach Black Boys*, edited by Eddie Moore, Jr., Ali Michael, and Marguerite W. Penick-Parks (2018)

Originally printed in Moore, E., Michael, A., and Penick-Parks, M. *The Guide for White Women Who Teach Black Boys* (2018). Corwin Press, Thousand Oaks, CA.

Virtuous. Enthusiastic. Ready. If I had to pick three words to characterize the feelings I had when I chose to become a teacher in the Cambridge Public Schools, these would be the words.

After a number of years with two children in the Cambridge school system, its everyday happenings had become central to my life. The school community sparked curiosity and energy in me. I couldn't seem to get enough of it. What drew me to this district rather than schools in general was the level of racial integration. Raised in an affluent white suburb, I didn't want for my children the kind of racial or class isolation that I'd found so limiting in my own childhood. The racial diversity in the Cambridge schools intrigued me and drew me closer.

One cold December morning as I left my daughters' school, I stopped in my tracks with the thought, "I wish I were a teacher." Then, in mid-stride, it occurred to me, "Mid-life career change is a thing. I wonder what it would take to change careers?" One month later, I found myself as a teaching assistant at my daughters' school, one of the city's most successful and cherished elementary schools. My idea was to test the teaching waters before committing to the graduate education I'd need to qualify as a lead teacher.

As my start day neared, I imagined "My love of kids makes me a natural," and "I'll be able to make a real difference!" What I didn't yet know was that although I was a "natural" with children who looked like me, this didn't translate as I thought it would with children who did not look like me. I didn't understand that loving kids would not be nearly enough and that my ideas about "making a difference" smacked of historical

(Continued)

(Continued)

patterns about "saving" and "helping" and "fixing" that held in place the very issues I envisioned conquering. My sense of entitlement to help, and my assumption that I was equipped to do so, were manifestations of my lack of cultural competence. Although cultural competence wasn't even a term in my white world, deep-seated ideas about being competent just by being white were.

I entered teaching fancying myself color-blind, and therefore able to love and teach each student equally. The truth, however, is that I did see color. In fact, race was very much on my mind. Despite a universally loved staff deeply committed to serving *all* children, I'd observed stark racial patterns emerge year after year at my daughters' school. White parents flocked to school events, sat on various committees, and occupied the rom-parent positions. Integrated kindergarteners who'd once held hands and bounced gleefully through school hallways slowly but surely got racially segregated into hierarchical reading and math groups. While my daughters' friend groups grew whiter over the year, once-bright-eyed Black and Brown five-year-olds grew to ten-year-olds whose downcast eyes avoided mine. The principal's bench, where recalcitrant students awaited their fate, disproportionately housed angry- or despondent-looking Black boys. Meanwhile, the white kids disproportionally maintained their youthful exuberance while advancing through reading and math levels and assuming leadership roles in the school.

These racial observations mixed and mingled with subconscious racial ideas I'd unknowingly absorbed in childhood. In my 1960s suburban life, white was my normal, the entirety of my visual backdrop. Immersed in a world of white families, white teachers, white books and TV characters, white presidents, white doctors, white dolls, whiteness became so normal as to be invisible. Although I consciously noticed race only when a person of color appeared, the reality is I subconsciously noticed whiteness every minute of every day. Far from benign, my racial observations packed unspoken ideas about inherent human difference along skin color lines. Without knowing it, my childhood belief system developed around a complex, better-than/worse-than value scheme in which white people were smarter, more responsible, harder-working, safer, and superior human beings.

So when I thought to myself "I'll be able to make a difference," it's pretty clear who I had in mind. I wasn't going into teaching to "make a difference" for the white kids. And I was far from color-blind. My unspoken assumption was that I, as the mother of two high-achieving white kids, had what it took to "help" the Black and Brown kids. The tragedy here is that despite my best intentions, without knowing my own racial history or culture, I was destined to undermine the success of the very students I most wanted to "help."

A crucial aspect of dominant white culture was, and continues to be, an unspoken agreement that Black people are not just "non-white others"; Black people are "troubled others," and these troubles are somehow self-inflicted and/or biologically based. Integral to this silent narrative is a ubiquitous freedom-and-equality narrative: "Life, liberty, justice for all," "level playing field," and "land of the free." Language like this exalts U.S. ideals while ignoring U.S. discriminatory policies and practices. This skewed messaging allowed us to quietly buy into distorted ideas about Black people as less-than and go on to use these ideas to explain away not only the divergent educational outcomes and parent engagement I observed at school but also the Black/white wealth gap and those scary "inner city" neighborhoods. My hushed explanations included thoughts like "they must not care about education," "they don't know how to make and save money," and "they have no regard for personal property." Having grown up in a white world where a white-authored history and version of current events shaped my worldview, I was oblivious to the way Black people told their own history. White history and narratives saturated not only my formal education but also information I soaked up through the media and my own white family's stories. Amid this onslaught of one-sided history rumbled the unspoken understanding that talking about race was rude.

In that information void, I remained unaware that from the get-go, U.S. public and private programs and policies have disproportionately diverted resources toward white people, economically castrating communities of color, and then blaming them for their circumstances. Without knowing U.S. racial history, I couldn't consider the kind of frustration and anger it might engender, which further undermined my aspirations to be that awesome, loving, color-blind, pied piper of a teacher I imagined I would be. Not only did I subconsciously judge people of color for their circumstances; I judged their attitudes and behaviors. I cannot stress enough how deep beneath the surface of my consciousness this was. Nor can I stress how damaging and perverse a mind-set it is, because really, my approach to making a difference was not about discovering policies and practices that were differentially impacting students along color lines; rather, my approach was rooted in wanting to teach "those" kids to have more "appropriate" attitudes and behaviors. I wanted to teach them to think and act more like me, to be more white.

I had no idea of the history I was repeating. Although consciously I scoffed at historical phrases such as "taming the heathens" and "civilizing the savages," subconsciously I was trapped in exactly that mind-set. Beneath my color-blind fantasy, I was deeply invested in the white way as the right way. What's more, I'd bought into ideas about women being the cultural torchbearers, both in the family and in society at large.

Without conscious memory of seeing the painting *American Progress*, depicting a white woman floating over the western plains, a Bible tucked under her arm, I essentially swallowed whole the narrative she conveyed: The white woman's role was to model how to be good, right, moral, and compliant. Choosing a career first in nonprofit management and later in elementary education fit right into the historically accepted role of white women doing society's "helping" and "fixing" charity work for the destitute and the young. And, like past tamers and civilizers, my actions would mostly make me feel good about myself while disempowering those on whom I imposed my ill-conceived ideas about right and wrong.

As I entered the classroom with these unexamined ideas, I unknowingly fueled the very racial divide I imagined I would bridge. I congratulated Black and Brown students for simply completing an assignment while pushing

(Continued)

(Continued)

white students to make corrections. I worked closely with Black and Brown students to adhere to rules yet excused white students' rule-breaking with thoughts like "gotta love her confidence" or "what spunk!" I bonded with the white parents who showed up at drop-off and parent-teacher conferences yet did little to connect with the parents of color who showed up less often, assuming their lack of engagement was due to external challenges such as work or transportation.

A key question I never asked myself was this: Is there anything about me that contributes to the outcome that parents or students of color engage more or less? What I didn't know was that the sight of white me could trigger historical feelings of mistrust and trauma for people of color. Nor did I understand that my cultural values around punctuality, efficiency, and independence were not similarly valued in all cultures. While I saw punctuality as a mark of ethical behavior, for instance, Black families may have seen my emphasis on punctuality as an indication that I value time more than I value human beings or relationships. By perceiving emotional restraint and conflict avoidance as a sign of good character combined with good rearing, I evaluated anger and agitation as character flaws combined with poor parenting, never as valuable feedback directed at me. Because my culture taught me to look for deficits in others, not to reflect on myself, I gathered evidence in support of Black people's shortcomings, while never questioning my own.

Take Rosie, a first-generation Haitian girl I spent a year "helping" with all my white might. Rosie had a pattern of getting up in the middle of an assignment and walking to a classmate's desk. With the best of intentions, my white colleagues and I believed this was a serious self-control issue and created a behavior plan that offered the incentive of earning stars by staying in her seat. My job was to implement it. Her response to my daily interceptions was to look devastated, return to her seat, and put her head on her desk, crushed that she'd failed again and too disheartened to focus on her schoolwork. For eight months, I blamed noncompliance as the source of her behavioral and academic troubles. Not once did I consider how my white cultural expectations could be playing a role.

Toward the end of the school year, a course I was taking helped me to wonder if a culture clash might be in play. As I learned that Haitian culture values group functionality over individual achievement, I began to get in touch with my own socialization around individualism and the lens it had given me in judging Rosie's behavior. One day, after watching Rosie get up in the middle of a math problem, I refrained from intercepting her. Free from my demands, she walked to a classmate's desk across the room and began rubbing her back. When I checked in with her later, she told me how she'd heard Kendall (who is white) crying. I'd been closer to Kendall's desk and not heard a thing. This hit me like a thunderbolt. Rosie's connectedness and compassion put into relief my lack of both. Did I have something to learn from Rosie and her culture?

As the course pushed me to consider how different cultures develop different sides of our human capacities, I wondered what sensibilities and impulses I might have developed in my culture. As I reconsidered the pity I'd felt when I learned Rosie shared a bed with five siblings and cousins,

I reimagined the human connectedness she would also develop from that experience. I rethought the insistence I'd had years earlier that my daughters "have their own space," each with her own bedroom. Had I set my own children up to thrive in the culture of individualism at the expense of human connectedness? Had my own lifetime of individual orientation left me communally challenged?

One manifestation of my lack of connectedness was the way I engaged with the idea of diversity. I was drawn to racially integrated communities because they felt exciting *to me*. A more connected, culturally aware person might have wondered: How does this community feel having me become a part of it?

If I could redo one part of my life, I would have become more culturally aware and competent before entering the classroom. Without either quality, I stepped into the role of educator with the only cultural training I'd had, the one centered on white, patriarchal cultural norms and social roles. Although I'd experienced the oppressiveness of men dictating what was best for me, thinking less of my abilities, and labeling me too emotional as a woman I turned around and imposed these very tendencies on students and families of color. My own ignorance about my culture both obfuscated my capacity to look for value in other cultures and allowed me to impose mine.

Reminding myself that I did not invent America's racial caste system has helped me move quickly through feelings of guilt and defensiveness and onto the more productive feelings of mutual responsibility. Connecting with people and ideas with fearless vulnerability and humble curiosity has been the hardest and most rewarding endeavor of my life. How I wish I'd had the opportunity to cultivate this human capacity earlier. What I would give to turn back the clock and have decades of racial consciousness ahead of me. May young educators continue to unearth and expose the toxic ideology that reproduces racial inequity every day and leave the old-fashioned ways of denial and dominance where they belong—in the past.

Reflect on This

What's Happening in Your School?

Reflect on the following questions in your journal:

1. Do you have teachers on your staff who are focused on "saving" the students rather than knowing them for who they are?

2. How can you lead them to know their students racially and build relationships with them? Do they have the skills to instruct students from where the students are?

3. Do some of your teachers already use race-conscious strategies in the classroom? What are they?

(Continued)

(Continued)

4. Can your students see themselves in the curriculum? If not, how can you guide your teachers to know the students racially and allow them to engage with materials that reflect their race and culture?

Source: Originally printed in Moore, E., Michael, A., and Penick-Parks, M. *The Guide for White Women Who Teach Black Boys* (2018). Corwin Press, Thousand Oaks, CA.

The Cycle of Socialization. Our social identities—our gender, sexual orientation, class, religion, cultural group, age, and ability status—come to bear in the roles we are socialized to play throughout our lives. As Harro (2000) explains, "These social identities predispose us to unequal *roles* in the dynamic system of oppression" (p. 15). Powerful elements of society socialize us to play these roles to keep the inequitable system intact. As school leaders, unless we examine how these forces have shaped our attitudes, assumptions, and beliefs about race, we will perpetuate racism in our schools. Our lifelong training in who we are supposed to be according to the social identities listed above is part of our cycle of socialization (Harro, 2000). This process, from the original sources of our socialization to the ways it perpetuates itself, is found in Figure 1.4.

The cycle of socialization is based on a system in which the dominant group establishes itself as the "norm" and defines everyone else in terms of that identity. In the United States, the most precise definition of the norm is a white, middle- or upper-class, heterosexual, gentile (and arguably Christian) male. Everyone else—women, people of color, youth and the elderly, people of other faiths, the poor—are a subordinate group. "Both groups are dehumanized by being socialized into prescribed roles without consciousness or permission," Harro writes (2000, p. 17). Yes, the dominant class is also harmed in this system, since, as Paolo Freire (1970/2000) explains, they lose their humanity in the act of oppressing others. When the subordinate group removes the dominant group's power, they also restore their humanity. From this perspective, the act of this abolishing racial inequity in our schools transforms everyone and switches off the engine that drives the detrimental, status-quo cycle of socialization.

Examining how the educational system has socialized us helps us understand ourselves as leaders. Understanding the cycle of socialization and doing the work to transform assumptions and beliefs is essential. White leaders can unpack how they have become blocked by "the fear and insecurity" they have been taught by being "kept ignorant and confused by the myths and misinformation" they have been fed (Harro, 2000, p. 20). Leaders of color who may have resigned themselves to surviving the cycle rather than confronting the additional pain that goes with fighting such a powerful and pervasive system can find the courage to align with all antiracist allies for making change. The following "My Cycle of Socialization" exercise will guide you through this process.

Figure 1.4   The Cycle of Socialization

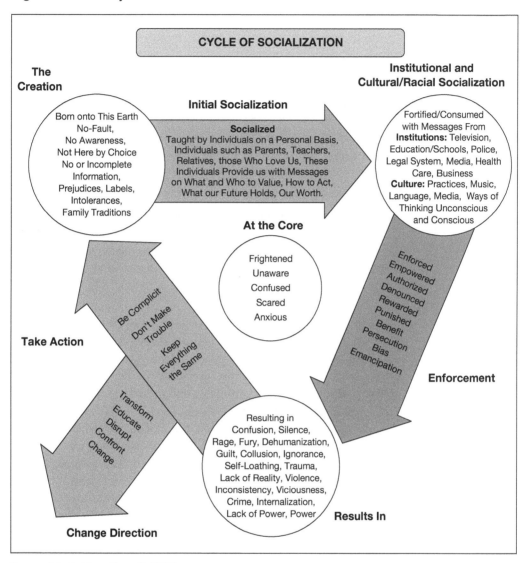

Source: Adapted from Harro, B. (2000).

Reflect on This
My Cycle of Socialization

Describe your first socialization in the blank document, Figure 1.5, by following the cues in Figure 1.4. This process helps you grapple with realizations that your upbringing, for example, did not fit well with the dominant culture that sent so many messages ("Black boys don't do well in school") telling you that your "beginning" was wrong and made you feel guilty, isolated, and so on.

(Continued)

(Continued)

White leaders must acknowledge that they've been socialized into whiteness and need to interrupt these patterns by consciously making a change instead of perpetuating the status quo.

1. In the circle "The Beginning" and arrow "First Socialization" describe the following: What was your situation/environment growing up? Who were your key teachers, and what were your key messages?

2. What events or experiences reinforced those messages and values for you ("First Socialization")?

3. What institutions reinforced your socialization (upper right circle)?

4. What were the results for you given those messages, experiences, and events (bottom circle)?

5. How will you move forward on your own personal racial journey— what changes will you make ("Direction for Change" and "Actions")?

Knowing My Strengths. Like the students in our schools, we need to learn what we are good at. Knowing our strengths builds our competence, which in turn increases the confidence we need to lead. When we see the benefits of using our strengths, the neurological feedback of that positive experience stimulates the pleasure centers in the brain and expands our feeling of well-being (Jackson & McDermott, 2015). Strengths-based leadership embraces the model that activates student strengths instead of focusing on deficits. Understanding our strengths and how they impact our leadership also helps build a leadership team based on a variety of signature strengths that complement each other.

Our institute uses Gallup's StrengthsFinder program, available online for a nominal fee, but you can find free strength assessments online such as positive psychologist Martin Seligman's (2019) "Brief Strengths Test" on his Authentic Happiness website. Learning happens when we use our strengths, not our deficits, so we invite you to start your journey of leading for equity by discovering your strengths.

Try this simple exercise suggested by the Gallup program to feel the difference between using your strengths and your weaknesses: Take a sheet of paper and write your name five times. Now, switch your hand and sign your name five times. What did it feel like to sign with your dominant hand? What words describe the feelings associated with signing your name with your nondominant hand? Imagine what you can do with the competence and confidence that comes from making decisions, taking action, and leading your staff when you use your dominant strengths. This helps you envision the effectiveness of a leadership team that is balanced by a collection of unique strengths.

The StrengthsFinder method uses theme words, both nouns and adjectives, to describe strengths that fall into the broad categories of

Figure 1.5 Fill-in Template for My Cycle of Socialization

CYCLE OF SOCIALIZATION

The Creation

Institutional and Cultural/Racial Socialization

Initial Socialization

At the Core

Take Action

Enforcement

Results In

Change Direction

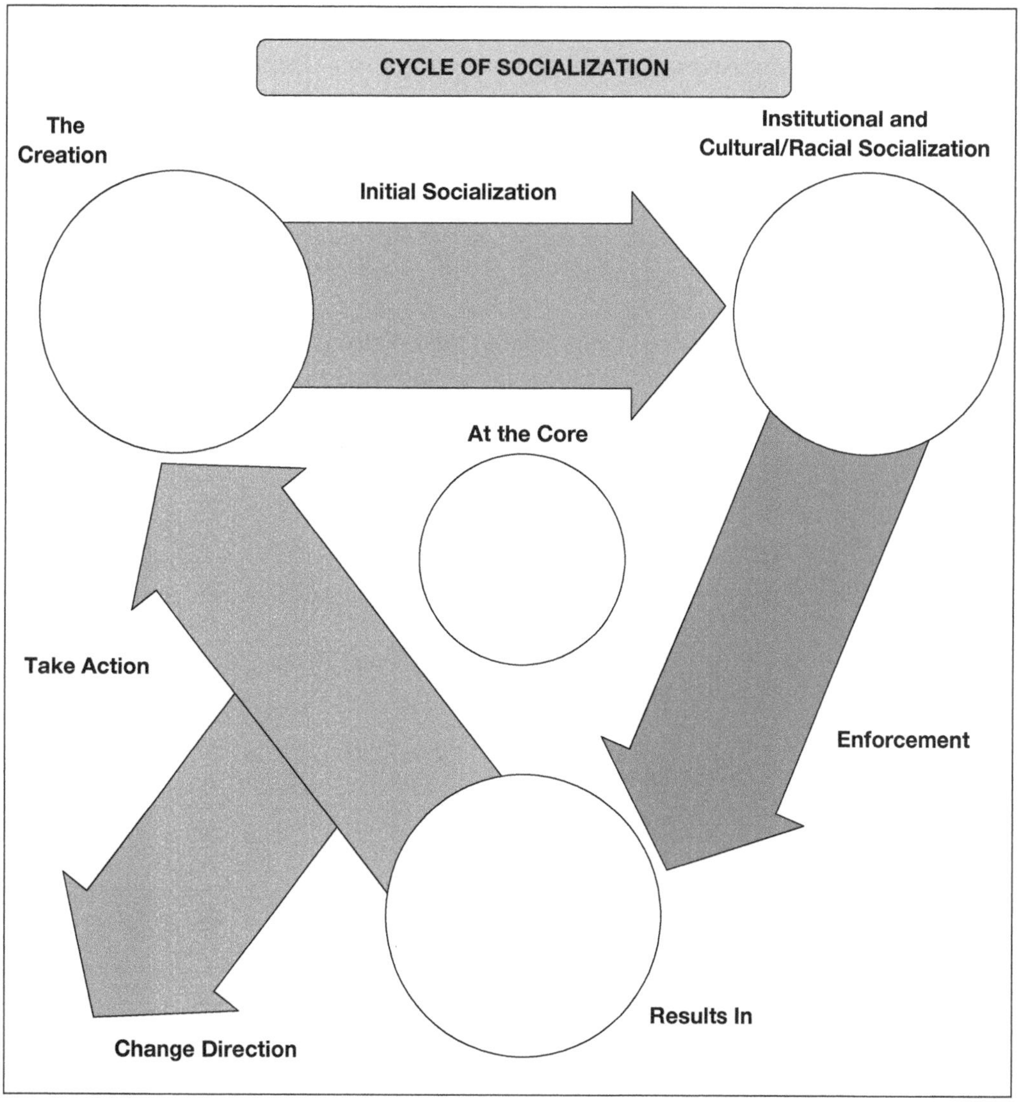

Source: Adapted from Harro, B. (2000).

executing, influencing, relationship building, and *strategic thinking. Discipline, consistency, responsibility,* and *focus* are a few of the words associated with the executing domain of leadership. Someone who identifies with the discipline theme, for example, thrives on creating order and structure. The communication theme includes strengths of communication, activator, competition, and significance. Leaders with communication strengths can easily put their thoughts into words and present them with impact. Relationship-building words such as *positivity, empathy, connectedness,* and *adaptability* describe the strengths of people who have, for example, an uncanny ability to understand what others are feeling. *Analytical, ideation, learner,* and *context* are just a handful of the words around the strategic-thinking domain. People with the strength of ideation are creative thinkers who can connect the dots between different subjects, experiences, and ideas (Rath & Conchie, 2008).

Positive psychology uses words such as *authenticity, courage, emotional intelligence, hope and optimism, social intelligence, gratitude, perseverance, self-regulation* (staying with a personal plan such as diet or exercise), *kindness, appreciation of beauty and excellence, creativity,* and *forgiveness* and *mercy* to name character strengths (Rashid, 2015).

We find it helpful to also identify our least-strong traits, or blind spots, to recognize when we are returning to those in a critical moment so that we can shift direction and tune into one of our strengths. An excellent way to uncover your top five strengths (Kachru, 2012) and blind spots is to recall successful and not-so-successful events in your leadership life, as directed in the following exercise. The journaling activity gives you an opportunity to analyze and reflect on what you have learned about your strengths and blind spots.

Reflect on This

Finding My Strengths and Blind Spots

Strengths

List three of your professional achievements:

_____

_____

_____

Write a brief summary of each of these and then list words that describe the strengths you can identify in your actions.

Blind Spots

List three situations in which your leadership did not result in the outcome you hoped for:

_____

_____

_____

Write a brief summary of each of these and then list words that describe the blind spots you can identify in your actions. Now consider which of these strengths and blind spots come up most often in your leadership and list them here:

Top 5 Strengths	Top 5 Blind Spots
_____	_____
_____	_____
_____	_____
_____	_____
_____	_____

Source: Adapted from Rath, T., & Conchie, B. (2008).

My Journal

Journaling About My Strengths and Blind Spots

In your journal, reflect on your journey as a leader for racial equity by answering the following:

1. How do your strengths support your leadership?

2. How do your blind spots impact your leadership?

3. Who do you need on your team based on what you learned about your strengths?

Now that you understand the Theory of Action pathway that begins with knowing yourself and cycles through several stages that will repeat throughout your life, you have a roadmap for becoming a leader for equity in your school. Your honest and thoughtful work throughout this chapter, from writing your "I Am From" poem and racial autobiography to examining your socialization, strengths, and blind spots, has taken you through Step 1, Knowing Self. Your attention to these activities should make you aware of your commitment to this journey and remind you that such commitment is a strength in itself, one that will support you every step of the way. Now we turn to the next stage of self-knowledge, Discovering my "Why."

References

Baldwin, J. (1962, January 14). As much truth as one can bear. *The New York Times Book Review*.

Fleming, C. L. (2018). *How to be less stupid about race: On racism, white supremacy, and the racial divide*. Boston: Beacon Press.

Freire, P. (2000). *Pedagogy of the oppressed* (30th anniversary ed.). New York: Continuum.

Harro, B. (2000). The cycle of socialization. In M. Adam, W. J. Blumenfeld, R. Castañeda, H. W. Hackman, M. L. Peters, & X. Zúñiga (Eds.), *Readings for diversity and social justice*. New York: Routledge.

Irving, D. (2014). *Waking up white and finding myself in the story of race*. Cambridge, MA: Elephant Room Press.

Irving, D. (2018). Ready to make a difference, the old-fashioned way. In E. Moore, Jr., A. Michael, & M. W. Penick-Parks (Eds.), *The guide for white women who teach black boys*. Thousand Oaks, CA: Corwin.

Jackson, Y., & McDermott, V. (2015). *Unlocking student potential: How do I identify and activate student strengths?* Alexandria, VA: ASCD.

Kachru, B. (2012). *The success of failure: A self-help guide to convert failures into success*. New Delhi: V & S.

Minnesota Department of Education. (2017). *2017 Minnesota Assessment Results Presentation*. Retrieved from https://content.govdelivery.com/accounts/MNMDE/bulletins/1af5eb1.

Moore, E., Jr., Michael, A., & Penick-Parks, M. W. (2018). *The guide for white women who teach black boys*. Thousand Oaks, CA: Corwin.

National Center for Education Statistics. (2017). *National Assessment of Educational Progress: National Report Card 2017*. Retrieved from https://nces.ed.gov/nationsreportcard/.

Rashid, T. (2015). Positive psychotherapy: A strength-based approach. *The Journal of Positive Psychology, 10*(1), 25–40.

Raskin, C., Krull, M., & Thatcher, R. (2015). Developing principals as racial equity leaders: A mixed method study. *AASA Journal of Scholarship & Practice, 12*(2), 4–19.

Rath, T., & Conchie, B. (2008). *Strengths based leadership: Great leaders, teams, and why people follow*. New York: Gallup.

Seligman, M. (2019). *Brief strengths test*. Retrieved from https://www.authentic happiness.sas.upenn.edu/user/login?destination=node/504.

Discovering My "Why"

CHAPTER 2

Essential Self-Reflection for Leadership

By choosing to resist racial constructions, we may emancipate ourselves and our children.

—Ian F. Haney López (1995)

Leaders make the impossible possible.

—Linda Cliatt-Wayman (2015)

Self-knowledge, the first step in our Theory of Action framework for becoming a principal for racial equity, includes understanding the purpose, or "why," that motivates our leadership.

High school principal Chris Hester, a Black woman graduate of our Institute for Principal Leadership who has been an educator at both the K–12 and college levels, solidified her purpose of being a student-focused equity leader during an incident when she was a seventh-grade science teacher. That core mission has stayed with her throughout her administrative career. "My 'why' started hitting home when I had a colleague who, while they were doing cuts in our school, had a friend who was let go," she said. "I had already been hired before that, but he came to me and said that the only reason I had my job was because I was Black. *Wow*, I thought, *if that's happening to me, what's happening to kids?*" (C. Hester, personal communication, August 1, 2019). Chris's equity-focused "why" evolved out of her long-standing sense of purpose as a college basketball coach who wanted to prepare young women for the world, "to make sure they're equipped," she said. Her "why" is the constant that continues to evolve as she develops new practices. It is also the engine that drives her ability to inspire others in her building.

Knowing My "Why"

We work with Simon Sinek's (2009) insights about finding your "why" in the first weeks of our institute to help principals clearly define their purpose. In *Start with Why: How Great Leaders Inspire Everyone to Take Action*, Sinek (2009) compares the mathematical relationship of proportion called the golden ratio to a natural pattern of human behavior he calls the Golden Circle. The center of Sinek's target-shaped model, labeled Why, represents the belief that motivates what a company or individual does. When the organization's messaging is about that belief instead of what it is selling or offering or how it makes its product, the message goes directly to the emotional part of the potential customer's brain to make a bigger impact. "When a company clearly communicates their WHY, what they believe," Sinek (2009) writes, "and we believe what they believe, then we will sometimes go to extraordinary lengths to include those products or brands in our lives . . . because they become markers or symbols of the values and beliefs we hold dear" (p. 54).

As leaders for equity in our schools, communicating our "why" allows us to share our beliefs with others at a deep and inspiring level. We tap into the emotional and gut-decision-making part of the brain, the limbic system, where the majority of decision-making takes place. Sinek's (2009) Golden Circle of Why, How, and What aligns with the basic outlines of the limbic system and neocortex, where we process rational thought and language, as illustrated in Figure 2.1.

The limbic brain is a collection of structures that deals with emotional responses and memory. Our decision-making is largely based on the unconscious processes happening here (and other networked areas), where the emotional memories of past experiences are instantly factored

Figure 2.1   Sinek's Golden Circle (Why, How, What) Aligns With the Brain's Limbic System and Neocortex

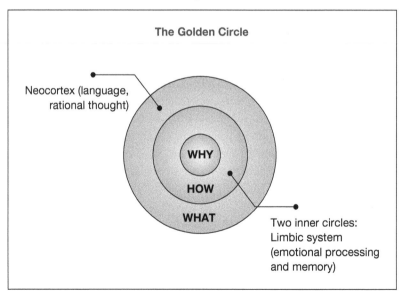

Source: Created by Antonia Felix based on Sinek's (2009) Circle.

into the situation at hand (Gupta, Koscik, Bechara, & Tranel, 2011). We can't explain why we "feel" that a gut-level decision is right because the limbic system works outside the brain's language region (a more recently evolved area).

Neuroscience aside, the point is that knowing our "why" empowers us to stay centered on our values as we make decisions and communicate our mission. Sinek's (2009) mantra, "People don't buy what you do, they buy WHY you do it" (p. 41), drives home the idea that knowing our "why" ramps up our impact—people are drawn to leaders who can express what they believe. "Their ability to make us feel like we belong, to make us feel special, safe and not alone is part of what gives them the ability to inspire us," Sinek writes (2009, p. 55).

Reflect on This

What I Do Versus Why I Do It: What Is My "Why"?

Does My "Why" Align With What I Do?

Watch Simon Sinek's 18-minute TEDx Talk, "Start with Why," linked on this book's website at racialequityleadership.com (Chapter 2 section). Now that you are familiar with this concept and the impact of knowing your "why," ask yourself the following and respond in your journal:

1. What is my "why"?

2. How does it align with what I do daily?

Reflect on This

My "Why," My Simple Slogan

Philadelphia principal Linda Cliatt-Wayman's (2015) TED Talk, "How to Fix a Broken School? Lead Fearlessly, Love Hard" shows us, for one, the power of the equity slogan for school leaders. Creating a slogan helps us home in on our "why," the essence of our leadership. After watching Cliatt-Wayman's 17-minute video linked on this book's website at racialequityleadership .com (Chapter 2 section), write your personal slogan below.

What slogan dedicated to your leadership and your equity commitment will you own and be known for?

My Equity Slogan:

_____

The Construction Process: From Stating Your Mission to Achieving Results

The Theory of Action pathway to courageous leadership for equity expands our self-knowledge by exploring our "why" and our beliefs. What we believe about children, learning, and our school culture is the foundation of our actions as leaders and feeds our mission—our dedication to our "why."

To accomplish results for your students, you must understand your beliefs and change your behaviors to match those beliefs. Your beliefs lie at the core of your mission and are the foundation of the vision you create for your school. Building this leadership through what we call the construction process, as shown in Figure 2.2, begins with stating your mission, forming that into a vision of what your school will become, examining and articulating your beliefs, and aligning those beliefs with your behaviors. Those behaviors can then lead to the positive results you envision for all your students.

We have seen that principals with beliefs that drive their behaviors can achieve results. When we fulfill our mission and vision by carrying out specific actions (behaviors) that reflect our beliefs, we create the change that builds achievement for all students.

Your Mission. Your purpose for existence. As a leader for racial equity, your mission statement expresses your commitment to advocating for all students, such as the following:

I ensure access, fairness, equity, and opportunity for every student, every day.

When your mission becomes your school's mission, your work will include empowering every teacher to fulfill this mission, and as a result of your behaviors your data will reflect that your school advocates for all children.

Your Vision. Where you are headed and envision yourself being in light of the mission you have set before you. What broad problems do you seek to solve, where are you heading, and how would you describe your school as a place and culture that reflects your mission? In stating your vision as a school leader, consider how this vision is a link between the present and the future, how it serves to energize and motivate, and how it provides meaning for racial equity work. Consider this example:

Figure 2.2 The Construction Process

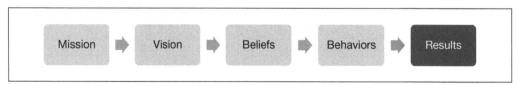

Source: Compiled by authors.

In an era of unprecedented educational challenge, I am committed to my continuous development to lead with fearlessness, skill, self-knowledge, and racial competence so that under my leadership, *every* child fully achieves.

Your Beliefs. The beliefs you hold about your leadership, students, learning, and school culture. These beliefs, such as the following examples, will drive the behavior you express to reach your goals as expressed in your mission and vision.

I believe that *all* students can learn at high levels.

I believe I can and will generate better achievement than I currently do, specifically on behalf of children of color.

I believe that I must model the racially conscious courageous leadership that I expect of the adults in my school community.

Your Behaviors. Your beliefs are a blueprint for defining the behaviors that will put those beliefs into action to create change. Being specific is the key to building a set of behaviors to own and act on. Note how the behaviors in the following examples align with the beliefs that motivated them. Use these examples from our institute participants to guide how you state your own beliefs and behaviors.

BELIEF	BEHAVIORS
• I believe that all students can learn at high levels.	• I will put equity work at the center of everything I do. • I will create a mind-set and environment that equity work is not "what we do" but rather "who we are." • I will analyze data to identify areas of access for students of color and teacher growth. • I will ensure that all advanced courses include students of color proportionately.
• I believe we must interrupt systemic racism/biases in order to provide safe and equitable learning environments.	• I will analyze data to recognize racial discrepancies in order to interrupt current practices and behaviors. • I will challenge inequitable beliefs, behaviors, and assumptions to create an equitable learning space.
• I believe I must model the actions or behaviors that we expect of the adults in our school community who work directly or indirectly with our students.	• I will operate with a growth mind-set. • I will learn and be open to others' perspectives. • I will anticipate "pushback" from unexpected places and help everyone become centered in the conversations.

(Continued)

(Continued)

BELIEF	BEHAVIORS
• As a white woman, I believe I must find the courage to speak about race and the inequities I see in my school, district, and community.	• I will foster and participate in discussions, especially when it is uncomfortable for me.
• I believe that adults should take charge of their own learning.	• I will educate and properly manage adults who are in charge of shaping our educational future.
• I believe I must be willing to put student needs first over adult comfort when it comes to racial equity.	• I will challenge my own and others' personal beliefs and biases to disrupt racial disparities and outcomes.
• I believe this work is the right work and I must do it.	• I will realize that courage means being scared and moving forward anyway.
• I believe that systems are designed to advantage white persons and must be interrupted to eliminate the racial opportunity gap.	• I will respond to systemic practices with courageous conversations and courageous actions.
• I believe that culturally responsive teaching is not *in addition* to best instruction practice, but *crucial* to best instructional practice.	• I will ensure that teachers know and understand culturally responsive teaching practices. • I will provide our staff development, PLCs, evaluations, courageous conversations, etc., that emphasize cultural responsiveness as a key factor in the successful instruction of every student.

Your Behaviors. Thinking about and clarifying your beliefs is critical, but it is not enough. Change happens when we live the behaviors that turn those beliefs into action. Owning and committing ourselves to the actions that align with our beliefs gets results.

Activity

Establishing My Mission, Vision, Beliefs, and Behaviors

Use this space to define your pathway to successful results based on the construction process shown in Figure 2.2. Your mission—founded on your "why" as a leader for racial equity—forms your vision, which in turn helps you describe your beliefs. Your beliefs are a roadmap for creating specific behaviors that will put those beliefs into action. What behaviors will you carry out today that reflect your beliefs?

My Mission

_____

_____

_____

My Vision

_____

_____

_____

My Beliefs and Behaviors

1) If I believe _____,

   then I will _____.

2) If I believe _____,

   then I will _____.

3) If I believe _____,

   then I will _____.

Single-Story Perceptions: Reshaping Our Beliefs

While we can transform our beliefs about our leadership, students, and learning by working with the cycle of socialization and other reflective methods, a single pivotal experience can also shift our understanding in a profound way. One conversation or observation can bring a narrow point of view to light and invite us to expand our perspective. Novelist Chimamanda Ngozi Adichie calls a person's limited perspective a "single-story perception" and relates how she came to recognize this limitation and transform one of her own limited beliefs.

Growing up in Nigeria reading British and American books, Adichie brought those worlds into the stories she began writing when she was 7 years old. Her crayon-illustrated tales were all about white children with blue eyes who ate apples and drank ginger beer. What this reveals, Adichie (2009) said in her TED Talk "The Danger of a Single Story," "is how impressionable and vulnerable we are in the face of a story, particularly as children. . . . I had become convinced that books, by their very nature, had to have foreigners in them. . . . I did not know that people like me could exist in literature." Her perception shifted when she began reading African authors like Chinua Achebe, which saved her from "having a single story of what books are." Later, this experience and others allowed her to understand why her white American college roommate was startled to find that Adichie shattered all the conceptions she had about Africans. Her roommate's single-story perceptions of Africa made her expect Adichie to be a poverty-stricken young woman from a remote village, an object of pity who had never seen modern appliances or heard any kind of music but tribal drumming. To her amazement, here was a well-read 19-year-old from a middle-class family who spoke perfect English, was raised by a professor and an administrator, and carried the latest Mariah Carey tape in her bag. The roommate's "default position" toward an African, Adichie said, "was a kind of patronizing, well-meaning pity. . . . [she] had a single story of Africa: a single story of catastrophe."

Adichie was forced to confront her own single-story outlook years later on a trip to Guadalajara in Jalisco, Mexico, where her conceptions of Mexicans clashed with the reality she witnessed. Having been immersed in the anti-Mexican U.S. media climate in which stories flowed about illegals sneaking into the country and gaming the health care system, she soon realized she was as single-minded about Mexicans as her former roommate had been about Africans. On her first stroll through the city, she was surprised to see people working, laughing, and shopping, and was immediately struck with "overwhelming shame." Her surprise at the ordinary lives she witnessed came from the fact that Mexicans had become one thing in her mind—"the abject immigrant," she said. "I had bought into the single story of Mexicans and I could not have been more ashamed of myself."

Adichie's story invites us to consider the single-story views about students of color that may be impacting what happens in our schools, especially in our classrooms. The latest figures show that 78% of U.S. school principals are white; 11% are Black; 8% are Latinx; and Asian, American Indian/Alaska Native, and those of two or more races each made up 1% (National Center for Education Statistics, February 2019). In the classroom, 80% of public school teachers are white, 9% are Latinx, 7% are Black, 2% are Asian, 1% are of two or more races, and less than 1% are American Indian/Alaska Native (National Center for Education Statistics, April 2018).

Not only are the vast majority of our school leaders and teachers white, but a white-centered curriculum has traditionally dominated the "stories" that all children learn about the world, knowledge, and how knowledge is made. Principals who challenge their single-story perceptions of Black, Latinx, and other students of color and lead teachers and other staff to do the same hold the key to narrowing our persistent teaching gaps and making education equitable for all children.

Reflect on This
My Single-Story Experiences

After watching Chimamanda Ngozi Adichie's 18-minute TED Talk, "The Danger of a Single Story," linked on this book's website, racialequityleadership .com (Chapter 2 section), ask yourself the following and respond in your journal:

1. Have I ever met someone who surprised me the way Adichie was surprised by the people she observed in Guadalajara? How did I respond in that situation?

2. How can I share this TED Talk with my teachers and staff to start a conversation about racial bias?

Activity
Racial Isolation

Find and visit a place where you are clearly in the racial minority. In this space, you will experience racial isolation instead of a power differential such as those that exist when a white teacher, for example, leads a classroom in which the majority of students are Black and Latinx. Here are a few suggested places:

- An African American hair salon or barbershop (you needn't get your hair done—just observe)

- A Latino Zumba class

- A church, mosque, or temple whose members are predominantly of a race other than your own

- A bar, coffee shop, or ethnically themed mall frequented by a race other than your own

- Any other venue or experience in which you are racially isolated

Write a reflection about your visit in your journal.

Introducing Racial Affinity Work

Deepening our self-knowledge by examining and transforming our "single-story perceptions," beliefs, and behaviors can be uncomfortable.

When working with groups, we have found that organizing members into racial affinity groups creates environments that feel safer. In racial affinity groups, people of the same racial group meet to discuss racism, oppression, and privilege within their workplace or organization. Our institute conducts racial affinity groups in advance of combined discussions about race and educational equity. Affinity sessions are not intended to be used as stand-alone meetings but are designed to add to a community-wide dialogue on racism.

We all have gateways into affinity groups—for white women, it's gender, their level of oppression, and their inclination to start this kind of work. Without oppression issues to draw on, white men typically don't undertake the work, so a white male racial affinity group needs to include at least one white man who understands white privilege. Any dominantly white institution (with its predominantly white male leadership) may be challenged to understand why equity work in general, and racial affinity groups in particular, are important. In research on social service agencies, for example, Blitz and Kohl (2012) reported that racial affinity groups are rarely conducted and state that the literature on antiracism efforts in organizations reveals a pattern of downplaying the concept of white privilege, pulling toward color-blindness, and discouraging conversations about white identity.

In our work, however, we have found that people of color and white people seriously committed to racial equity work find great value in racial affinity groups. Individuals who consider themselves multiracial may choose any affinity group in which they feel they belong. Holding racial affinity group dialogues can be a valuable part of racial equity work among your principal colleagues and in your school because of the following:

- Through talking with people who are like us, we can gain new insights into our own beliefs as well as others'.

- We can practice talking about difficult issues before we join discussions in a mixed racial group.

- We can unpack our own "baggage" before joining dialogues with mixed racial groups.

- Participants gain mutual support and learn that they have a voice in making a difference. Participants build new relationships and trust.

- Participants explore different ways to work with others.

In the following Learning From Mentors section, four graduates of our institute offered their reflections on the impact of participating in the racial affinity groups that were part of our program.

Learning From Mentors

The Value of Racial Affinity Groups

Carla Hines

Principal of a middle school in the Minneapolis metropolitan area, Carla Hines said, "As an African American woman leading a building, it is critical to be a part of a racial affinity group in the field of education. As a leader, I understand that I am not given much room to make a mistake" (C. Hines, personal communication, October 6, 2019). She described the group as a sheltering place for her as a leader who faced the pushback and obstacles that go with racial equity work:

> "The racial affinity group allows me to be in a safe space where I can practice my work as a racial equity leader without the scrutiny of feeling like a failure or that I am not meant to do the work. When I am with my racial equity group, I feel supported, encouraged, and challenged. I am able to learn from my colleagues from their experiences as an African American leader. I can provide coaching and be coached myself in order to continue to persist through the challenges I face in the workplace" (C. Hines, personal communication, October 6, 2019).

***

Todd Goggleye

The principal of a magnet school in a metropolitan district, Todd Goggleye believes that participating in racial affinity groups taught him more about himself as part of his Native American community:

> "For me, racial affinity group work provides an understanding of the historical trauma that has happened with my people, the Ojibwe Nation, and all Native Americans for centuries. It gives me an understanding of other cultural groups: how we are different yet all the same. As a Native American male, I have often been invisible to many white-face people. When I'm invisible I'm not looked at as being a human being or an equal in the human race. Affinity group work has helped me understand the historical trauma, mental health problems, and complex stories we have experienced. They have allowed me to continue to explore how race has shaped my life as an Ojibwe male."

> "The racial affinity group in the principal institute assisted me in understanding the similarities and the differences we experience every day. As an educator, this helps me provide ongoing support in my work with students and staff while coming to an understanding of cultural differences—and an understanding of when we are not yet ready for agreement/closure. As Sitting Bull said, "Let's put our minds together to see what life we can make for our children" (T. Goggleye, personal communication, November 1, 2019).

***

(Continued)

(Continued)

Nan Yurecko

Nan Yurecko, who was working as the executive director of teaching and learning in a metropolitan district when she attended the institute, reflected on her experiences as a white woman leader and member of our white women affinity group with these insights:

> *"Racial affinity groups are an essential component in the identity development of white women and in the process of cultivating our courageous leadership. As females, most of us have experienced some form of oppression. The shared personal experience of oppression provides an avenue for us to connect to the racism experienced by people of color through an emotional linkage."*

For example, one of our white female leaders was working diligently in her district to interrupt predictable disparities for students. She was passionate about this work and it resonated deeply with her because of her Judaism lineage. However, her inability to recognize her privileged position as a white person undermined her sensitivity to racial oppression based on her heritage. Her white female positioning within the American racial hierarchy maintains a persistent racial disconnect as our bonds to whiteness keep us from examining that oppression through the intersection of race.

The group also gave Nan and other white women a closer understanding of the construct of "whiteness":

> *"A frequent misconception is that the social construct of race only applies to people of color. White females are socialized in a manner that tucks away our true racial privilege and entitlement into our subconscious. The racial affinity group provides a space for us to come together in dialogue and better understand ourselves as a racialized group. It becomes a place for us to honestly unpack that socialization, deconstruct segregationist and assimilationist conditioning, and bring to our consciousness those experiences that have intentionally or unintentionally inhibited our ability to see racial inequities. Being able to do so in the absence of white males enables white females to engage in conversations about race without the presence of power, and without the fear of imperfection in front of colleagues of color, thereby creating a safe harbor for unlearning and relearning."*

She then shares the example of a principal in the group who was struggling with a painful new realization:

> *"As white females discover the normalcy in which we have been racialized, it requires us to dig deeper to forgive ourselves for not recognizing this system, for unconsciously or consciously participating in it, and for perpetuating it further through silence even after increasing our understanding of the impact of race on our own lives and the lives*

of others. During one group session, a leader broke down in tears when she shared how her daughter adversely reacted on the first day of preschool when being introduced to her new Black female teacher. The leader had not realized until observing the behavior of her child that, although she demonstrated a certain level of racial consciousness in her daily work for students, she had actually been isolating her own family from having meaningful interactions and relationships with people of color. Our racial affinity group helped her resolve the cognitive dissonance in that lived experience."

Nan continues with insights about the healing and new sense of responsibility and empowerment she experienced by participating in the group. She concludes with a statement about her understanding that as a white person, she "is the system":

"Since white females are encultured to associate blatant and horrific acts with racism rather than indirect and subtle daily occurrences, the racial affinity group is a means for resolving feelings of guilt, shame, and embarrassment that often accompany our perceived immunity to the consequences of racism. It serves as a forum for healing as we try to make sense of and work through those tensions that both prevent us and propel us to effect change within ourselves, our families, our communities, and the educational systems in which we work. And then after my racial consciousness has been raised and I have grappled with my part in it, I am changed so I have a responsibility to act. The racial affinity group empowers white females to move beyond awakening and into action. The group becomes a supportive network where we thoughtfully examine our roles as allies to people of color and determine how we can responsibly, with care and dignity, exercise the white privilege that we have inherited."

The racial affinity group deepens my racial purpose and nurtures my confidence so that I can successfully implement the leadership strategies necessary to dismantle the racial inequities in my system. I am the system, and communicating my own challenges and listening to the experiences of other white female leaders strengthens my fortitude to push forward through uncharted waters. I am no longer willing to sit idle on the shore, and I now know I am capable of steering through the waves along the way (N. Yurecko, personal communication, October 7, 2019).

***

Michael Elston

A high school assistant principal from a medium-sized district, Michael Elston attributes significant development in his racial consciousness to affinity group work:

(Continued)

(Continued)

"As a white man committed to equity and antiracism, I believe it is crucial to understand the importance of racial affinity groups as a place where two critical things occur. One is the space created for Black and Brown people to have an honest dialogue with one another without the need to code switch, placate, or try to make white people feel comfortable. This allows a freedom of thought and an ability to challenge and hone thinking and understanding without the stress, anxiety, or toxicity that exist in our racialized society. The "good chemicals" that are released in the brain in a safe space allow for the highest level of thinking and learning. As a white man, I need to give up the idea that I should be entitled to know what everyone else is talking about while often keeping my own thoughts and feelings private. As a principal, this means setting up structures for people in racial groups that are not white to openly discuss their experiences with no need for me to be a part of it or to dictate that they report to me. The point of a racial affinity group is to be a space for free conversation, and giving up my potential need or want to control the thoughts and minds of others is a step toward freedom."

The second critical aspect of racial affinity groups is what occurs when white people get together to discuss race and racism. Not only does this help white people understand their own racialization, but it can be a place where white people learn to bond through antiracism. This runs counter to the status quo in which white people bond in a dream world where they pretend that racism doesn't exist. White affinity groups provide a space and a context for white people to deconstruct and understand the role and presence of whiteness in their lives. Many of my most meaningful learning experiences have come from confronting and discussing whiteness with other white folk. The problem of racism must be owned by white people, and the onus to change falls on the shoulders of white people like me. Ensuring the space for racial affinity groups is one place to start (M. Elston, personal communication, November 26, 2019).

Knowing yourself, your purpose and "why," mission and vision, and beliefs and behaviors has moved you through a large section of the "knowing" phase of the Theory of Action pathway. The final work in this phase focuses on knowing the research-proven best practices in education that will guide your leadership with a strong foundation.

References

Adichie, C. N. (2009, July). *The danger of a single story* [Video file]. Retrieved from https://www.ted.com/talks/chimamanda_adichie_the_danger_of_a_single_story/transcript#t-292433.

Blitz, L. V., & Kohl, B. G., Jr. (2012). Addressing racism in the organization: The role of white racial affinity groups in creating change. *Administration in Social Work, 36*(5), 479–498. doi:10.1080/03643107.2011.624261 or https://doi.org/10.1080/03643107.2011.624261

Cliatt-Wayman, L. (2015, June 5). *How to fix a broken school? Lead fearlessly, love hard* [Video file]. Retrieved from https://www.youtube.com/watch?v=Xe2nlti47kA.

Gupta, R., Koscik, T. R., Bechara, A. & Tranel, D. (2011). The amygdala and decision making. *Neuropsychologia, 49*(4): 760–766.

López, I. F. H. (1995). The social construction of race. In R. Delgado (Ed.), *Critical race theory: The cutting edge* (pp. 191–203). Philadelphia: Temple University Press. (Original work published 1994)

National Center for Education Statistics. (April 2018). *Characteristics of public school teachers.* Retrieved from https://nces.ed.gov/programs/coe/indicator_clr.asp.

National Center for Education Statistics. (February 2019). *Characteristics of public school principals.* Retrieved from https://nces.ed.gov/programs/coe/indicator_cls.asp.

Sinek, S. (2009). *Start with why: How great leaders inspire everyone to take action.* New York: Portfolio/Penguin.

Research Reality Check

CHAPTER 3

Key Frameworks for Understanding Ourselves, the System, and Best Practices in Teaching and Leading

Anti-oppression education is a lifelong commitment. . . . The nature of anti-oppression begs one to re-examine one's power relations, one's privilege(s) in relation to other groups, to consider how our multiple locations may shift and change depending on the spaces we occupy.

—Junie Désil (2005)

To reverse segregation in the district's math program, Astein Osei, his teaching and learning team, and math design team members built a strategy based on years of racial equity work in education. The Black male superintendent of a suburban district bordering Minneapolis, Astein recognized that the majority-white middle school honors math classes contained basically the same curriculum as the grade-level math classes in which the majority of the students were children of color. The only real difference was the racially segregated spaces in which they were taught. In 2019 he and his team revised the course sequence, which brought all the students together at grade level and gave students access to the same rigorous math opportunities. He and his team also created a structure that allowed any student to grade-level accelerate, which was an instructional practice that had not been offered in the past.

Once this strategy was set, Astein knew he had two basic options for explaining the change to the district's stakeholders, particularly its white teachers and families. One approach would call out the segregated programs for what they were, to announce that the district was "blowing up" the racist math structure because such systems would not be tolerated. "While that's a very truthful pathway, I anticipated that we would eventually hear from people in our community concerned about what these would mean for the rigor students would experience in class. I also recognized that this pathway could lead to the mental model that we are dumbing down the curriculum for 'those kids,' which often comes up in these types of program/curricular changes," he said (A. Osei, personal communication, December 20, 2019). Instead, he chose to talk about the district-wide change connected to the strategic direction of the district and how it aligned with the math programs in some of the metro area's most affluent suburban schools. Since many considered those schools academically rigorous environments, the community would be more likely to embrace the structural change. Rather than frame the change as a disruption of racial segregation, the message emphasized the benefits—that all children would now have access to highly rigorous academic courses and the opportunity for grade-level advancement if they were able to demonstrate proficiency at grade level—just like the schools in the wealthiest suburbs.

Astein recognized that racism had upheld the segregated math sequence, since racism is embedded in education just as it is throughout American society. "Sometimes it's not the intentional, outwardly blatant racism that upholds inequity," he said, "but unconscious racism. We have to undo that in our schools because segregated tracking systems are harmful not only to students of color and Indigenous students but also to white students." He believes the type of messaging he used about the change will ultimately serve all the students best. "Option A about reversing a racist practice evokes emotions that can undermine the work," he said. "Leading with Option B, talking about the benefits as positive comparisons to other schools, gives us more time to implement the plan and get it in place."

Astein firmly believes that there are other ways to approach racial equity work more along the lines of Option A but that this type of change is only possible when people have developed their racial awareness. The strategy he is using may be more incremental in nature, he says, but it appears to be more sustainable as it allows for the interest of students and families to converge:

> I have colleagues in other districts who choose to address racist systems full-on, calling out racism while leading change. As a leader, I believe there are instances where that is necessary as that is a more liberating approach to the work. I chose an interest convergence approach in this situation because I don't have evidence that a more intensive, completely disruptive approach would have been sustainable over time. Due to the permanence of racism in American society, as a leader I have to make strategic decisions that interrupt racist practices while considering the sustainability of the interruption. Systems are made up of people, and people have to do their own work. In our district we believe that the more we can help people increase their own racial consciousness first, the more we will be able to sustain and deepen our racial equity work. The first

thing you have to do as an educator is to learn about the impact of race and culture on your personal lived experience and how you navigate through the world, whether you are a person of color, Indigenous, or white (A. Osei, personal communication, December 20, 2019).

The new math structure in Astein's district gives students of color access to a rigorous math experience. His messaging strategy was based on what he has learned from experience and, as you will see in this chapter, his understanding of critical race theory, implicit bias, and the ways white people respond to racial equity issues.

As white women educators (authors Raskin and Krull) who have led school districts, we understand why Astein is strategic about his messaging in his equity work. When we took a more aggressive approach in our districts, describing our strategies with language around "race," "racial equity," and undoing "racist practices," we met strong, ongoing resistance from many in the white community. We have observed that leaders of color face this and the additional burden of being tagged as "the race leader" and are often perceived as combative and antiwhite. This can shut down much of the work of building racial capacity. We discuss how to deal with resistance in Chapter 6, but it is important to recognize in Astein's story that navigating white perceptions is always part of building capacity for racial equity and is doubly challenging for leaders of color.

While resources about principal leadership for racial equity are scant, we have built much of our work on four key areas of theory and research. This foundation begins with critical race theory, the blueprint for understanding and addressing issues of race in many fields. Next, white fragility gives us detailed insights into the challenges of talking about race and how to overcome them. Finally, the visible learning and Pedagogy of Confidence models of teaching and learning offer groundbreaking alternatives to educational paradigms that have perpetuated underachievement for students of color.

Critical Race Theory

Developed by legal scholars in the 1970s (Delgado & Stefancic, 2012), critical race theory (CRT) is a framework for analyzing and addressing the connections among race, racism, and power. Equity-minded scholars frustrated with the slow gains of racial equity formulated the theory to examine how the "regime of white supremacy and its subordination of people of color" has been created and perpetuated through the law (Crenshaw, Gotanda, Peller, & Thomas, 1995, p. xvi). Since then, this form of critique has spread to other fields, including education, and transformed how we discuss and understand race and strategize ways to create equity.

Critical race theory includes a social justice focus that gives it a central place in learning to lead for racial equity. The tenets of CRT help us not only understand what is happening in our schools and communities (and inside ourselves in terms of our beliefs and assumptions) but also empower us to challenge the status quo. When we are aware of the power dynamics of racism and how they are constructed, we can deconstruct them and make real change.

The key tenets of CRT include the theme that racism is ordinary in our society. Rather than an atypical or unusual phenomenon, racism is business as usual, the way things are, a fact of life that oppresses people of color every day. In the words of the late legal scholar Derrick Bell (1992), considered the intellectual father of the theory, racism "lies at the center, not the periphery; in the permanent, not in the fleeting; in the real lives of Black and white people, not in the sentimental caverns of the mind" (p. 198). Because white experience/perspective permeates and dominates society as the "norm" and white Americans do not face disadvantages based on their race, racism is largely unacknowledged. As we discussed in Chapter 1, people are socialized about race throughout their lives in conscious and unconscious ways, and white people can spend their entire lives unconscious of their role in perpetuating racism (or their white privilege, which we will get to later).

Many white people who are consciously unaware of systemic racism and adopt the color-blind ideology ("I do not see race, only people") believe that treating everyone as equal, without regard to race or ethnicity, will end discrimination. By declaring that race doesn't matter, this outlook is a form of racism itself, as it denies the negative racial experiences of people of color. Sociologist Bonilla-Silva (2006) contends that color-blind racism is a "new powerful ideology" that has emerged "to defend the contemporary racial order" (p. 25). In our schools as in all our institutions, the injustices of the racial order cannot be remedied until racism is acknowledged.

A second key tenet of CRT is the theory of interest convergence, which holds that civil rights victories for Blacks are achieved only when the interests of Blacks and whites converge. Examples abound to support this theory that white people will *only* promote racial justice for Blacks and other nonwhite people when they see some benefit in it for themselves. Astein Osei applied this tenet when he developed his messaging to his white stakeholders about desegregating his district's math program, emphasizing the benefits for all (including white) students.

In another famous example, Bell (1995) contended that three factors of interest to whites led to the Supreme Court's 1954 *Brown v. Board of Education* decision that prohibited segregation in public schools—and a sudden moral awakening about racial equity was not one of them. In reality, U.S. policymakers in the 1950s Cold War era were competing with the Soviet Union to win the hearts and minds of people from developing nations. Ending school segregation—a sudden break from the "separate but equal" doctrine that had blocked desegregation efforts in the courts for decades—sent a global message that the United States respected all races. The Court's landmark decision also came at a time of rising anger and resentment among southern Black World War II veterans who had come home to violent attacks and discrimination. A major civil rights action like *Brown v. Board* could possibly quell some of that sentiment or at least prevent it from spreading. Finally, Bell (1995) observed that some southern whites were eager to end the conflict over school segregation in order to prioritize a shift from rural agriculture to a more profitable industrialized economy. Legal arguments to ban segregation in the schools had been brought to the courts for 60 years, with no impact. But in 1954 these three white concerns combined to create a perfect storm of opportunity for whites to promote a civil rights victory like *Brown v. Board of Education.*

A more recent example of interest convergence in education comes from the University of Missouri, where racial tensions that had existed for decades exploded into white shouts of racial slurs and other incidents targeting Blacks and Jews in 2014. Students and faculty protested and demanded action from the white university president for 3 months, but the president did nothing to address the problem. Not until the football team—which brought in millions of dollars in revenue for the university—boycotted practices and games did the administration take action: the president resigned and the chancellor stepped down to another role.

The theme of race as a social construct, a third tenet of CRT, asserts that race and races are categories invented and manipulated by society. Skin color and hair texture may be common traits of people with shared origins; however, these very small fractions of our genetic makeup do not biologically define a fixed "racial" category. In spite of this scientific reality, society creates races—groups with pseudo-permanent characteristics—to manufacture difference. Human beings share virtually the same genetic endowment other than the minuscule physical variations noted above, and as Delgado and Stefancic (2012) explain, these variations have no connection to "distinctly human, higher-order traits, such as personality, intelligence, and moral behavior" (pp. 8–9). Perhaps more than any other tenet, this "social construction" theme of CRT defines race—and its origins—as a relationship of power. Pulido (2006) describes the "idea of race" as an ideology that arose with imperialism and colonization:

> A justification was needed to help rationalize taking over other countries and peoples, whether by usurping their resources, appropriating them as colonies, or enslaving them. The . . . notions of biological inferiority and superiority gave conquering forces ideological tools to dehumanize their victims and legitimize their actions. That racial ideologies are still with us . . . suggests that they are still useful in shaping contemporary power relations. (p. 22)

One way these ideologies have persisted in "shaping" power relations is through another social construct, the fear of Black people, or negrophobia. Like the invention of race, white society's history of equating Blackness with being criminal results in discrimination and violence targeting people of color. Writing about the fatal shooting of Trayvon Martin by a white male member of Neighborhood Watch, George Zimmerman, in Sanford, Florida, in 2012, Tyrone Howard (2014) states, "What has been persistent for the better part of four centuries is that Black maleness in all of its totality has often been viewed as a menace. . . . The idea that . . . a 17-year-old Black male wearing a hoodie must be guilty of some type of criminal activity has become normalized" (pp. xi–xii). Critical race theory's focus on social constructions invites us to analyze this normalization from the historical context Howard (2014) describes, such as through a comparison of the lists in Figure 3.1. A police-shooting database adds another dimension to these lists, revealing that an unarmed Black man is about 4 times more likely to be killed by police than an unarmed white man (Fox, Blanco, Jenkins, Tate, & Lowery, 2019). The social construct of fear also asks us, How would you feel if society taught everyone to fear you?

Related to the theme that race is a social construct, another key tenet of CRT addresses the way the dominant group racializes groups differently over time to serve its own needs. This phenomenon, called

Figure 3.1   Racial Comparison of Fatal Police Shootings

SHORT LIST OF UNARMED BLACK MALES FATALLY SHOT BY POLICE	
• Oscar Grant, 2009	• Alton Sterling, 2016
• Trayvon Martin, 2012	• Philando Castile, 2016
• Michael Brown, 2014	• Stephon Clark, 2018
• Tamir Rice, 2014	• Botham Jean, 2018
• Jamar Clark, 2015	• Atatiana Jefferson, 2019 (female)
• Walter Scott, 2015	• Breonna Taylor, 2020 (female)
	• Dijon Kizzee, 2020

ARMED WHITE MALES ARRESTED WITHOUT INCIDENT	
• Timothy McVeigh, 1995, "Oklahoma bomber," killed 168	• James Holmes, 2012, shot up a movie theater in Aurora, CO, killing 12 and wounding 70
• Ted Kaczynski, 1995, "Unabomber," killed 3, wounded 23	• Dylan Roof, 2015, shot and killed 9 Black people having a Bible study in a South Carolina church
• Jared Loughner, 2011, shot Congresswoman Gabrielle Giffords and killed 6	• Jason Dalton, 2016, randomly shot and killed 6 in Kalamazoo, MI
• Nikolas Cruz, 2018, shot and killed 17 in Parkland High School, FL	

differential racialization, affects the shifting way a group is treated legally, socially, and economically. Consider how Mexicans were stereotyped by white farm owners in the nineteenth century as lacking ambition or skills beyond fieldwork, willing to work for low wages, and better able to tolerate stooping to pick crops than whites because they were shorter in height. That set of stereotypes justified the landowners' view of Mexicans as ideal workers who could be exploited as cheap labor (Pulido, 2006). In recent years, a different set of Mexican stereotypes flooded American society to promote a political stance on immigration policy. The president of the United States (and, by their silence, members of his political party also in power) propagated stereotypes of undocumented Mexican immigrants as criminals, drug dealers, rapists, and "animals" (Korte & Gomez, 2018). In both examples, negative stereotypes supported the aims of the dominant group.

Another key tenet of CRT is *intersectionality*, the idea that the multiple aspects of a person's identity (e.g., race, gender, class, sexual orientation) create overlapping experiences of discrimination. Kimberlé Crenshaw (1989), one of the founders of CRT, coined the term to describe the compounded ways that Black women are unjustly treated in society. Crenshaw (1989) argued that the courts, feminist scholars, and civil rights thinkers have approached Black women's issues in one-dimensional ways that do not capture the reality of their lives: "Black women's experiences are much broader than the general categories that discrimination discourse provides. . . . Often they experience double-discrimination—the combined effects of practices which discriminate on the basis of race, and on the basis of sex" (p. 149). The concept of intersectionality helps us understand that the "unique compoundedness" (p. 150) of identity creates experiences of oppression that are greater than the sum of their parts. A Black woman who works a minimum-wage job, for example, may regularly face racial, gender, and class discrimination, such as being a) the target of racist comments by coworkers or customers, b) passed over for better work opportunities because her supervisor prefers men in those roles, and c) unable to access health care in her low-income neighborhood. These combined experiences impact the woman's life in a way that only she and perhaps other Black women in the same circumstances can describe, which leads us to the final tenet.

The unique voice of color principle of critical race theory challenges the dominant white narrative within our laws and policies, including the policies we put forth in our schools. This tenet asserts that the lived experiences of people of color give them knowledge that white people do not possess, and that this knowledge is "appropriate, legitimate, and an integral part to analyzing and understanding racial inequality" (Lee, 2008, p. 14). Voices of color, traditionally silenced in our "racism is ordinary" society, are put center stage in CRT because they carry a "presumed competence to speak about race and racism" (Delgado & Stefancic, 2012, p. 10).

Without the perspective of people of color in our institute (or in this book), our knowledge of how implicit bias and systemic racism impact teaching and principal leadership is incomplete, to say the least. White people of privilege cannot begin to see and feel the depth of systemic racism and the pain, violence, and lack of voice/agency that goes along with it. We can only get an accurate picture of what is happening from the voices of people of color. Black scholar David Stovall (2014) describes this tenet as "critical race counter storytelling, where the lives of people of color are contrasted against mainstream assumptions on our lives" (p. 9).

Derald Wing Sue's (2015) work on racial dialogues compares "white talk," statements of white beliefs about society, and "Back talk," statements that counter those assumptions. Examples of "White Talk: The Master Narrative," include "Anyone who works hard enough can succeed in society," "People should be color-blind and not judge one another by the color of their skin," and "Racism is abhorrent, but is now a thing of the past" (slide 10). This narrative maintains white people's innocence and naiveté about systemic racism and perpetuates the racial status quo. Sue (2015) explains that "ultimately, the function of white talk is to justify inaction" (slide 10). "Back Talk: The Counternarrative" contains statements designed to challenge this master narrative:

- We live in a society that advantages some groups while disadvantaging others.

- It is ordinary white people, not the white supremacist, who do the most harm to people of color.

- Whites often do not treat others with fairness and respect, but in prejudicial and discriminatory ways.

- White people seem adverse to seeking the truth about racism and engage in self-deception.

- Equal access and opportunity are falsehoods.

- Meritocracy is a myth.

- Color-blindness is impossible and it perpetuates inequities.

- Racism is alive, well and thriving in the current times.

  In other words, we do not live in a post-racial era. Back talk threatens to reveal the ugly racist White secrets of society. (Sue, 2015, slide 14)

This type of counterstorytelling by people of color and their white allies can create dialogues that chip away at false beliefs and move the story forward to social change.

The six key themes of critical race theory described here give us a scheme for recognizing, discussing, analyzing, and finding solutions for systemic racism. Each element helps school leaders understand that society has framed racism as an individual and not a social problem—a fact borne out in educational paradigms that blame students of color for low achievement scores and high suspension rates rather than the adults who teach them and lead their schools.

Reflect on This

"Just Being a Tiny Bit Racist Is Enough"

In 2017, the New Zealand Human Rights Commission launched an anti-racism campaign with a video featuring one of its biggest celebrities, actor and movie director Taika Waititi, who is of Maori descent. Waititi uses comic irony to drive home a message about the persistence of racism. Watch the less-than-2-minute video linked to the Chapter 3 section of this book's website at racialequityleadership.com and ask yourself these questions:

1. How do tiny bits of racism enter your life?

2. How have you been just a tiny bit racist?

3. As leaders, if you don't *plan* to keep racism out of your schools, it *will* get in. At this point in your equity journey, what's your plan?

White Fragility

The first tenet of critical race theory, the idea that racism is embedded as the normal, permanent state of our society, speaks to the largely unconscious, complicit relationship white people have with racism. Robin DiAngelo (2011) has supplied us with a broader understanding of that relationship with her work on white fragility, the term she coined for a specific aspect of white privilege. If white privilege is "an invisible package of unearned assets" (MacIntosh, 1988, p. 1) that most white people are unaware they possess, white fragility is the inability to talk about race or acknowledge that privileged status. Due to white fragility, the slightest challenge to a white person's racial worldview creates intolerable stress, as if the person's identity as a good, moral person has been questioned or attacked. In short, DiAngelo (2011) writes, "Socialized into a deeply internalized sense of superiority that we either are unaware of or can never admit to ourselves, we become highly fragile in conversations about race" (p. 2).

When white people live a segregated white existence throughout their childhood and adulthood and are never told they are missing something in that isolation, they also internalize this message: There is no inherent value in the perspective or experiences of people of color (DiAngelo, 2017). This "knowing," however deep below the surface, perpetuates the status quo of racism as ordinary in society. DiAngelo (2011) describes the segregated lives of most white people as one of seven factors that lead to white fragility.

The second factor is the dual category of universalism and individualism. When white people view themselves as "universal humans," the representation of "people" in general (DiAngelo, 2011, p. 59), they can adopt the view that we should see everyone as the same (colorblindness). This distances them from reality by denying issues of race and the privileges of being white. Whites are also taught to value themselves as individuals and be oblivious of belonging to a "racially socialized group" (p. 59), which distances them from the actions of white society. Another factor underlying white fragility is white people's sense of entitlement to racial comfort. Having never been challenged about their race, they have not built up a tolerance for racial discomfort and are triggered into a variety of responses. Shutting down or blaming and retaliating against whoever caused the discomfort ensures that nothing will change. "White insistence on racial comfort ensures that racism will not be faced" (p. 61). The fourth factor, racial arrogance, stems from a strong sense of entitlement based on a positive perspective of the white self and negative perspective of nonwhites. Ignoring white privilege, whites believe they have built their success on their own efforts. While they have little or no understanding of racism, their racial arrogance gives them no qualms about debating the subject with experts and then trivializing that expertise.

As members of the dominant society, white people see their own racial image everywhere. This creates another factor underlying white fragility: a sense of racial belonging. This largely unconscious sense is taken for granted, and on the rare occasion that it is interrupted, the experience is "destabilizing and frightening" (DiAngelo, 2011, p. 62). Placed in a white affinity group, for example, people can feel "a curious sense of loss" over the "disorienting sense of themselves as not just people, but most particularly white people" (p. 62). The sixth factor, psychic freedom, comes from not having to take on the social burden of race. By perceiving race as an issue only for people of color, white people can dismiss it and expend their psychological energy elsewhere. As a result, they do not gain the stamina necessary to talk about the uncomfortable subject of race.

Finally, white fragility grows out of the constant messages that white people are more valuable—through representation in everything. Whites as the central figures in TV shows and textbooks, on magazine covers and in films, as teachers, and in religious imagery are some of the ways "we receive constant messages that we are better and more important than people of color" (DiAngelo, 2011, p. 63). The message of white superiority becomes internalized, regardless of how genuinely someone believes they are not better than someone else.

The previous factors prevent white people from having productive, self-reflective conversations about race. Instead, when our assumptions and behaviors are challenged we react emotionally, feeling attacked, shamed, insulted, outraged, judged, frightened, or accused (DiAngelo, 2018). Common behaviors that go along with these feelings include physically leaving the scene, denying, arguing, avoiding, emotionally withdrawing, and crying. We then make claims in an attempt to prove that we've been falsely accused, such as "I just said one little innocent thing," "I know people of color," "That is just your opinion," "Some people find offense where there is none," "You misunderstood me," "You're playing the race card," or "You don't know me" (pp. 119–120).

Each of these behaviors and defenses cancels out the opportunity for dialogue and accomplishes one thing: perpetuating racism. Understanding this crucial, challenging aspect of talking about race helps school leaders prepare for the responses they will encounter in their buildings and communities.

Reflect on This
Exploring White Fragility

Robin DiAngelo presents a valuable and accessible overview of white fragility in the video, "Deconstructing White Privilege with Dr. Robin DiAngelo," which you can view via the link in the Chapter 3 section of racialequityleadership.com. After watching this 22-minute presentation, answer the following in your journal:

1. As a leader, where do you see white fragility in your work?

2. What does responding to white fragility look like to you?

Visible Learning: Part I

In addition to the theoretical areas of critical race theory and white fragility, the key foundations of our work for training leaders for racial equity involves the instructional models put forth by John Hattie and Yvette Jackson.

For the past 25 years, John Hattie of the University of Melbourne, Australia, has done groundbreaking research to identify the most effective teaching practices. His first book, *Visible Learning* (Hattie, 2009), offered a synthesis of over 800 meta-analyses about factors that impact achievement. As of 2019, his expanded research is based on more than 1,600 meta-analyses involving more than 95,000 studies examining the achievement of 300 million students around the world (Corwin Visible Learning, 2020). This evidence-based research into what actually does and does not work to improve learning presents one overall principle: The most successful learning occurs when teachers see learning through the eyes of the student (visible teaching) and students see themselves as their own teachers (visible learning).

Visible teaching means teachers regularly evaluate the effects of their teaching and adjust their methods accordingly. The critical point is that teachers see themselves as evaluators of their effects on students and develop a mind frame in which they see this as their primary role. The fourth item about progress in the brief overview of actions involved in visible learning in Figure 3.2 addresses this concept. The greatest influence on student achievement is not a teacher's specific methods or ideas but her beliefs and commitments. To transform schools to places where the primary focus is on learning and impact rather than on teaching and inputs we need to work with our ways of thinking—or mind frames—about teaching and learning, because these underlying thoughts affect the decisions we make as educators.

Figure 3.2 The Art of Visible Teaching and Learning

WHAT EXPERT TEACHERS DO . . .	SO THAT STUDENTS
• Provide clear learning intentions	• Understand learning intentions
• Develop challenging success criteria	• Are challenged by success criteria
• Create a range of learning strategies	• Develop a range of learning strategies
• Know when students are not progressing	• Know when they are not progressing
• Provide feedback	• Seek feedback
• Visibly learn themselves	• Visibly teach themselves

Source: Moffat, J. (n.d.). What is visible learning? Ealing Education Authority, ealing.gov.uk

Hattie (2012) argues that a school principal's beliefs about his or her role is "the core lever with which to create schools that lead to enhanced impact" (p. 174). Principals who assume the role of creating a collaborative learning environment of achievement, which encompasses several of the mind frames listed below, encourage teachers to "engage in evaluating their impact and then using this evidence to enhance their teaching" (p. 174). Education consultant and author Peter DeWitt (2016), who has worked with Hattie as a visible learning trainer, provides the following overview of Hattie's mind frames (the italicized texts are our additions).

The 10 Mind Frames of Visible Learning

As a teacher or school leader . . .

1. **I am an evaluator.**

   Teachers/leaders believe that the "best" teaching does not mean employing the top teaching methods; rather, it involves altering instruction "on the fly" based on feedback about the effects they are having on students.

   Evaluation isn't just about the formal evaluation that comes down from the state education department and district offices. As educators we all have to evaluate whether our practices are bringing out the best learning in our students. After all, in Hattie's words, we have to *"know thy impact."*

2. **I am a change agent.**

   Teachers/leaders believe that success and failure in student learning is about what they as teachers/leaders did or did not do. They are the change agents who take responsibility for enhancing student learning and setting high expectations.

   In these days of more accountability and more on the plates of teachers and leaders, it's easy to feel as though we are victims of our present educational situations. Hattie believes we have to change our mind-sets to understanding we are change agents. This is important, because research shows that when teachers have a low level of efficacy they feel as though they don't have any impact on student learning, which doesn't put them in the role of change agent at all. It's important for leaders to establish a school climate that fosters an increased sense of teacher efficacy so that they can build collective teacher efficacy as a staff and help teachers realize they may be one of the only change agents in a child's life.

3. **I talk about learning and not about teaching.**

   Teachers/leaders need to recognize that they mostly talk about teaching, and instead they need to learn how to discuss student learning.

   When we talk about teaching we are focusing on the adult in the room and very often forget about the students. The adult is important, but focusing on the student is more important. In *The Politics of Distraction*, Hattie wrote that school stakeholders, policymakers, and politicians talk a great deal about the adult issues in school, such as unions, prep time, and teacher evaluation, but not enough time discussing learning.

4. **I see assessment as feedback to me.**

   Of course assessment is about the student, but teachers/leaders need to begin to see classroom assessment as feedback for the

(Continued)

(Continued)

teacher as well. Who did you teach well and who not so well? What did you teach well and not so well?

Ward et al. wrote that schools are awash with data, but very often the data that we all have access to is not used at the depth that it could be because data has been used as a *"gotcha"* instead of a tool that could lead to deeper conversations. What sort of formative assessment are we doing to make sure that what we are doing in the classroom is actually working?

5. **I engage in dialogue, not monologue.**

   Currently, classrooms are dominated by teacher talk. There is a major need for teachers/leaders to see their role as listeners. They should listen to students' questions, their ideas, their struggles, their strategies of learning, their successes, and their interactions with peers.

   Do we engage in dialogue where we listen to the thoughts of the person on the other side of the conversation, or do we use the conversation to merely get our own self-interests across? In the classroom with students, do teachers listen to students or just lecture and talk at students without giving them enough time to debate and discuss?

6. **I enjoy challenge.**

   Teachers/leaders enjoy the challenge and never retreat to "doing their best." The teacher's/leader's role is not to decide on a challenge and break it into small pieces for the student but rather to engage the student in the challenge.

   Hattie believes we spend too much time giving students answers to questions that they struggle with in the classroom instead of taking the opportunity to teach them that error is the best way to learn. It's through error that they dig deep within themselves. This will work better if, at a young age, we teach students that learning is not always easy, which is one of the greatest parts of it.

7. **I engage in positive relationships.**

   Teachers/leaders believe it is their role to develop positive relationships with students. Classrooms are safe harbors for error, and staff rooms are safe places for teachers to talk about their impact on student learning.

   Hattie's work has shown that teacher–student relationships have an effect size of .72, which is nearly double the hinge point (.40) he found through his research that offers a year's worth of growth for a year's input. Positive relationships, whether through teacher–student relationships or the relationships students have with peers, can have an enormous benefit.

8. **I use the language of learning.**

   To enhance the engagement of students in their learning, educators/leaders must bring parents into the experience as well. Teachers/leaders inform families about the language of learning.

   The focus on learning is important, which is why we need to talk about it more than we talk about teaching. However, having common language around learning is the crucial next step.

9. **I see learning as hard work.**

   All of the above mind frames come together in this mind frame. Engaging in dialogue, diving deeply into assessment data, teaching students about learning dispositions, and becoming change agents is no easy task, which is why learning is hard work.

10. **I collaborate.**

   Hattie not only has 10 mind frames, but within his research he found 150 influences on learning, which continues to grow. "I collaborate" is crucial to the influence that is near the top spot, which is collective teacher efficacy. We, as adults, teach students about the importance of collaboration. . . . Unfortunately, adults still don't collaborate as grade levels and departments nearly as often as they should.

We explore Hattie's (2019) influences more fully and discover strategies for working with the mind frames in Chapter 6. For now, examine how your leadership and the teaching in your school aligns with the visible learning ways of thinking in the following exercise. The reflection exercise that follows it, "My Mind Frames," invites you to delve more deeply into each mind frame from your current perspective.

Activity
Mind Frames in My School

1	2	3	4	5	6
STRONGLY DISAGREE	GENERALLY DISAGREE	PARTLY DISAGREE	PARTLY AGREE	GENERALLY AGREE	STRONGLY AGREE

In this school, the school leaders

a) believe that their fundamental task is to evaluate the effect of their teaching on students' learning and achievement.	1 2 3 4 5 6
b) believe that success and failure in student learning is about what they, as teachers or leaders, did or did not do. . . . We are change agents!	1 2 3 4 5 6

(Continued)

(Continued)

1 STRONGLY DISAGREE	2 GENERALLY DISAGREE	3 PARTLY DISAGREE	4 PARTLY AGREE	5 GENERALLY AGREE	6 STRONGLY AGREE
c) want to talk more about the learning than the teaching.					1 2 3 4 5 6
d) see assessment as feedback about their impact.					1 2 3 4 5 6
e) engage in dialogue not monologue.					1 2 3 4 5 6
f) enjoy the challenge and never retreat to "doing their best."					1 2 3 4 5 6
g) believe it is their role to develop positive relationships in classrooms/staffrooms.					1 2 3 4 5 6
h) inform all about the language of learning.					1 2 3 4 5 6
In this school, the teachers					
a) believe that their fundamental task is to evaluate the effect of their teaching on students' learning and achievement.					1 2 3 4 5 6
b) believe that success and failure in student learning is about what they, as teachers or leaders, did or did not do. . . . We are change agents!					1 2 3 4 5 6
c) want to talk more about the learning than the teaching.					1 2 3 4 5 6
d) see assessment as feedback about their impact.					1 2 3 4 5 6
e) engage in dialogue not monologue.					1 2 3 4 5 6
f) enjoy the challenge and never retreat to "doing their best."					1 2 3 4 5 6
g) believe it is their role to develop positive relationships in classrooms/staffrooms.					1 2 3 4 5 6
h) inform all about the language of learning.					1 2 3 4 5 6

Source: Adapted from Hattie (2012).

Reflect on This

My Mind Frames

Mind frames work is not a step-by-step program but a philosophy of the most effective ways of thinking about teaching and learning, based on rigorous research. How many of the mind frames do you already embrace in your leadership? In the following spaces, note where you currently stand with each mind frame. Do you already think this way? Is the idea new to you? Do you agree with, disagree with, or question the idea? Do some mind frames strike you as more impactful than others?

1. I am an evaluator. _____

_____

2. I am a change agent. _____

_____

3. I talk about learning and not about teaching. _____

_____

4. I see assessment as feedback to me. _____

_____

5. I engage in dialogue, not monologue. _____

_____

6. I enjoy challenge. _____

_____

7. I engage in positive relationships. _____

_____

8. I use the language of learning. _____

_____

9. I see learning as hard work. _____

_____

10. I collaborate. _____

_____

High Operational Practices: Pedagogy of Confidence: Part I

The Pedagogy of Confidence, Yvette Jackson's approach to urban education, is based on her experiences as a teacher in Yonkers, New York, where she observed the high intellectual performance of her urban students; her expertise in gifted education that includes her service as the director of gifted programs for the New York City Public Schools; and her studies in cognitive psychology and neuroscience. The Pedagogy of Confidence rejects the deficit culture of urban education with its focus on student weaknesses and high rates of enrolling students of color in special education programs. In contrast, Jackson's approach focuses on student strengths and empowering teachers to fearlessly stand up against traditional practices. With "confidence in their ability to inspire, elicit, and build on [student] strengths," teachers enable "the high intellectual performance that encourages self-directed learning and self-actualization" (Jackson, 2011, p. 4). As the CEO of the National Urban Alliance for Effective Education, founded at Teachers College at Columbia University, Jackson presents the Pedagogy of Confidence throughout the world and consults with school districts across the country.

To reverse student underachievement and cultivate their high intellectual performance, the Pedagogy of Confidence adheres to three beliefs gleaned from cognitive psychology:

1. Intelligence is modifiable.

2. All students benefit from a focus on high intellectual performance.

3. Learning is influenced by the interaction of culture, language, and cognition (Jackson, 2011, p. 72).

Jackson's (2011) model, reflective of gifted education and based on neuroscience, enhances learning in ways that increase competence, confidence, resilience, and high intellectual performance. These stimulating experiences affect the neurological system, making students feel more confident and deeply engaged in the endorphin-induced pleasure of learning. Teachers derive the same neurological benefits when student achievement affirms their teaching methods, strengthens their positive relationships with their students, and releases the endorphins of pleasure that increase their enjoyment in their work (Jackson, 2011). In this 180-degree turn from an environment of low expectations, Jackson's model creates a cycle of increasing enrichment, confidence, and self-directed learning in which "the innate potential of all students can be realized" (Jackson, 2016).

The neuroscience behind Jackson's approach begins with identifying and activating students' strengths, which stimulates the brain's pleasure centers as just mentioned. In turn, these neurotransmitters also spark memory, a core factor in learning. These neurological activities motivate students to be proactive in learning. Two types of thinking maps, the bubble map and tree map (see Figure 3.3), acknowledge student strengths and are effective classroom practices based on Jackson's work. The same learning-enhancing brain activity results when students form positive bonds with their teachers. Relationships are a critical piece of helping adolescents feel connected to school, and the neuroscience of emotional connectedness "can provide fertile ground for social and cognitive development" (Jackson, 2011, p. 93). This relationship building requires that teachers understand child and adolescent development and the cultural references of all students. Because adolescents "can discern (and are deeply affected by) teachers' behaviors that are not equitable," teachers who connect to their students' frame of reference make an investment in the positive relationships that impact learning (Jackson, 2011, p. 81). By understanding students' different cognitive styles that are shaped by their racial and adolescent cultures, teachers can develop the bonds that have a positive effect on the learning brain. Positive relationships built on a cultural frame of reference make student learning more efficient due to "the brain's use of existing neural patterns that have been strengthened by repeated use from cultural experiences" (p. 82).

Figure 3.3 A Student's Bubble Map, Listing Her Strengths

Sasha's first attempt at the map was left blank, but when her teacher helped her become more introspective, she listed a full page of adjectives. The bubble map enforces a student's strengths while it directs her to "precision in word usage for language development" (Jackson, 2011, p. 103).

Jackson's (2011) model also incorporates the brain science that validates prominent learning theories about high intellectual performance. Neuroscience shows us that high-level activities that require high cognitive functions are the engine for increasing intellectual performance. Brain scans reveal that "when the brain is engaged and encounters challenging tasks and 'complex environments' supported by mediated feedback, new neural patterns are established" (Jackson, 2011, p. 94). This is the science behind setting goals for high intellectual performance for all students and bringing enrichment into the classroom that pushes students to the "frontier of their intelligence" (p. 95).

Neuroscience has also validated the cognitive benefits of putting instruction into the context of students' lives. Students learn best in environments that hold relevance and meaning and are hindered by instruction that comes from the cultural context of "a community to which they do not belong" (Jackson, 2011, p. 98). This is borne out in brain scans that show how a familiar context triggers the expansion of neural networks.

We explore how to put this science-backed model into practice when we delve into Jackson's (2011) High Operational Practices in Chapter 6.

By now you probably recognize overlaps in some of the key ideas found in critical race theory, white fragility, visible learning, and the Pedagogy of Confidence. Their unique perspectives on courageously challenging the status quo and honoring and amplifying voices of color, for example, come together to establish a foundation of ideas that will underpin strategies for transforming our schools in the second half of the book. In the next chapter, we continue to explore the psychological shifts we are challenged to make in leading for racial equity and examine racism in more detail.

References

Bell, D. (1992). *Faces at the bottom of the well: The permanence of racism*. New York: Basic Books.

Bell, D. (1995). *Brown v. Board of Education and the interest convergence dilemma*. In K. W. Crenshaw, N. Gotanda, P. Teller, & T. Thomas (Eds.), *Critical race theory: The key writings that formed a movement* (pp. 20–29). New York: New Press.

Bonilla-Silva, E. (2006). *Racism without racists: Color-blind racism and the persistence of racial inequality in the United States* (2nd ed.). Lanham, MD: Rowman & Littlefield.

Corwin Visible Learning. (2020). *Visible learning research*. Retrieved from https://us.corwin.com/en-us/nam/the-visible-learning-research.

Crenshaw, K. (1989). Demarginalizing the intersection of race and sex: A black feminist critique of antidiscrimination doctrine, feminist theory and antiracist politics. *University of Chicago Legal Forum, 1*(8), 139–167.

Crenshaw, K. W., Gotanda, N., Peller, P., Thomas, T. (Eds.). (1995). *Critical race theory: The key writings that formed a movement*. New York: New Press.

Delgado, R., & Stefancic, J. (2012). *Critical race theory: An introduction*. New York: New York University Press.

Désil, J. (2005, March 31). Anti-oppression in anti-capitalist movements. *Upping the Anti 1*(1), p. 85. Web archive retrieved from http://web.archive.org/web/20070415072944/http://oat.tao.ca/~tom/journal/uta1_sequential.pdf.

DeWitt, P. (2016). *John Hattie's 10th mindframe for learning*. Corwin Connect. Retrieved from https://corwin-connect.com/2016/02/john-hatties-10th-mindframe-for-learning/.

DiAngelo, R. (2011). White fragility. *International Journal of Critical Pedagogy, 3*(3), 54–70.

DiAngelo, R. (2017). *Deconstructing white privilege with Dr. Robin DiAngelo* [video file]. Retrieved from https://www.youtube.com/watch?v=DwIx3KQer54.

DiAngelo, R. (2018). *White fragility: Why it's so hard for white people to talk about racism*. Boston: Beacon Press.

Howard, T. (2014). Foreword. In K. J. Fashing-Varner, R. E. Reynolds, K. A. Albert, & L. L. Martin (Eds.), *Trayvon Martin, race, and American justice* (pp. xi–xiii). Rotterdam, Netherlands: Sense.

Fox, J., Blanco, A., Jenkins, J., Tate, J., & Lowery, W. (2019, August 9). What we've learned about police shootings 5 years after Ferguson. *Washington Post*. Retrieved from https://www.washingtonpost.com/nation/2019/08/09/what-weve-learned-about-police-shootings-years-after-ferguson/?arc404=true.

Hattie, J. (2009). *Visible learning*. New York: Routledge.

Hattie, J. (2012). *Visible learning for teachers: Maximizing impact on learning*. New York: Routledge.

Hattie, J. (2019). *Visible learning 250+ influences on student achievement*. Retrieved from https://www.visiblelearningplus.com/sites/default/files/250_influences_chart_june_2019.pdf.

Jackson, Y. (2011). *The pedagogy of confidence: Inspiring high intellectual performance in urban schools*. New York: Teachers College Press.

Jackson, Y. (2016, February). Transformational pedagogy: Cashing the promissory note of equity for all students—especially those who are marginalized. *Equity-centered Capacity Building*. Retrieved from https://capacitybuildingnetwork.org/article8/

Korte, G., & Gomez, A. (2018, May 16). Trump ramps up rhetoric on undocumented immigrants: "These aren't people. These are animals." *USA Today*. Retrieved from https://www.usatoday.com/story/news/politics/2018/05/16/trump-immigrants-animals-mexico-democrats-sanctuary-cities/617252002/.

Lee, J. M., Jr. (2008, November 9). *Toward a new educational framework of critical race theory*. Presented at the ASHE Annual Conference, Louisville, KY. Retrieved from https://www.slideshare.net/cloganwashington/critical-race-theory-13359782.

MacIntosh, P. (1988). *White privilege: Unpacking the invisible knapsack*. Retrieved from https://www.intergroupresources.com/rc/knapsack.pdf.

Moffat, J. (n.d.) What is visible learning? *Ealing Grid for Learning*. Retrieved from https://www.egfl.org.uk/sites/default/files/School_effectiveness/5a%20What%20is%20Visible%20Learning.pdf.

Pulido, L. (2006). *Black, brown, yellow, and left: Radical activism in Southern California*. Berkeley: University of California Press.

Stovall, D. (2014). Killing you is justice: Trayvon Martin as metaphor for the continual disposability of black life in the eyes of the law. In K. J. Fashing-Varner, R. E. Reynolds, K.A. Albert, & L. L. Martin (Eds.), *Trayvon Martin, race, and American justice* (pp. 9–13). Rotterdam, Netherlands: Sense.

Sue, D. W. (2015). *Talking race: Lessons from the Obama presidency* [Power-Point slides]. Retrieved from division45.org › Talking.Race_.D.-Sue-Obama .shortened.version.pptx.

Racism at Work

Mental Models, Implicit Bias, Microaggressions, and Internalized Racism

Your body responds to racism like a physical assault.

—**William A. Smith (2017)**

In his many interviews and writings, University of Utah professor of Education, Culture & Society, and African American Studies William A. Smith discusses *racial microaggressions* and their lifelong effect, *racial battle fatigue*, the term he coined. In a 2017 interview, he shared a personal story to illustrate these phenomena from his experience as a Black male. The scene is the dentist's office in December 2009, where Smith went for a routine checkup. After getting a clean bill of health from his dentist, he stopped at the reception desk to make his next 6-month appointment. When he got to the counter, a man sitting in the waiting room called out, "Oh my gosh!" Smith and the receptionist turned to look at the white man, who Smith figured to be about 60 years old. "I didn't know colored people came to the dentist's office," the man said. Jerking his arms like he was gripping a tool with both hands, he said, "I thought your teeth were so strong that you needed a wrench to pull them out!" Smith was in shock, as was the lady at the desk, whose mouth was agape. The man wasn't finished. "What's the problem with those Utes?" he said next, referring to the University of Utah basketball team. "You need to go up there and tell Coach Majerus a thing or two and get that team right." As Smith (2017) explained, "He went from an animalist stereotype to an athletic stereotype, thinking that just because I'm Black and six-foot-three I must be doing something sports related." Smith turned back to the receptionist to make his appointment and the man kept talking, this time about the Utah Jazz professional basketball team. As Smith was leaving, the man finally said, "Merry Christmas and may God bless you!"

Smith believed that the man "probably didn't understand the level of racism he had just engaged in. Those were racial microaggressions." Each microaggression a person of color experiences, he explained, is like Hank Aaron taking a bat and hitting their body:

> Your body responds to racism like a physical assault. These are violent acts he committed against my body, my humanity. But guess what? After I leave, I carry that with me. He doesn't. He doesn't even remember. He goes on about his life. Even as

I tell this story, my blood pressure probably increased, my heart rate probably increased. . . . That's just a small example of what people of color carry with them every day. (Smith, 2017, n.p.)

In this chapter we identify several ways racism manifests in society as well as in the inner lives of people of color—including many types of microaggressions and the racial battle fatigue that results from them. First, however, we'll look into the embedded mind-sets that can motivate such assaults.

Mental Models

Our deepest attitudes are formed over years of making assumptions and conclusions about what we see around us. Although our conclusions may not be reliable in face of the facts, they are such deeply set ways of thinking that we act on them unconsciously. Senge (2010) defines these thinking patterns, or mental models, as "deeply ingrained assumptions, generalizations, or even pictures or images that influence how we understand the world and how we take action" (p. 8). The mental pathway of this process, which Senge (2014) and others refer to as a *ladder of inference*, starts with an observation and advances toward conclusions, beliefs, and the actions we take based on those often-misguided beliefs. As shown in Figure 4.1., the ladder of inference becomes more abstract as we go higher up each rung until we make generalizations based on nothing more than our untested assumptions.

Working from the bottom of the ladder upward, imagine this scenario: On the first day of the school year, a white teacher may observe two Black male students sitting beside each other in the back row of her history classroom. The teacher notices the boys' loose jeans and bright hoodies and unconsciously associates them with a Black rap musician she has briefly seen in music videos and whom she considers offensive, violent, and antisocial. She then assumes that the two students are fans of that artist and concludes that they harbor angry thoughts and aggressive attitudes toward her and the white students in the classroom. Her belief that the two Black students are simmering with anger makes her fearful, and she avoids looking them in the eye or calling on them in class. Each time she sees a Black male student in the building her belief that Black males are dangerous loops her unconscious thinking back to her selection of the specific "data" she will focus on in that moment, causing her to scan them for expressions or gestures that appear angry or aggressive. In the classroom or hallway, her mental models of Black males flash through her mind in a second or two, below her conscious awareness.

Our mental models keep us in a cycle of behaviors that spring from unexamined, inaccurate data and simplistic explanations of what we see and hear. We believe that the truth we construct in our mental models is

Figure 4.1   Ladder of Inference

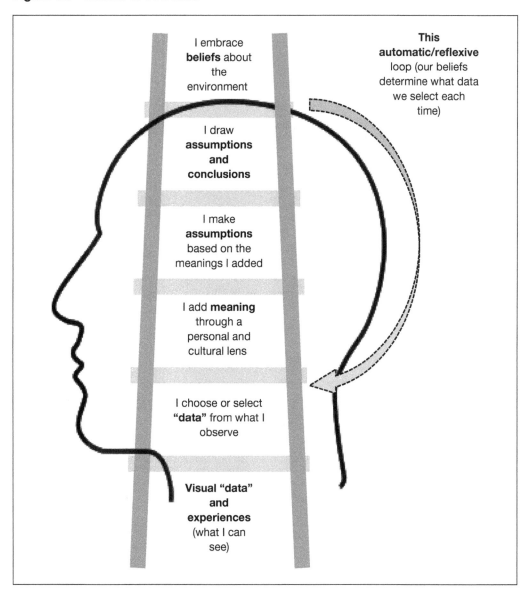

Source: Adapted from Senge (2014).
Image Source: pixabay.com/GDJ.

the obvious, self-evident truth, so when confronted with other versions of events we enter a confused situation filled with misunderstanding. The iceberg model seen in Figure 4.2 illustrates how we process our mental models below the surface of consciousness. When unaware of our mental models, we cannot examine them, and without examining them we cannot change them. This perpetuates the behavior that supports racism in all its forms. "As the world changes," Senge (2010) writes, "the gap widens between our mental models and reality, leading to increasingly counterproductive actions" (p. 166). Fortunately, we can take apart our mental models by reflecting on our own thinking and reasoning. When we do the equity work of analyzing our beliefs and behaviors about people, learning, teaching, and leading, we can disarm the limiting, automatic behaviors that have held us back and evolve our mental models in a positive way.

Characteristics of Mental Models

- They are often unexamined.

- They are incomplete and constantly evolving.

- They are usually not accurate representations of a phenomenon; they typically contain errors and contradictions.

- They provide simplistic explanations of complex phenomena.

- Most often we are not consciously aware of our mental models or the effects they have on our behavior. (Culatta, 2019)

Figure 4.2 The Iceberg Model for School Leaders

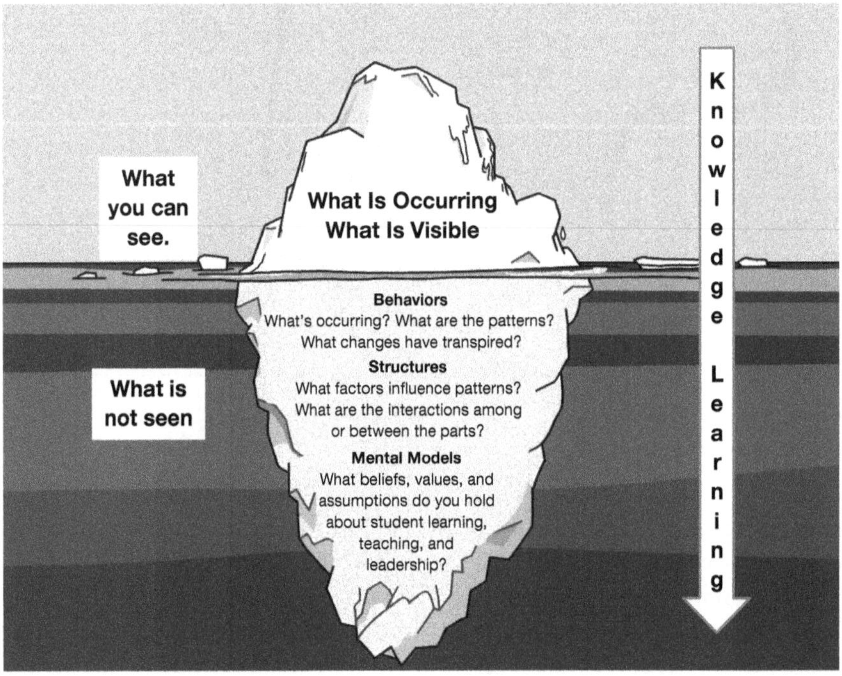

Source: Adapted from the Association for Supervision and Curriculum Development (n.d.).

Image Source: pixabay.com/MoteOo.

Reflect on This

Two Short Films That Illustrate Mental Models

Jon M. Chu's (2006) award-winning 5-and-a-half-minute film *Silent Beats* shines light on the mind frames stimulated in our everyday encounters. After watching the film, linked in the Chapter 4 section of this book's website at racialequityleadership.com, refer to Figures 4.1 and 4.2 as you consider the following:

1. What mental models can you identify in the film?
2. What values?
3. What beliefs?
4. What patterns?
5. What else?

Adam Davidson's (Springboard Schools, 2008) 10-minute film *The Lunch Date*, filmed in New York City's Grand Central Station, has a surprise twist ending that also illuminates the largely unconscious elements that motivate our behavior. Use these questions to study the message in the film:

1. What were the woman's unexamined mental models?
2. What mental models were not accurate representations of a phenomenon?
3. How did the woman's mental model provide a simplistic explanation of complex phenomena?
4. Did the woman's mental models evolve in a positive way? What is the evidence for your answer?

The examples in these films clarify how our unexamined mental models can drive our behavior. As a school leader, what is one mental model you now recognize in yourself that you would like to disrupt?

Assumptions and beliefs in my limiting mental model:

_____

_____

One example of an action/response I made based on this mental model:

_____

_____

How I can more positively and productively act/respond in the same situation:

_____

_____

The unconscious nature of our mental models explains why we can inadvertently cause harm with our language and behaviors. As explored in the following section, many of the everyday racial assaults, or microaggressions, experienced by people of color are motivated by mental models and other unconscious bias.

Racial Microaggressions

White nationalist marches and police shootings of unarmed Black men are highly visible and violent forms of racism in America, but they are not the broadest examples of how racial discrimination manifests in our society. Racism occurs most consistently in the form of racial microaggressions, the small, everyday insults targeted either overtly or covertly at people of color. Pierce (1974) suggests that the "subtle, cumulative, mini-assault is the substance of today's racism" (p. 516). "Simply stated," write Sue, Bucceri, Lin, Nadal, and Torino (2007), "microaggressions are brief, everyday exchanges that send denigrating messages to people of color because they belong to a racial minority group" (p. 72). These messages are "subtle, stunning, often automatic, and non-verbal exchanges which are 'put downs' of Blacks by offenders" (Pierce, Carew, Pierce-Gonzalez, & Willis, 1978, p. 65). People can commit microaggressions unconsciously, such as eliciting subtle facial expressions or tones of voice that can be intrusive if that tone or expression feels negative to the receiver. The tendency to overlook these subtle and seemingly innocuous behaviors is so common that microaggressions are virtually invisible to white people.

Breaking down microaggressions into three forms—microinsults, microassaults, and microinvalidations (Sue, 2010)—helps us understand these racial assaults in more detail. *Microinsults*, while often unconscious, are rude, insensitive, and demeaning words and behaviors directed at particular groups. Repeating or laughing at a joke that stereotypes people of color or ignoring a person of color as she waits in line and serving a white person before her are two examples.

Microinvalidations, often unconscious, are "subtle communications that exclude, negate, or nullify the psychological thoughts, feelings, or experiential reality of . . . people of color" (Sue, 2010, p. 37). When a Latinx person who speaks English hears "Wow, your English is really good," the invalidation is the presumption that this person should not speak English well. A common theme of invalidation is the belief in the myth of meritocracy, which asserts that everyone has an equal opportunity to succeed, regardless of one's race or gender. This belief invalidates the reality of systemic racism and sexism and instead attributes success and failure to individual characteristics. The often hidden messages of microinsults and microinvalidations diminish, offend, or emotionally weaken the person of color on the receiving end.

Finally, *microassaults* are the direct, deliberate, and obvious discriminatory actions that most people associate with "true racism" (Sue, 2010, p. 30). Explicit racial assaults can be verbal, such as yelling racial epithets; in the form of images, such as confronting Blacks with a Confederate flag or drawing swastikas on Jewish temples; or manifest in actions such as participating in white supremacy parades. Sue (2010) explains that because microassaults create a public outcry, perpetrators try to commit these assaults anonymously (secretly drawing swastikas in a bathroom or writing them online), engage in them in a setting with like-minded people in which they feel safe, or only display their racist attitudes when they lose control (such as when actor Mel Gibson made anti-Semitic remarks while intoxicated).

Microaggression forms, themes, and categories and their relationships with one another are shown in Table 4.1.

A 2019 Pew Research Center survey shed light on some of the most common microaggressions and acts of discrimination targeting people of color. The researchers asked Blacks, Hispanics, and Asians about their racist experiences and found that "Blacks are much more likely than other racial and ethnic groups to report that people have acted as if they were suspicious of them or as if they thought they weren't smart; that employers

Table 4.1 Types and Characteristics of Racial Microaggressions

TYPE OF MICROAGGRESSION	EXAMPLES	THEMES
Microinsult Insensitive, often spur-of-the-moment snub that debases a person's racial identity, often made without the perpetrator's conscious awareness of the insulting message conveyed.	• A white teacher acts surprised rather than congratulatory when a Black girl informs her she is in an honors class. • A white administrator questions a school leader of color about where she earned her doctorate.	**Ascription of Intelligence:** Labeling a person of color's intellectual capacity based on their race. **Second-Class Citizen:** Treating a person of color or racial group as less-than. **Pathologizing Cultural Values/ Communication Styles:** Perceiving white values and communication styles as the ideal and others as abnormal. **Assumption of Criminal Status:** Presuming a person of color to be deviant, dangerous, or a criminal based on their race.
Microinvalidation Statements that invalidate or undermine the thoughts, feelings, or lived experience of a person of color by excluding, negating, or nullifying those realities, often made unconsciously.	• A white teacher tells a principal of color that he is being oversensitive about a microaggression he experienced. • A white parent advises a principal of color that if she was more polite, people would not discriminate against her.	**Alien in Own Land:** Assuming Asian Americans and Latinx Americans to be foreign born. **Color-Blindness:** Declaring to not see color as race as a way to ignore and avoid acknowledging racism. **Myth of Meritocracy:** Asserting that race does not play a role in life success. **Denial of Individual Racism:** Renouncing personal racial biases.

(Continued)

Table 4.1　(Continued)

TYPE OF MICROAGGRESSION	EXAMPLES	THEMES
Microassault Explicit racially denigrating words or actions purposely meant to harm, typically in the form of a violent verbal or nonverbal attack. Made deliberately and consciously by an individual, therefore considered the "old-fashioned" form of obvious, undeniable racism.	• Students paint swastikas on a school wall or use racial epithets when talking about students of color on social media. • A high school theater director rejects the boy of color who gave the best audition for the lead role because, as she explains to him, she did not want to cast him with the white girl who would be his romantic interest in the play.	

Source: Adapted from Sue, Capodilupo, et al. (2007).

have treated them unfairly in hiring, pay or promotion; and that they have been unfairly stopped by police" (n.p.). In the same survey, 45% of whites reported that people have assumed they were racist or prejudiced. The results of this section of the survey are found in Figure 4.3.

Figure 4.3　Excerpt From *Key Findings on Americans' Views of Race in 2019*

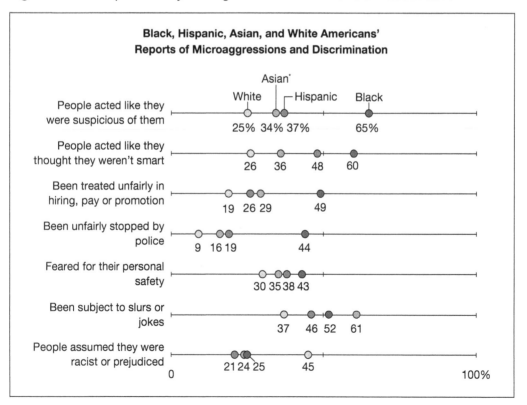

Source: "Key findings on Americans' views of race in 2019." Pew Research Center, Washington, DC (2019). https://www.pewresearch.org/fact-tank/2019/04/09/key-findings-on-americans-views-of-race-in-2019/

Our research on Black principals' experiences with microaggressions and racial battle fatigue reports the prevalence of microaggressions and the extensive variety of ways in which they occur, as shown in Table 4.2 (Krull & Robicheau, 2020).

Table 4.2 Specific Principals' Survey Responses to Questions Related to Microinsults, Microinvalidations, Microaggressions, and Microassaults

PRINCIPALS' REPORTED MICROAGGRESSIONS	
MICROINSULTS	**%**
Hidden insulting messages	100.0
Rude communication	96.9
Insensitive communication	96.9
Experienced your heritage in demeaning ways	90.0
Experienced your race in demeaning ways	87.9
Experienced your identity in demeaning ways	87.9
Experienced insults made that are unknown to the perpetrator	84.8
MICROINVALIDATIONS	
Being nullified or neutralized for your feelings or experiences	93.8
Being negated	87.5
Experienced being excluded	84.4
MICROAGGRESSIONS	
Being the only person of color	97.1
Being dismissed or ignored	97.1
Unaddressed stereotypes	97.1
Offer the "person of color perspective"	94.3
Hearing inappropriate comments made	91.4
Hearing stereotypes used within the context of the workplace	88.6
Hostile reaction to your participating in group discussions	76.5
Excluded from participation	61.8
Being discouraged during meeting with your supervisor	60.0
Racial jokes or teasing	54.3
MICROASSAULTS	
Avoidance by others	94.1
Nonverbal derogatory remarks	76.5

(Continued)

Table 4.2   (Continued)

PRINCIPALS' REPORTED MICROAGGRESSIONS	
MICROASSAULTS	
Overhearing racist conversations	74.3
Purposeful discrimination	70.6
Verbal racial derogatory remarks	50.0
Name-calling	35.0

Source: "Racial Microaggressions and Racial Battle Fatigue: Work-Life Experiences of Black School Principals." Melissa Krull and Jerry Robicheau. *Journal of Education Human Resources 38*(4), 301–328. Reprinted with permission from University of Toronto Press (https://utpjournals.press). https://doi.org/10.3138/jehr-2019-0003

Racial Battle Fatigue

Over time, microaggressions and other race-related negative impacts experienced by people of color take a toll that Smith (2017) compares to post-traumatic stress syndrome (PTSD). While beginning his research on the impact of microaggressions on Black males in the 1990s, Smith (2017) recognized some of the manifestations of stress reported by his study participants. Their descriptions resonated with the "butterflies, headaches, and back pain" (n.p.) he regularly experienced, adding a subjective dimension to the analysis of his data. At that point he coined the term *racial battle fatigue* to echo the stress-overload nature of PTSD suffered by veteran servicemen and servicewomen. Veterans can begin to show symptoms of PTSD such as nightmares, sleep problems, difficulty concentrating, and irritability after they return home to their "normalized" environment. Smith (2017) points out, however, that Blacks and other people of color don't have a "post-traumatic" environment but instead suffer the stressors of trauma continuously. "When have Black people been in a post-racial condition? We are always living that stress . . . those symptoms are constantly occurring across our lifespan" (n.p.). He adds that the physiological impact of that lifetime stress shortens the lives of Black males, who die "on average between sixty-five and sixty-eight years of age, younger than any other major racial/ethnic population in the country" (n.p.).

Racial battle fatigue is, then, "the constant use or redirection of energy for coping against mundane racism which depletes psychological and physiological resources needed in other important, creative, and productive areas of life" (Smith, Hung, & Franklin, 2012, p. 40). Further, these researchers describe the condition as "the result of constant physiological, psychological, cultural, and emotional coping with racial microaggressions in less-than-ideal and racially hostile or unsupportive environments" (p. 40). Examples of how this stress manifests are found in Figure 4.4.

Figure 4.4 Stress Responses to Racial Battle Fatigue

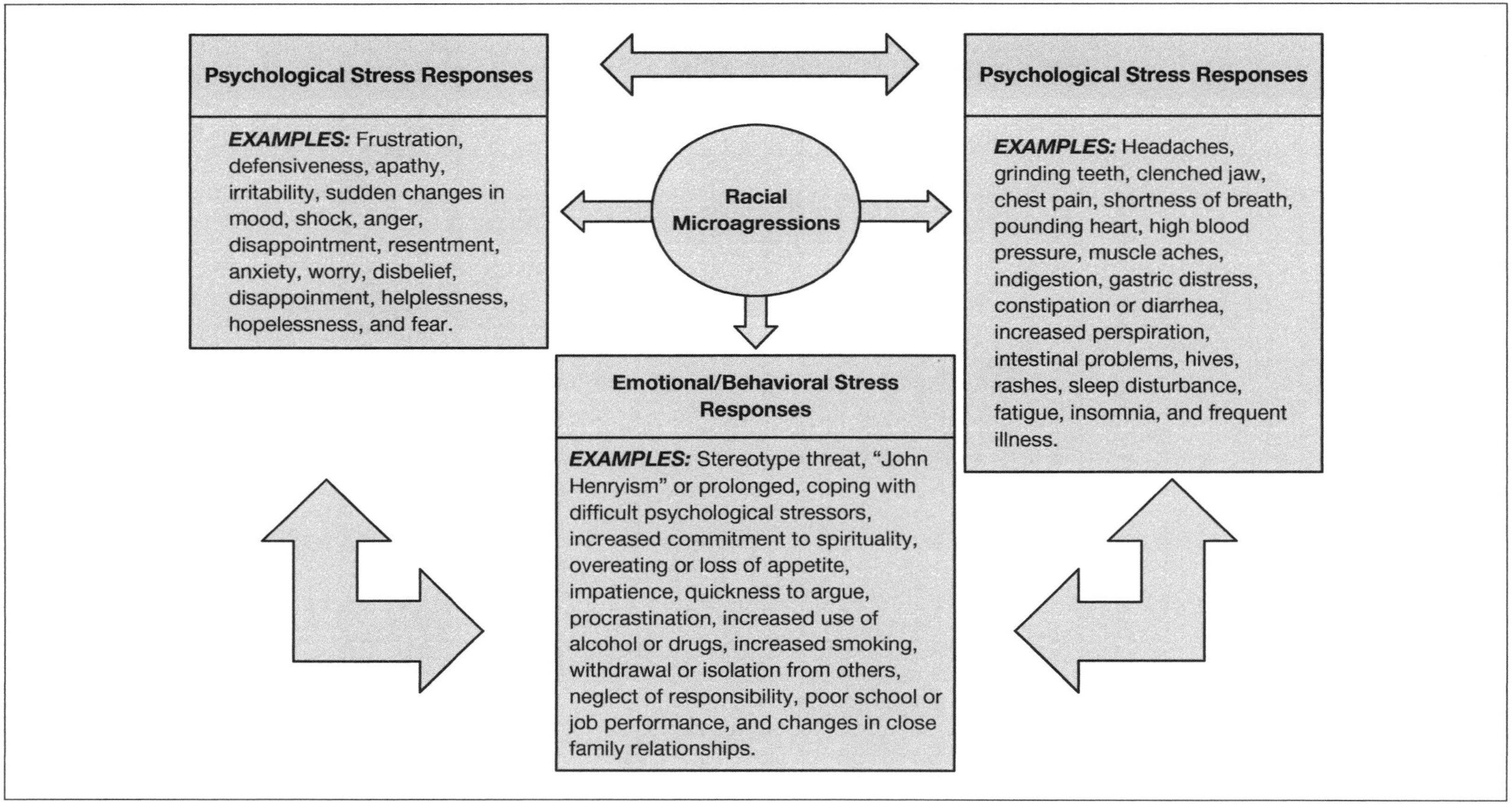

Racial Microagressions

Psychological Stress Responses

EXAMPLES: Headaches, grinding teeth, clenched jaw, chest pain, shortness of breath, pounding heart, high blood pressure, muscle aches, indigestion, gastric distress, constipation or diarrhea, increased perspiration, intestinal problems, hives, rashes, sleep disturbance, fatigue, insomnia, and frequent illness.

Psychological Stress Responses

EXAMPLES: Frustration, defensiveness, apathy, irritability, sudden changes in mood, shock, anger, disappointment, resentment, anxiety, worry, disbelief, disappoinment, helplessness, hopelessness, and fear.

Emotional/Behavioral Stress Responses

EXAMPLES: Stereotype threat, "John Henryism" or prolonged, coping with difficult psychological stressors, increased commitment to spirituality, overeating or loss of appetite, impatience, quickness to argue, procrastination, increased use of alcohol or drugs, increased smoking, withdrawal or isolation from others, neglect of responsibility, poor school or job performance, and changes in close family relationships.

Source: Smith, Hung, & Franklin (2011), p. 68.

87

The majority of principals in our study of microaggressions and racial battle fatigue validated Smith, Hung, and Franklin's (2011) research shown in Figure 4.4. In survey responses, 87.9% of principals reported experiencing psychological stress, 54.4% reported physiological stress responses, and 51.1% reported emotional/behavioral responses (Krull & Robicheau, 2020). The same study examined the impact of those experiences in terms of Black principals' psychological, physiological, and emotional/behavioral stress responses, as shown in Table 4.3.

Figure 4.5   Theory of Action

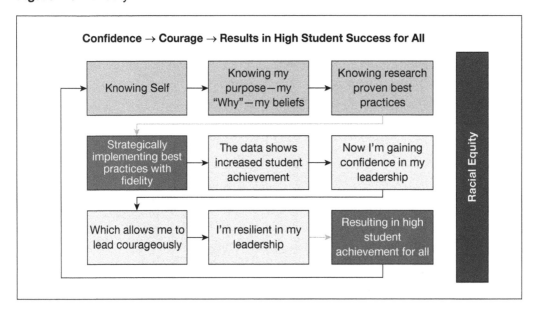

Table 4.3   Specific Principals' Survey Responses to Questions Related to Psychological, Physiological, and Emotional/Behavioral Stress Responses

PRINCIPALS' REPORTED STRESS RESPONSES TO MICROAGGRESSIONS	
PSYCHOLOGICAL STRESS RESPONSE	%
Disbelief	100.0
Disappointment	100.0
Frustration	96.8
Defensiveness	96.8
Anger	96.8
Irritability	96.7
Sudden changes in mood	93.5

PRINCIPALS' REPORTED STRESS RESPONSES TO MICROAGGRESSIONS	
Resentment	93.5
Anxiety	93.5
Worry	90.0
Apathy	87.1
Shock	86.7
Helplessness	71.0
PHYSIOLOGICAL STRESS RESPONSE	
Fatigue	93.5
Sleep disturbance	90.3
Pounding heart	80.6
Headaches	74.2
Insomnia	71.0
Muscle aches	69.0
Gastric distress	58.1
Increased perspiration	58.1
Shortness of breath	56.7
Indigestion	54.8
Clenched jaw	48.4
High blood pressure	48.4
Chest pains	45.2
Intestinal problems	41.9
Constipation/diarrhea	40.0
Grinding teeth	35.5
Frequent illness	35.5
Hives	16.1
Rashes	16.1
EMOTIONAL/BEHAVIORAL STRESS RESPONSE	
Commitment to spirituality	96.8
Procrastination	90.3
Impatience	87.1
Loss of appetite	74.2

(Continued)

Table 4.3   (Continued)

PRINCIPALS' REPORTED STRESS RESPONSES TO MICROAGGRESSIONS	
EMOTIONAL/BEHAVIORAL STRESS RESPONSE	
Prolonged coping with difficult psychological stress	71.0
Withdrawal or isolation from others	71.0
Overeating	67.7
Stereotype threats	61.3
Quickness to argue	58.1
Changes in close relationships	56.7
Neglect of responsibilities	38.7
Poor school or job performance	38.7
Increased smoking	35.0
Use of alcohol and drugs	25.8

Source: "Racial Microaggressions and Racial Battle Fatigue: Work-Life Experiences of Black School Principals." Melissa Krull and Jerry Robicheau. *Journal of Education Human Resources 38*(4), 301–328. Reprinted with permission from University of Toronto Press (https://utpjournals.press). https://doi.org/10.3138/jehr-2019-0003

Reflect on This

Microaggressions and Racial Battle Fatigue in My School

Now that you are familiar with microassaults, microinsults, microinvalidations, and racial battle fatigue, consider where you see these occurring in your school. List your examples in the following table.

Microassaults	
Microinsults	
Microinvalidations	
Racial Battle Fatigue	

Microaggressions and their cumulative effect as racial battle fatigue are challenges for students of color as well as their teachers and school leaders of color. After identifying some of these assaults in your school, how can you respond as a school leader? The following examples, written by principals in our institute, offer up some ideas (we work on practice in more detail in Chapter 6).

RACIAL MICROAGGRESSIONS WE SEE IN SCHOOLS	LEADER RESPONSES NEEDED
Adults not listening to students' perspectives, minimizing student concerns	Listening to and validating students' feelings and perspectives, creating a space where their voices can be heard
Assumptions made about families (e.g., parents not doing homework with students, providing no structure at home)	Building relationships with families to work in partnership to better serve students
Microinsults/microinvalidations committed against students regarding their religion or other cultural practices	Showing private and public value for individual religious or cultural practices
Lack of student representation in the curriculum and curricular materials	Intentionally identifying curriculum and materials that include and represent multiple perspectives and content
Students of color not being called on in class	Intentionally including voices of all students by specifically reaching out to students of color, assigning leadership roles equitably, and showing confidence in the abilities of all students
Students of color addressed for behaviors while white students are not addressed for the same behaviors	Calling out these inequities; overtly modeling equitable responses to behavior issues; learning about behavior challenges with race in mind to inform staff of counterstories

Implicit Bias

Implicit bias is responsible for many of the microaggressions just described. This unconscious prejudice, which can be held by anyone, drives our involuntary perceptions, decisions, and actions. The Kirwin Institute for the Study of Race and Ethnicity (Staats, Capatosto, Tenney, & Mamo, 2017) defines five key characteristics of the attitudes and stereotypes that make up implicit bias. These mind-sets have the following characteristics:

1. Are unconscious and automatic: They are activated without an individuals' intention or control.

2. Are pervasive: Everyone possesses them, even those avowing commitments to impartiality.

3. Do not always align with explicit beliefs: Implicit and explicit biases are generally regarded as related but distinct mental constructs.

4. Have real-world effects on behavior: Significant research has documented real-world effects of implicit bias across domains such as employment, education, and criminal justice, among others.

5. Are malleable: The biases and associations we have formed can be "unlearned" and replaced with new mental associations (p. 10).

Joy DeGruy (WorldTrustTV, 2011), author of *Post Traumatic Slave Syndrome: America's Legacy of Enduring Injury and Healing*, illustrates the characteristics of implicit bias in a story about the treatment she received one day on a trip to the grocery store with her 10-year-old daughter and her sister-in-law, Kathleen. Joy and her daughter were standing in line behind Kathleen, who is half Black and half white but whose blue eyes and white skin make her look "whiter than most white folks" (WorldTrustTV, 2011, n.p.). The young white female cashier cheerfully greeted and chatted with Kathleen as she wrote out her check for her groceries. When she finished, Joy moved ahead and the cashier's expression dropped. She did not greet Joy or engage in any chatter but instead checked out her items in silence. When Joy began writing her check, the cashier said she would need two forms of ID. Joy saw that her daughter had noticed the cashier's changed behavior and was getting upset. Joy's mind raced with options as she tried to "second guess all the drama"—if she asked the cashier why she needed the ID, she may come off as the angry Black woman and at the very least annoy the cashier and the two elderly women in line behind her. Deeply humiliated and also concerned about her daughter, she decided to simply hand over her identification. The cashier, however, was not done. She pulled out the "bad-check-writers book" and began scanning the names, which made Joy's daughter cry with embarrassment. As Joy deliberated about what to do, Kathleen intervened.

"Excuse me, why are you doing this?" Kathleen asked the cashier.

"What do you mean?"

"Why are you taking her through all this?"

"Well, um, this is our policy."

"No, it's not your policy because you didn't do that with me."

"Oh, well, I *know* you, you've been here—"

"No, no. *She's* been here for years; I've only lived here for three months."

At that point, the two white women behind Joy chimed in to echo Kathleen's sentiment. "Ugh!" one of them said. "I can't believe what this checker has done with this woman—it is totally unacceptable!"

The manager then came over and Kathleen explained what had happened. In this example of the automatic nature of implicit bias and its real-world consequences, one "white" person's challenge of that bias made a transforming impact on the white people around her. Kathleen used her white privilege to point out the injustice and influence others to see it the same way. "Kathleen knew that she walked through the world differently than I did and she used her white privilege to educate and make right a situation that was wrong," Joy said (WorldTrustTV, 2011, n.p.).

As an element of the racism that is ordinary in our society, implicit bias is also a reality in our schools. In its latest overview of studies on implicit bias, the Kirwin Institute (Staats et al., 2017) discussed research showing that white teachers identified Black students as engaging in disruptive behaviors such as arguing and fighting to a much greater extent than they identified other students exhibiting those behaviors. The researchers attributed their findings to "differences in teachers' perceptions of student behavior rather than changes in the behaviors themselves" (p. 30). Another study in the overview reported the biased perceptions of teachers as they were asked to look for challenging behaviors in a video of Black and white preschool boys and girls. Although none of the children were misbehaving in any way, an eye tracker measured that the teachers "looked longer at Black children compared to white children" and that "this finding was most pronounced for Black boys" (p. 27). The overview also discussed a study in which white instructors' anxiety about and decreased lesson quality for Black students resulted in lower test scores for those learners. Another study analyzed 10 years of school discipline data to find that Black girls were overrepresented among disciplined girls by a factor of three. This rate of inequity was larger than the other significantly overrepresented group of Black males who were 2.65 times more represented among the population of disciplined male students.

This collection of recent studies (Staats et al., 2017) reveals how implicit bias impacts teachers' perceptions of the behavior and learning capacities of Black students. How does this bias impact students of color in your school? Hearing from a group of Black male high school students in a video produced by ColorLines (2014), the news website of the research and advocacy organization Race Forward, can help us reflect on the experiences of Black students in our schools. As you'll see in the following exercise, these students' comments about teachers' low expectations and stereotyped perceptions of them help us understand how implicit bias affects their identities and experiences in school.

Reflect on This

"They Put You in This Box"

Responding to the Life Experiences of Young Black Males

Watch the 7-minute "Chapter 1: High School" video from *Life Cycles of Inequity: A ColorLines Series on Black Men* (2014 — found on racialequityleadership .com, Chapter 4 section) and reflect on the following in your journal:

1. Have you created a space in your school in which Black male, Black female, or other students of color (by gender) can discuss the impact of implicit bias on their lives?

2. Do any of the boys' comments sound similar to what you have heard from students of color in your school?

3. Which comment surprised you the most, and why?

As a crucial element in knowing ourselves, facing our implicit bias is an intrinsic, early step in the Theory of Action framework introduced in Chapter 1. Leading for racial equity begins with knowing ourselves, from examining our cycle of socialization to uncovering the unconscious biases that affect our beliefs and behaviors. Diversity and inclusion expert Verna Myers (2014) suggests three phases of implicit bias work that have been powerful tools for reflection and discussion in our institute. First, Myers (2014) urges us to leave our comfort zone by seeking out the facts: "Just get out of denial and go looking for disconfirming data that will prove that in fact your old stereotypes are wrong" (n.p.). Next, she challenges us to stop avoiding those we have been taught to view with suspicion and fear and instead expand our social and professional circles. Consciously and intentionally "move toward young Black men instead of away from them. . . . Walk toward your discomfort," Myers (2014) states. Without taking this action, white educators can ignore their implicit bias indefinitely and continue to assume that their good intentions are enough. Black educational policy scholar Bettina L. Love (2019) discusses the importance of this step based on her own experience: "My K–12 schooling was filled with white teachers who, at their core, were good people but unknowingly were murdering my spirit with their lack of knowledge, care, and love of my culture" (n.p.). The "unknowing" nature of white teachers, principals, and others in the school environment must be transformed before any other equity strategies can begin in earnest.

Third, Myers (2014) asks us to respond to racist talk and behavior instead of letting it pass. At family gatherings, for example, when the people we love make comments we know are wrong and damaging, we need to say something. The next generation is sitting at the same table, and without speaking up, we help ensure that these biases don't die. "We've got to be willing to say, 'Grandma, we don't call people that anymore.' . . . We've got to be willing to not shelter our children from the ugliness of racism when Black parents don't have the luxury to do so, especially those who have young Black sons" (Myers, 2014).

The following activity is an opportunity for you to learn more from Myers's (2014) work and begin uncovering your implicit bias through direct, intentional action.

Reflect on This
Walking Boldly Toward Your Biases

Watch Verna Myers's (2014) 17-minute TED Talk, available at the link on this book's website, racialequityleadership.com (Chapter 4 section). Reflect on your relationships in and outside your school by asking yourself the following and writing your responses in your journal:

1. How will you move toward young Black men rather than away?
2. How will you help your teachers move toward young Black men rather than away?
3. Who is in your circle, who is missing, and why?
4. How many authentic relationships do you have with Black men or your Black male students?

Related to Myers's (2014) message to move out of denial and call out racism, Ibram X. Kendi (2019) draws a stark contrast between the terms *not racist* and *antiracist*. When white people try to deny their implicit bias and other racist beliefs and behaviors by calling themselves color-blind or not racist, Kendi (2019) explains, they perpetuate the status quo. The "not racist" response is an attempt to sound neutral, as if neutrality were a positive stance, but "there is no neutrality in the racism struggle. The opposite of 'racist' isn't 'not racist.' It is 'anti-racist'" (p. 8). The neutrality mask of "not racist" is actually a form of racism that contrasts with the mind-set and actions of someone who is "antiracist," as shown in the following table (based on Kendi, 2019, p. 8):

NOT RACIST (MASK FOR RACIST)	ANTIRACIST
Endorses the idea of a racial hierarchy (i.e., supports racist leaders and policies)	Supports racial equality
Believes race-issue problems are rooted in people of color	Locates the roots of race-issue problems in power and policies
Allows racial inequities to persevere through actions and inaction	Confronts racial inequities
Considers the word *racist* a slur or pejorative (which freezes white people into inaction)	Considers the word *racist* a usefully descriptive term

Founder of the Antiracist Research & Policy Center at American University, Kendi (2019) calls denial the "heartbeat of racism" (p. 9). He acknowledges that he, a Black man, "used to be racist most of the time" but is changing, "no longer speaking through the mask of racial neutrality" (p. 10). "We know how to be racist," he writes. "We know how to pretend to be not racist. Now let's know how to be antiracist" (p. 11).

Internalized Racism

Race-based oppression occurs not only on the institutional level (i.e., laws and business practices) and through personal actions such as microaggressions and hate crimes but also as a manifestation within people of color as internalized racism (Jones, 2000). As the counterpart of white privilege, internalized racism arises when people of color "develop ideas, beliefs, actions and behaviors that support or collude with racism" (Bivens, 2005, p. 44). Bivens (2005) places these types of support and collusion into four categories: inner, interpersonal, institutional, and intercultural.

The inner dimension relates to the limited sense of self that results from living in a society in which race is a social and political construct devised to oppress people of color. A limited sense of self can manifest in people of color feeling

- inferior to other people;

- like a victim and disempowered to transform a situation;

- overwhelmed by the emotional toll of navigating life with a limited identity; and

- drained of time, energy, and resources due to a focus on trying to "read" and change white people.

Bevins (2005) states that the inner dimension of internalized racism "can undermine people of color's belief in our full humanity and disrupt our understanding of our inner life" (p. 46), which resonates with W. E. B. Du Bois's (1907) notion about the conflicted consciousness of people of color. Because they see the world through the lens of the dominant white culture, Du Bois contends, people of color sense themselves as two separate identities, one as an American and one as a person of color. Instead of developing a "true self-consciousness" (p. 3), people of color can develop the limited sense of self that is one aspect of internalized racism. In Du Bois's (1907) words, this conflicted sense of self

> is a peculiar sensation, this double-consciousness, this sense of always looking at one's self through the eyes of others, of measuring one's soul by the tape of a world that looks on in amused contempt and pity. One ever feels his two-ness,—an American, a Negro; two souls, two thoughts, two unreconciled strivings; two warring ideals in one dark body, whose dogged strength alone keeps it from being torn asunder. (p. 3)

Recent writing about this inner challenge comes from Kendi (2019) in *How to Be an Antiracist*, in which he shares his experience as the only Black student in his eleventh-grade International Baccalaureate classes:

> Rarely opening my lips or raising my hand, I shaped myself according to what I thought they believed about me. . . . I saw myself through their eyes: an impostor, deserving of invisibility. My drowning in the supposed sea of advanced intelligence was imminent. I internalized my academic struggles as indicative of something wrong not just with

my behavior but with Black behavior as a whole, since
I represented the race, both in their eyes—or what I thought
I saw in their eyes—and in my own. (p. 99)

Bevins (2005) suggests that people of color can address the inner dimension of internalized racism by strengthening their sense of agency and personal power. "Drawing on the strengths of one's culture" to develop a "clear sense of one's racial identity" (p. 46) can begin to heal the interior wounds of internalized racism.

On the interpersonal level, internalized racism creates challenges in the relationships people of color form between each other and with white people. People of color may project their sense of inferiority on other people of color, resulting in a lack of trust and confidence. This projection, as well as feelings of inadequacy, can erode interpersonal relatedness and communication, setting up roadblocks to the consensus building essential for creating change (Bevins, 2005). The interpersonal dimension can also bring about "uncontrolled and inappropriately expressed rage at white people for their unwillingness and/or inability to be aware of and take responsibility for their privilege" (Bevins, 2005, p. 47). People of color can undo the challenges brought on by this level of internalized racism, Bevins (2005) suggests, by learning new methods for communicating and resolving conflicts across differences.

The institutional dimension of internalized racism refers to subverting one's own power in white-controlled institutions (Bevins, 2005). In a racist system that prevents people of color from making crucial decisions about their lives and resources, people of color may "assume white people know more about what needs to be done for us and for society than our own people do" (Bivens, 2005, p. 48). Similar to the interpersonal element discussed, the institutional level may lead people of color to reject the authority and power of other people of color, particularly when a challenge to white privilege is at stake. "Structurally, there is a system in place that rewards people of color who support white supremacy and power and coerces or punishes those who do not" (Bevins, 2005, p. 48). Former national security advisor and secretary of state Condoleezza Rice, for example, has been described as being rewarded as a Black supporter of white-controlled institutions based on her work on corporate boards and role in the George W. Bush administration. During her service on the Chevron board of directors, the oil company (that named a tanker in her honor) became embroiled in a human rights lawsuit involving two Nigerians who were shot and killed during a peaceful protest. Chevon was charged with paying Nigeria's military police to crush the peaceful demonstration against Chevron's exploitation of the nation's oil resources. When asked about her affiliation with "big oil" in general, Rice defended American oil companies—and implicitly, their behavior—as "important to our security" (Felix, 2010, p. 193). In contrast to Rice's career rise in government, the Black NFL players who rejected "white supremacy and power" by peacefully protesting police shootings of Blacks were punished by being silenced by NFL leadership and publicly ridiculed by the president of the United States.

According to Bivens (2005), people of color can counter the institutional level of internalized racism by a demand for more education and awareness about systemic racism and its workings, all while "holding onto and sharing our own core values, wisdom and understandings" (p. 48).

Finally, the cultural dimension of internalized racism involves suppressing the deepest values of one's culture to align with the dominant white culture. The nation's history of racial inequity and oppression continues to live side by side with its promotion of key ideals such as the right to life, liberty, and the pursuit of happiness, and this clash creates a struggle for people of color. How can people "align our culture with the ideals of U.S. culture, and yet avoid the minefields of a society founded on our oppression" (Bevins, 2005, p. 49)? Internalized racism manifests as people of color accepting white, Eurocentric norms such as light-colored skin as the universal standard to which they must confirm to be valued. Black girls, for example, may feel inferior to other Blacks and to whites based on the darkness of their skin. As one young woman shared in a media interview, "Adolescent angst is bad enough without the extra stress of knowing that you live in a skin that is intrinsically and inexplicably considered less attractive. People of color make up the majority of the world, yet somehow, from Beijing to Bahia, women aspire to whiteness" (Anyangwe, 2017, n.p.).

The cultural aspect of internalized racism also shows up when people of color embrace the myth that issues of race are caused by people of color rather than the oppressive system itself. For example, people of color may internalize the belief that people of color are more violent than white people. To address this type of internalized racism, people of color are challenged to clarify "the distinction between race, ethnicity and culture" and actively raise awareness about and deconstruct "the false culture of race" (Bivens, 2005, p. 50).

Through internalized racism, Blacks, Latinx, Asians, and Indigenous people accept society's negative messages about the "abilities and intrinsic worth" of people of color (Jones, 2000, p. 1213). Understanding this phenomenon allows school leaders to recognize when internalized racism is impacting the lives of students of color.

Reflect on This
Looking Into Internalized Racism

As you watch Kiri Davis's (2007) 7-minute video, "A Girl Like Me" (linked in the Chapter 4 section of racialequityleadership.com), think about the girls of color in your school and other implications of internalized racism that impact students of color. Reflect on your understanding of internalized racism in your journal with the following questions:

1. Can you now identify examples of internalized racism that you did not perceive as such before learning what internalized racism is?

2. How do you see internalized racism as affecting learning?

3. As a leader, what will you do when you see internalized racism in motion?

We now move on from learning about ourselves to learning about our schools—their culture, data, and practices—along the Theory of Action pathway. We continue, however, to reflect and expand our awareness throughout our journey as racial equity leaders in every phase of this process, as outlined in the Theory of Action diagram.

References

Anyangwe, E. (2017, April 14). A moment that changed me: Rejecting the white "prettiness" ideal. *The Guardian*. Retrieved from https://www.theguardian.com/commentisfree/2017/apr/14/moment-that-changed-me-white-prettiness-racist-beauty.

Association for Supervision and Curriculum Development. (n.d.). *The iceberg model*. Retrieved from http://www.ascd.org/ASCD/pdf/journals/ed_lead/el200910_kohm_iceberg.pdf.

Bivens, D. (2005). What is internalized racism? In M. Potapchuk, S. Leiderman, D. Bivens, & B. Major, *Flipping the script: White privilege and community building*. Silver Spring, MD: MP Associates. Retrieved from https://www.racialequitytools.org/resourcefiles/potapchuk1.pdf.

Chu, J. M. (2006, October 17). *Silent beats* [Video file]. Retrieved from https://www.youtube.com/watch?v=76BboyrEl48.

ColorLines. (2014). *Life cycles of inequity: Chapter 1: High school* [Video file]. Retrieved from https://www.youtube.com/watch?v=ezZn_N43Jdw.

Culatta, R. (2019). *Mental models* [Web log post]. Retrieved from https://www.instructionaldesign.org/concepts/mental-models/.

Davis, K. (2007). *Kiri Davis: A girl like me* [Video file]. Retrieved from https://www.youtube.com/watch?v=z0BxFRu_SOw&ab_channel=4TruthAndJustice.

Du Bois, W. E. B. (1907). *The souls of black folk: Essays and sketches*. Chicago: A.C. McClurg & Company.

Felix, A. (2010). *Condi: The Condoleezza Rice story*. New York: Newmarket Press.

Jones, C. P. (2000). Levels of racism: A theoretic framework and a gardener's tale. *American Journal of Public Health, 90*(8), 1212–1215.

Kendi, I. X. (2019). *How to be an antiracist*. New York: One World.

Krull, M., & Robicheau, J. (2020). Racial microaggressions and racial battle fatigue: Work-life experiences of black school principals. *Journal of Education Human Resources, 38*(4), 301–328.

Love, B. L. (2019, March 18). Dear white teachers: You can't love your black students if you don't know them. *Education Week, 38*(26). Retrieved from https://www.edweek.org/ew/articles/2019/03/20/dear-white-teachers-you-cant-love-your.html.

Myers, V. (2014). *How to overcome our biases? Walk boldly toward them* [Video file]. Retrieved from https://www.youtube.com/watch?v=uYyvbgINZkQ.

Pew Research Center. (2019). *Key findings on Americans' views of race in 2019.* Retrieved from https://www.pewresearch.org/fact-tank/2019/04/09/key-findings-on-americans-views-of-race-in-2019/.

Pierce, C. (1974). Psychiatric problems of the black minority. In S. Arieti (Ed.), *American handbook of psychiatry* (pp. 512–523). New York: Basic Books.

Pierce, C., Carew, J., Pierce-Gonzalez, D., & Wills, D. (1978). An experiment in racism: TV commercials. In C. Pierce (Ed.), *Television and education* (pp. 62–88). Beverly Hills, CA: Sage.

Senge, P. M. (2010). *The fifth discipline: The art & practice of the learning organization.* New York: Crown.

Senge, P. M. (2014). *The fifth discipline fieldbook: Strategies and tools for building a learning organization.* New York: Crown.

Smith, W. A. (2017, May 1). *Challenging racial battle fatigue with Dr. William A. Smith* [Video file]. Retrieved from https://www.youtube.com/watch?v=f6weBHfD_Mc.

Smith, W. A., Hung, M., & Franklin, J. D. (2011). Racial battle fatigue and the miseducation of black men: Racial microaggressions, societal problems, and environmental stress. *Journal of Black Masculinity, 80*(1), 63–82.

Smith, W. A., Hung, M., & Franklin, J. D. (2012). Between hope and racial battle fatigue: African-American men and race-related stress. *Journal of Black Masculinity, 2*(1), 35–58.

Springboard Schools. (2008, July 14). *The lunch date* [Video file]. Retrieved from https://www.youtube.com/watch?v=epuTZigxUY8&list=RDepuTZigxUY8&start_radio=1.

Staats, C., Capatosto, K., Tenney, L., & Mamo, S. (2017). *State of the science: Implicit bias review.* Kirwin Institute for the Study of Race and Ethnicity. Retrieved from http://kirwaninstitute.osu.edu/wp-content/uploads/2017/11/2017-SOTS-final-draft-02.pdf.

Sue, D. W. (2010). *Microaggressions in everyday life: Race, gender, and sexual orientation.* New York: John Wiley & Sons.

Sue, D. W., Bucceri, J., Lin, A. I., Nadal, K. L., & Torino, G. C. (2007). Racial microaggressions and the Asian American experience. *Cultural Diversity and Ethnic Minority Psychology, 13*(7), 72–81.

Sue, D. W., Capodilupo, C. M., Torino, G. C., Bucceri, J. M., Holder, A. M. B., Nadal, K. L., & Esquilin, M. (2007). Racial microaggressions in everyday life: Implications for clinical practice. *American Psychologist, 62*(4), 271–286.

WorldTrustTV. (2011, September 20). *Cracking the codes: Joy DeGruy, "A trip to the grocery store"* [Video file]. Retrieved from https://www.youtube.com/watch?v=Wf9QBnPK6Yg.

Understanding My School/District

CHAPTER 5

Unwrapping Legacies of Policy and Practice

The No Child Left Behind Act was not supposed to make sense. It was the latest and greatest mechanism for placing the blame for funding inequities on Black children, teachers, parents, and public schools. . . . While misbehaving White children have received compassion and tolerance—as they should—misbehaving Black children have been more likely to hear "No Excuses" and to be on the receiving end of zero tolerance and handcuffs.

—Ibram X. Kendi (2017a)

Throughout her 30-plus-year career that spans student teaching as a Yale undergraduate to running schools and a district in three regions of the country and earning her doctorate at Harvard, Dr. Rhoda Mhiripiri-Reed has tackled many dimensions of racial injustice in public education. Her beginnings in a majority nonwhite school in New Haven, Connecticut, where she, a woman of color, was student teaching under the mentorship of a white male teacher was a wake-up call to the challenges she would be facing in her field. "It was very evident that some of the white teachers did not care about making sure that students were engaged in high levels of learning," she said (Personal communication, February 15, 2020).

In her first job as a social studies teacher in her home state of Minnesota, Mhiripiri-Reed began to see more clearly the challenges inherent within the public education system. In her subsequent roles as an assistant principal, principal, and superintendent of three districts, she has seen patterns of behavior in teachers and students that spell out the problem and point to how to address it. "We talk a lot in education about student 'behavior,'" she said. "I find that term very offensive because what I see is students acting out a rejection; they're demonstrating their opposition to racist practices in what can be experienced as an uncaring system. It's a manifestation of students' dissatisfaction, their refusal to conform." Where some see student behavior as destructive and nothing more, Mhiripiri-Reed sees it as an inevitable form of protest. "If teachers are not demonstrating a high level of care, why should students? Adults are the models for students."

Mhiripiri-Reed's leadership approaches to analyzing what's happening in her schools have always included student shadowing, which gives her firsthand insights into what needs to be changed. In every administrative position she has held, she has shadowed individual students for a full day each. While shadowing a Black girl in a northern California high school, for example, she counted only two instances in which the student was asked to use her voice either by responding to a question or talking through her thinking about a complex topic. "I remember thinking that our teachers are doing so much talking or there's so much time for independent work that students who need it most don't have those multiple opportunities to talk about their learning out loud," she said.

In private schools she has visited, she has seen students sit around a table talking about the text while the teacher is off to the side. "This is an exercise in voice and mastering your ideas and being skillful in how you articulate those ideas," she said. "In public school we're all about compliance, and there is a lot of teacher talk. Instead of teaching all our students through inquiry and a mind-set of 'I'm going to give you a little bit because I know your big brain can figure out the rest,' we save that kind of approach for the honor settings, the white settings, or the private settings."

As a young assistant principal in a suburban high school, Mhiripiri-Reed had her first encounter with a rigid, disproportionate discipline system and leadership's role in it. In that school, student fights were handled with student arrests for disorderly conduct—negotiation was not an option. "The principal, the other assistant principal, and I asked each other why we were criminalizing our students, especially Black boys," she said. "We knew that a large number of young African American men were already in the criminal justice system, and we had to ask ourselves why we were contributing to that." With an all-white staff and nearly 50% of the enrollment students of color, the school "was not a culturally peaceful environment because of that cultural mismatch," she said. "Teachers reminisced about the 'good old days' and a certain kind of student they used to teach, and students came to school just wanting to be seen and feel valued and learn. Instead, they were stereotyped and faced low expectations."

Mhiripiri-Reed's principal team worked to change their teachers' reference point, emphasizing that their focus should be on the present and the students in front of them. They showed their teachers the inequities of kids of color being put in basic classes and not represented in advanced placement or honors classes, and students of color receiving the majority of office referrals and suspensions. "It was a battle," she said, "because the entrenched system was, 'When a student does x, then they need y,' and y was always punitive—it wasn't an opportunity to shift or change behavior." If a student was being disrespectful to a teacher, Mhiripiri-Reed explained, she talked with that student to help them understand that they needed to present themselves differently, and then returned the student to class. "Sometimes that worked, but at other times teachers refused to take them back." Transforming mind-sets takes time, she learned again and again, whether they belong to teachers, leadership, school boards, or other members of the community. And the race of the leader is always a factor.

Over the years, Mhiripiri-Reed has found that leading as a woman of color is a balancing act that requires constant vigilance:

> You can't be too progressive with your social justice platform. You have to play both sides, which looks like softening your approach or sometimes acting white as you advocate for kids of color, rather than being resolute about the equitable approach. Contrary to what some assume, I'm not sticking up for these kids because I'm Brown; I'm sticking up for them because they're being criminalized and we're not treating them with respect. I want to stand up for that—even if I had green skin I would do that.
>
> So you are put in a strange space: You're on water with land on both sides and you have to figure out how to stay on top and not drown. You can't be seen as fully planted on one side versus the other. If you're too direct, you risk shutting down the conversation because you failed to create a comfortable enough space for some individuals to walk into. Others may give the eye roll and go along with it, but mentally they put you on their I'm-not-dealing-with-you list, so the partnership will not be there.

Since becoming the superintendent of a suburban district in Minnesota nearly 3 years ago, Mhiripiri-Reed has taken several approaches to disrupt inequity in her schools, including long-term leadership training and hiring more leaders of color. For a full day every month, every assistant principal, principal, district department leader, and cabinet member comes together for a courageous leadership program designed for the district and run by authors Krull and Raskin. The strength of the program, Mhiripiri-Reed believes, is the double impact of building a 37-member community of trust while also developing knowledge and awareness about race as individual learners.

> Two-and-a-half years ago when I was speaking to the leaders in our conference room, not only were there 36 poker faces, but very few voices contributed to what I had hoped would be a collective conversation. I'm used to that, but it was clear that there was so much work to do to build trust and an idea of who we were going to be together. Today, it is so different. We're not there yet, but the distance we've come is remarkable.

As a collective we're working through what we're going to do when we see racist practices. It's going to be a long road because there are racist practices across our system, but now our leaders are honing the tools they're going to use when they have to tackle a situation or speak to a staff member or not fold if they're presented with white fragility. That is huge.

Mhiripiri-Reed created a position called the director of principal leadership to specifically build principals' capacity through coaching and supervision, and in the past year she hired four principals of color. "Two out of our ten principals are now women of color, and that changes the game," she said. "Our group is really strong—we're not afraid to challenge each other, and we're all growing in being morally resolute for the kind of system we want to have." Four of her cabinet members are people of color, and "our white males are totally on board," she said. In addition, she describes the district's school board as very equity driven.

She reflected that her leadership group has been deeply thoughtful about the work. At the end of the first year, which involved their personal, internal exploration of biases and identities, she felt that the consensus was *Oh, we've got this. We don't need to do a year two.* But now that they are well into their second year, they see the need to stay in it together because, as Mhiripiri-Reed explained, "now it's about untangling and reimagining and right-sizing an entire system."

As her district continues its equity work, Mhiripiri-Reed anticipates a gradual yet broader awakening throughout the state. Her experience has shown her that mind-sets and practices begin to change when demographics reach a tipping point. Working in three districts where the percentage of students of color was less than 50% and three in which students of color made up more than 50%, she saw distinct perspectives on either side of the threshold. When white students become the minority, "you will find that the mind-set of 'Whatever it takes, we're here for the kids' is far more pervasive and observable than in districts where white students are still the majority." She observes that the attitude in Minnesota appears to be "Well, the achievement gap is really wide, but at least our white kids have the highest achievement scores in the country—we're still mostly doing good." But when students of color become 55%, she believes, Minnesotans will no longer be able to say they're mostly doing good. "Then the narrative is going to change," she said. "We'll have to say, 'We're mostly not doing good.' That is the reality that shifts for a lot of people here."

Those who have made the shift in advance of the tipping point, she said, include the white teachers in her district who "totally get it." She finds them in every school and understands that it is exhausting for them to continually be at odds with their colleagues. "It takes a lot of courage to have a different perspective," she said. "There's so much conformity. You hear, 'How dare you try to lead—you're not better than us. This is the way we do things here.' We're such a compliance-oriented system that that attitude is built into our DNA as public school educators."

While Mhiripiri-Reed's district has not yet reached the demographic tipping point, the progress of her equity-driven, fully-on-board leaders, teachers, and other staff inspire her to continue the work. She has steered her career in the same direction since her undergraduate days at Yale and is optimistic about her suburban district that reflects the realities facing similar districts across the country. "You need to put a stronghold in place to move the ship in a different direction," she said, "and I think a lot of the ingredients for that are starting to take shape here."

The first half of this book has addressed the need for school leaders to examine themselves and how their beliefs and behaviors are shaped by a society permeated by systemic racism. As leaders, we are challenged to face our personal facts and transform ourselves to set the stage for enacting practices that will transform education for every child in our schools. Socrates claimed that the unexamined life is not worth living, and we would say that the school leader's unexamined life not only holds her back but also impedes the lives and flourishing of everyone in her building.

The next step in knowing ourselves as school leaders is knowing our schools. In this chapter, we'll learn how to take a close and objective look at what's really happening in our buildings (or districts) that digs deeper than numerical data alone. Creating the eye-opening overview we call the data dashboard will be followed by an exercise in student shadowing, which Mhiripiri-Reed described as a powerful technique for witnessing the reality of student life. We'll then work with a tool for assessing where our teachers and staff align with our goals and how to effectively communicate with them when worlds collide around race in our buildings. Next, we take cues from the policy insights of Ibram X. Kendi to further examine how our leadership can disrupt old policy and usher in the new. Finally, a case study project invites us to delve into a specific incident/issue and find solutions based on our expanded knowledge of our schools and how to communicate around race.

Understanding Your School: The Data Dashboard

Who are the students in your school? What is your data? What is your culture? Pulling together elements of these three categories in one visual can be a critical step in knowing where to set your priorities and actions for leadership.

Knowing Your Students. As seen in the sample dashboard in Figure 5.1, knowing your students means documenting who they are racially, academically, and culturally. Recording students' racial demographics and the programs in which they are enrolled provides an all-in-one overview that can easily be compared to other sections of the dashboard. What is the racial makeup of your school? How many are English Language Learners, enrolled in special education, receive free or reduced lunch programs, or are homeless?

Figure 5.1 Sample Data Dashboard

Enrollment

1,154 students

52% females, 48% males

24% Hispanic

43% Black/African American

18% Asian

15% White

ELL: 23%

SPED: 12%

Free & Reduced Lunch: 82%

School Name: Elementary School

Mission: To equip every student with the knowledge, life skills, and global perspectives to contribute to society and respond to the needs of an ever-changing world.

Leadership Team

Principal:
- 1 Hispanic male

Assistant principals:
- 2 white males

Special education director:
- 1 white female

ESL coordinator:
- 1 Hispanic female

Initiatives and Programs

- Restorative justice practices
- Culturally responsive training
- NUA strategies
- Kagean strategies
- Backward design process
- Reciprocal teaching

Staff

Teachers: 87

Nonlicensed staff: 51

Total staff: 138

17% male

83% female

Experience

0–3 years: 32

3–10 years: 37

10 or more years: 18

Racial Background/ All Staff

Black/African American 2%

Hispanic: 3%

Asian: 2%

White: 93%

Native:

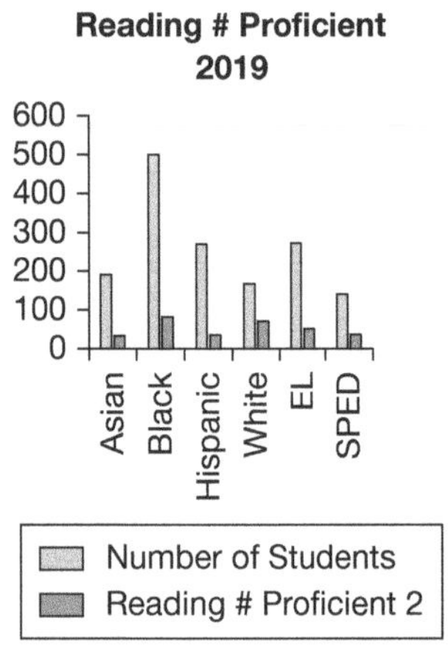

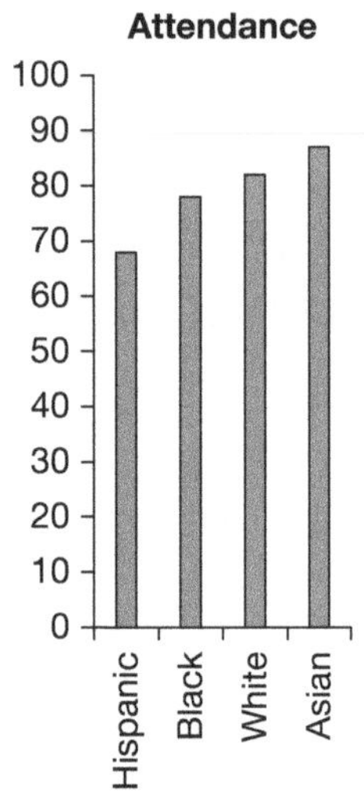

Reading # Proficient 2019

(bar chart: categories Asian, Black, Hispanic, White, EL, SPED; y-axis 0–600)

Legend:
- Number of Students
- Reading # Proficient 2

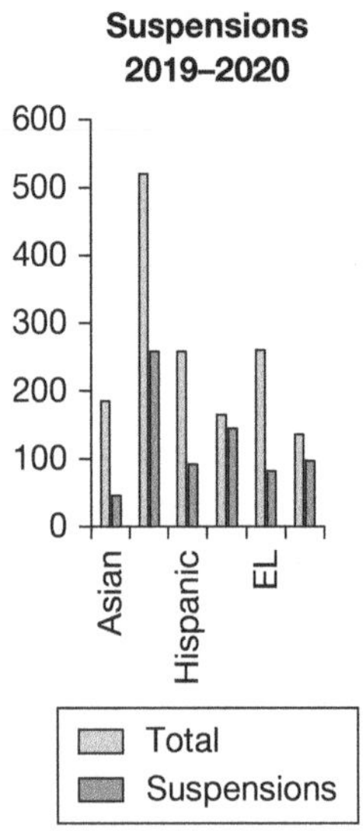

Suspensions 2019–2020

(bar chart: categories Asian, Hispanic, EL; y-axis 0–600)

Legend:
- Total
- Suspensions

Attendance

(bar chart: categories Hispanic, Black, White, Asian; y-axis 0–100)

Perceptions

- Challenging school that is no longer like it used to be.
- Significant behaviors occur without consequences or consistent follow-through.
- District and grant control instruction with huge demands of teachers.

Knowing Your Data. Seeing the full picture of your data involves multiyear proficiency data broken down by race as well as other criteria. Your data also include your attendance and discipline figures. Who's achieving? Who's not? Who's missing instruction by being out of school? What do your initiatives say about student access to learning? What programs are in place, and how many are directed at students of color?

Knowing Your Culture. Knowing your school culture means understanding the demographics and beliefs of your staff: What are their education and experience levels? What is the racial makeup of your teaching staff and leadership team? How does that align with the racial demographics of your students? How do your staff and faculty feel about working here? What do they say about the students and the school mission and environment? How do the adults in your school interact, and what do they believe?

Your school's data dashboard is a unique tool that lays out all the dots and shows where they do or do not connect. Principals in our institute have told us that their dashboards gave them insights, particularly about disconnects, that they would not otherwise have uncovered and helped them begin to improve the picture in their schools. One common disconnect we find are comments about teachers that don't align with the facts. A principal comment on the dashboard may state that "staff are known to call this school a hidden gem, a school of excellence, and describe us as a tight family," but a glance at the academic data shows that Black students are barely on the chart and Latinx kids are coming in very low. This tells us that the culture is unaware of what's really happening and therefore lacks a sense of urgency about what's at stake. In another corner of the chart a principal can list five initiatives designed to have a positive impact but that evidently are not benefiting students of color. One would think that students of color would thrive under certain programs, but the data show that something is happening in the classroom to prevent it, perhaps an absence of racial consciousness.

Studying your dashboard will bring up questions that will inspire reflection and new thinking about the changes that need to happen. If your school is racially diverse, for example, why are 90% of your teachers and 100% of your leadership team white? If you have used the same "multicultural" reading curriculum for 8 years but the scores of your students of color are not improving, why do you continue it? If people in your building say and believe positive things about achievement and culture, but the data do not reflect it, what's the next step? The following activity will guide you through the process of constructing your school's dashboard, including where to find a variety of templates.

Activity

My Data Dashboard

The Story of My School

Your school's data dashboard can include variations on the following template but should at least contain the following sections:

1. Student enrollment by total number, gender, and race. Additional student information such as ELL, special education enrollment, free and reduced lunch, homelessness, or other facts can be included in the gender and race section or in a separate section.

2. Leadership information by gender and race.

3. Staff information by position, gender, experience, education, and race.

4. Academic data by race (and gender, if available) and at least 2 years of reading and math.

5. Attendance data.

6. Discipline data.

7. Initiatives and programs.

8. Perceptions of staff and teachers: How do they describe the school? How do they feel about working here? What do they say about students?

You will find templates for Figures 5.1 and 5.2 as well as others to download on this book's website at racialequityleadership.com (Chapter 5 section).

Consider the following as you examine what your dashboard reveals about your school:

- Find patterns and linkages that contribute to the outcomes you see. What are possible cause-and-effect relationships that contribute to the student results?

- How do perceptions about the school, according to staff and teachers, align with other sections? How do those perceptions align with the school mission and your perceptions?

- Which mind frames align with this dashboard?

Figure 5.2 Data Dashboard Template

School Name

Vision

Mission

Staff

Teachers:

Paraprofessionals:

Nonlicensed staff:

Total staff:

% male, % female

Experience

>10 years: %

3–10 years: %

<3 years: %

Racial Background/All Staff

Black/African American:

Hispanic:

Asian:

White:

Native:

Perceptions

Enrollment # students

% female, % male

% Hispanic

% Black/African American

% Asian

% Two or more races

% White

% American Indian

ELL: %

SPED: %

Free & Reduced Lunch: %

Principal:

Assistant Principal/s:

Coaches:

LT:

Initiatives and Programming

Race	Math 2016	2017	Reading 2016	2017
American Indian				
Asian				
Black				
Hispanic				
White				
2+ Races				
SPED				

Discipline Data

Attendance

109

Student Shadowing: Lessons From a Day in the Life of a Student of Color

Truly knowing our schools requires qualitative data as well as the quantitative data that make up much of our data dashboards. Student shadowing, as Dr. Mhiripiri-Reed shared, uses direct observation to provide real-time qualitative evidence of what is happening in our schools.

When one of our institute participants, the principal of a diverse middle school, spent the majority of a school day shadowing a student from his town's Somali community, he unearthed some surprising data. The seventh-grader was a member of an immigrant family and learning English as a second language (ESL). After reviewing his notes, the principal tallied that the student had been given only two opportunities to speak the entire day. She had been spoken to in every class but invited to participate only twice. The principal was astonished to discover that despite the Title III language programs initiated in his school, an ESL student faced this kind of isolation rather than being engaged in her new language. Following a student to witness facts about their learning, interactions, relationships, and simple daily experiences uncovers the truth about our schools in exacting detail.

The key to student shadowing is staying objective, making low-inference observations and notes that stay with the facts without interpretation, opinion, or judgment. Watching and noting *what* occurs rather than inferring *why* creates an objective overview of the student's experience. The example in Figure 5.3 shows a principal's notes for shadowing a 7-year-old Black boy. After analyzing the data, the principal recorded a summary of the details and organized the facts on the second page. Using this or another template as discussed in the activity at the end of this section will help you shadow a student effectively and glean vital information from your observations.

After spending as much of your day as possible shadowing one student, your notes become a set of raw data that can pinpoint areas that need to be addressed. Do you need to discuss instructional practices with a teacher? Are some students expressing disparaging biases toward another student by smiling and glancing at friends when that student speaks? How will you deal with that behavior? The following activity is a guide for analyzing your notes and planning the changes that need to be made.

Figure 5.3 Student Shadowing Notes Example

SHADOW A STUDENT FOR A DAY—GRADE 2—BLACK MALE

Student Data

- 7 years old
- 1st year at ____ school
- The teacher described the student as "a younger second-grade student in age but a physically bigger student."
- Student ILP indicates that the student's strengths include love of reading, curious, determined, empathetic with genuine excitement.

Class Schedule

8:30–9:15 Breakfast
morning meeting
9:15–9:55 Focus time reading
10:00–10:45 Reader's Workshop
10:55–11:40 Science
11:45–12:15 Recess
12:15–12:45 Lunch
12:50–2:15 Math
2:15–2:45 ST Math
2:45–3:00 Snack

Breakfast/Morning Meeting

8:30–9:15

- The student arrived with breakfast in hand.
- Student ate breakfast.
- Students go to the library to change books individually.
- The student was the last one to return from the book exchange.
- Everyone was called to sit on the carpet.
- Students sat in a circle and greeted one another.

Focus Time 9:15–9:55

- Tiered reading intervention time.
- Switched teacher for service.
- The teacher worked with 2 groups, tiered 1 and 2 of about 14 or fewer students per group.
- 1st activity was to find the answers on a worksheet with teacher guidance.
- 2nd activity was to read individually and respond in writing.
- The student was highly responsive to small guided group learning in activity #1. He raised his hand 12 times and was called on 2 times.

Reading 10:00–10:45

- The student sat in the second row nearest the teacher on the carpet for whole-group instruction.
- Was the second-to-last student still looking for a book to read during independent reading.
- At guided small-group practice, the student sat next to the teacher and asked twice for the date to write on the clipboard (10 minutes).
- During independent reading time, he sat quietly at his desk and stared around the room until I reminded him to read. Read two books after I reminded him once

Science 10:55–11:40

- The student had a challenging time following the teacher's directions.
- He was in the "take-a-break" chair twice with several reminders to follow directions, sit still, and be quiet.
- Raised his hand to respond to questions.

Playground/Lunch 11:45–12:45

- He was the last in line during recess.
- He asked the teacher a question: "I thought we could only play tennis on Tuesdays and Thursdays, so how come you bring the equipment out on Friday?"
- He spent half his time walking alone until he finally joined a group to play in the sand toward the last 5 minutes of recess.

Math/ST Math 12:50–2:45

- Sat in the second row nearest the teacher on the carpet.
- As he continued to sit and wait, he began to hum softly (I couldn't hear from the back of the room). He was sent to take-a-break in the buddy room.
- At the buddy room, he sat still and looked around the room.
- Returned to math class after 11 minutes.
- Upon returning to class, he went to sit at his desk.

(Continued)

111

Figure 5.3 (Continued)

SHADOW A STUDENT FOR A DAY—GRADE 2—BLACK MALE

he got praise for being quiet even when a misbehaving student was distracting him.

- During pair-share, he was the only one who had no partner. He became frustrated by sighing loud enough for me to hear him from the back of the room. He started to slam his books on the table and let out more sighs. When the student walked by and bumped into him, he made a loud growl. The teacher talked to him.

- He was the first to wait in line when the whistle was blown, signaling the end of recess.

- He waited, but no students came to stand behind him. They formed a new line and indicated to him to go to the back of their line.

- Eventually, he fell asleep and slept from 12:38 to 12:45.
- I woke him up for ST Math after the teacher left with the rest of the class.
- Upon arrival at the computer lab, the teacher told him to go to the nurse for some rest. He rested until 2:40 and returned to class for a snack.

"Sitting in Place" Classroom Behaviors (Context of 1 period)

- 90% or more of the time, the student sat quietly at his desk or on the carpet.

- His eyes—50% of the time staring straight ahead, on the floor, or at his desk and work materials.

- Range of 10–20% hand-raising depending on the subject/teacher.

- 30% of the time doing the work or focusing on the teacher.

- The student demonstrated frustration usually toward the end of each subject period via letting out a frustrated sigh, slightly slamming books on the table, or getting emotional.

Hand Raised vs. Being Called On

Subject/ Teacher	Hand Raised	Called On
1	12	2
2	5	0
3	6	4
4	4	0

Note: The student was called on near the end after having raised his hand several times.

Percentage of Teacher/Student Talk

90%/10%

Student Attendance

97%

Source: Created by Halee Vang (2013). Reprinted with permission.

112

Activity

A Day in the Life

Shadowing a Student

Step 1: Download a student shadowing template from the website racialequityleadership.com (Ch. 5 section) and schedule a school day to spend the majority of your time shadowing a student.

Step 2: Choose a child of color to shadow.

Step 3 (Shadowing Protocol): As you observe your student, note facts about his or her experiences without filtering them through your interpretations or opinions. Describe actions such as body language, facial expressions, and teacher and fellow students' words and behaviors.

You can draw a diagram on a separate sheet to show where the student is sitting in class and create your own shorthand to record some statements verbatim (*T* for teacher, *S* for shadowed student, *WFS* for white female student, etc.). For example, one entry may note what happened with the student 15 minutes into the class: *15 min, T talking, S puts down her pencil and sits back. Stops looking at T and stares at the table.*

Collect and include perceptions of your school that you have heard from teachers, staff, students, parents, and community members:

- What do they say when they talk about your school?
- What words or phrases do you hear in the teachers' lounge?
- What do you hear students say about their teachers?
- In the grocery store, what do you hear community members say about your school?

Step 4: Briefly summarize your notes and organize your findings as shown in the example in Figure 5.3.

Step 5: Reflect on your findings:

- What essential insights around teaching and race emerged for you?
- In your specific circumstance, what adult actions concern you on behalf of instruction?
- How does your shadowing data inform you on the academic needs of students of color?
- What do you plan to do now that you have seen specific student experiences in action?

Retaining for Success and the Commitment to Excellence: Who's Willing and Able?

Bringing your teachers into alignment with your beliefs as a leader for equity is a challenge on several fronts, but we have learned that starting out with an assessment of where each of them stands on these issues can launch your work more efficiently. Some of your teachers may be willing and able to implement all of your equity initiatives, from those that impact the classroom to those that transform the building environment. Others may be on the other end of the spectrum, unwilling and incapable of doing any of the work.

Your standards as a leader set the roadmap for your teachers. As shown in Figure 5.4, your teachers take direction according to your stated "givens," such as "We do not remove Black and Brown students from the school" and "We believe all children can learn." The upper-right quadrant contains your standards as principal, listing the supports, feedback, and data you provide to lead your staff. The two lower quadrants illustrate the political landscape and other challenges that factor into your decision-making about retaining teachers.

Our leadership framework for developing teachers into a cohesive group of dedicated and proactive instructors for racial equity contains

Figure 5.4 Retaining for Results (RFR)

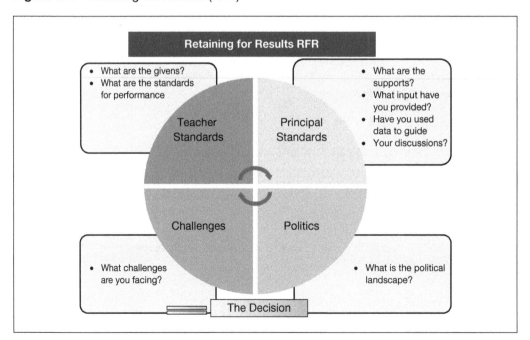

two models, the first for identifying your staff's dispositions about racial work and the second for holding critical conversations that lead to change.

Assessing Your Staff. The willingness/capacity quadrant, based on will/skill concepts and matrixes in organizational management and education (Jackson, 2013; Mayer & Dufresne, 2009), is an efficient framework for diving in to understand your staff specifically in terms of educating for racial equity. You will most likely be able to describe behaviors in each quadrant, as shown in the examples in Table 5.1. As leaders it is our responsibility to move our staff forward, regardless of where they fit in this quadrant. The quadrants are organized clockwise from most willing and able to least, as follows:

"Willing and Able": These teachers are skilled and motivated to do the work and improve. They are your equity allies, leading by example for their students and other staff.

"Willing but Unable": These are your biggest potential learners, currently lacking skills but open and enthusiastic about coaching and professional development.

"Unwilling but Able": For whatever reason, these equity-trained teachers have lost the motivation and passion for putting their skills to work. Their attitudes can be frustrating and cause a drop in morale as others may think *They were the gung-ho frontrunners and fizzled out, so what's the point in trying?*

"Unwilling and Unable": Teachers who show no interest in equity work and have not developed any skills can create a toxic environment.

After listing the behaviors that provide your evidence of these states of willingness and capacity, the following exercise asks you to fill out another quadrant that lists the teachers who fall into each category. You will then have four distinct groups to address with the appropriate action. Your teacher quadrant invites you to reflect on the basic call to action for each group. *My willing and able person needs to be challenged to gain a new skill level. I must provide professional development opportunities for my willing but unable people. My unwilling but able people need adequate stimulation to make change. More than likely, I should help my unwilling and unable person find a new job.* Removing staff is an absolute option, and frankly, we believe there is not enough removal. We're not saying it's easy, but when your intention is fixed on the best outcome for all students, this decision will increasingly feel justified.

When you complete the following activity, placing your teachers' names in each group, you will know who needs to a) upgrade their skills to the next level, b) begin professional development, c) be stimulated to integrate their skills and regain their passion, or d) have another chance to embrace equity or move on.

Table 5.1 Willingness/Capacity Quadrant: Sample List of Teacher Behaviors

	ABLE	UNABLE
WILLING	**Willing and Able** Good at everything and motivated to get better • Signs up for new initiatives and implements them • Teaches others • Shares new ideas • Serves as a coach	**Willing but Unable** Open to coaching and professional development but unable to transfer the professional development into practice • Tries but implements unsuccessfully • Attends all training • Unorganized and struggles with finding the time to employ new ideas with fidelity • Can speak to the new ideas but cannot carry out
UNWILLING	**Unwilling but Able** Has the skills to do it but has lost the motivation and passion • Avoids new learning • Does the minimum • Shows little faith in new ideas taking hold	**Unwilling and Unable** Not skilled to do the work and unwilling to engage in getting better • Avoids new learning • Incapable of employing new ideas successfully • Poor results with students • Does the minimum

Source: Adapted from Mayer & Dufrense (2009).

Activity

Coaching, Training, and Retaining/Removing for Success

Who's Willing and Able?

To begin uncovering where your teachers stand with equity work in your school, list the behaviors you've seen that fall under the categories in the quadrant below (see examples in Table 5.1).

Willingness/Capacity Quadrant for My School

	ABLE	UNABLE
WILLING	**Willing and Able** **(Challenge)** Good at everything and motivated to get better • • • •	**Willing but Unable** **(Coach)** Open to coaching and professional development but unable to transfer the professional development into practice • • • •

	ABLE	UNABLE
UNWILLING	**Unwilling but Able** **(Motivate)** Has the skills to do it but has lost the motivation and passion • • • •	**Unwilling and Unable** **(Remove)** Not skilled to do the work and unwilling to engage in getting better • • • •

Once you've listed the behaviors/actions that fall into the categories above, identify where each of your teachers belongs in the quadrant below.

Willingness/Capacity Quadrant for My School Teacher Groups (Names) and My Call to Action

	ABLE	UNABLE
WILLING	**Willing and Able** **(Challenge)** Good at everything and motivated to get better **MY TASK:** Challenge them to advance to a new skill level. _____	**Willing but Unable** **(Coach)** Open to coaching and professional development but unable to transfer the professional development into practice **MY TASK:** Provide coaching and professional development. _____
UNWILLING	**Unwilling but Able** **(Motivate)** Has the skills to do it but has lost the motivation and passion **MY TASK:** Stimulate them to regain their motivation and act on their passionate belief that all children can learn. _____	**Unwilling and Unable** **(Remove)** Not skilled to do the work and unwilling to engage in getting better **MY TASK:** Determine whether they should have another opportunity or help them move on. _____

Investing your time in this level of individualized action boosts the foundation of your equity work and shows your staff your commitment to excellence. You're showing everyone—including yourself—that you walk your talk. You're also challenging yourself to engage in conversations about the emotionally triggering topic of race. Our second model for leading your staff cuts to the chase with a step-by-step process for conducting these urgent conversations.

Holding Critical Conversations. Now that you know which teachers are unwilling to move ahead with transforming their school—and the level of their resistance—your plan for change begins with a conversation. Being skillful at talking about race takes practice, and in the beginning most of us take up precious time avoiding it. We try to figure out how to get our message across without annoying or upsetting anyone and making ourselves vulnerable to our own emotional responses. As Scott (2004) writes about her model of "fierce conversations," "While we often tell ourselves we are softening the message so as not to hurt someone else's feelings, we are really trying to protect ourselves. We do not look forward to dealing with our own emotions, much less someone else's" (p. 145).

The principals in our institute tell us that the first sign of change when they begin racial equity work is an increase in the number of conversations they must have. To help leaders get comfortable talking with people quickly and efficiently about change, we present Scott's (2004) 60-second opening-statement technique designed to launch a productive exchange that lowers the potential for an emotional confrontation.

When you have decided to speak to a teacher about his/her equity commitment, and before you prepare your opening statement, clarify your objective for the encounter through the following steps (Scott, 2004):

1. Identify your most pressing issue (concerning the teacher).

2. Clarify the issue. What's going on? How long? How bad is it?

3. Determine the current impact. How is this impacting me? What is being produced? How is it impacting others?

4. Determine the implications.

5. Examine your personal contribution to this issue.

6. Describe the ideal outcome.

7. Commit to action. What is the most potent first step for me? What will get in the way, and how will I get around it? When do I start? (p. 87)

For example, consider this scenario in which a principal is preparing to speak to an "unwilling but able" teacher about a current issue.

1. *Issue.* Mrs. Smith has "given up" on two Black girls in her tenth-grade English class and skipped the last two equity initiatives

staff meetings. After attending 2 years of equity training, she had confronted her bias and committed herself to respecting and calling on all the voices in her classroom, but now, a year later, she regularly calls out the two Black girls for talking in the back row and "punishes" them by ignoring them.

2. *Clarifying*. She sends them to the office for talking rather than calling on them during class or otherwise engaging them in discussion. The students said this has been happening since the beginning of the semester, and they claim some of their Black friends complain to them about the same thing. She also skips our equity meetings.

3. *Current impact*. Mrs. Smith's absence from our equity meetings waters down the equity mission for the rest of the staff. It sends a message that this work is not sustainable or really important to the school. The two students are angry that she doesn't do anything when the white students talk in class, and they feel betrayed by her.

4. *Implications*. Mrs. Smith can resent the work she had begun and spread her attitude to other staff. Morale can continue to erode and drive other teachers away from the work. Students of color can reject Mrs. Smith and not engage in her class.

5. *My contribution to the issue*. I did not check in with Smith about her commitment to our equity initiatives as often as necessary. I did not press her to share her concerns during our meetings. I did not act on signs that her racial consciousness was relapsing.

6. *Describe the ideal outcome*. Smith recommits to integrating her skills around race into practice. She has a restorative conversation with the two girls and expresses her willingness to listen to them.

7. *Commit to action*. What is the most potent first step for me? What will get in the way, and how will I get around it? When do I start? In my conversation with the teacher, I need to state my expectations and offer her the supports I have defined as my standards in leading and developing my staff.

After reaching this clarity around your issue with a teacher, you can prepare the critical opening of your conversation. This technique gets the full message across without leaving room for an immediate interruption that can throw things into a spiral. Organized and ready, you can confidently state your points and then listen to the teacher's response. The opening statement involves seven steps:

The 60-Second Opening Statement

1. Name the issue.

2. Describe a specific example.

3. Describe your emotions about the issue.

4. Clarify what is at stake.

5. Identify your contribution to this problem.

6. Indicate your wish to resolve the issue.

7. Invite your partner to respond. (Scott, 2004, p. 254)

Following the Mrs. Smith scenario earlier, here is our imaginary principal's opening statement:

> I understand you are disciplining Kim Tatum and Junelle Richards for talking in class but not the white girls in the back of the class who are doing the same thing.
>
> You sent Kim and Junelle to my office three times last week for this behavior but did not send anyone else. You are also ignoring the girls by not calling on them.
>
> I am concerned that you are repeatedly singling out these students, and I'm frustrated that you are going back to old behavior and not attending our equity meetings.
>
> When you step back from the work that you've become so skilled in, you set an example that it's not important. The students see it and feel it, and the staff feel less committed to our mission of teaching all our students with excellence.
>
> I regret that I didn't reach out to you often enough to check in on how you're doing with implementing the equity protocols you studied. I should have been more on top of that and talked to you after you missed your first meeting.
>
> I believe you can make a big difference here, and I want to help you get back on track as one of our leaders on our mission.
>
> I expect you to attend all equity meetings and to set up a meeting with me, Kim, and Junelle to restore your teacher–student relationship. I will be following up with you and these students. Would you like to add anything about resolving this issue?

In addition to the carefully thought-out initial statement, we have found that Singleton's (2015) seminal Courageous Conversations About Race (CCAR) protocol is an essential tool for tackling a conversation about a pressing issue as well as for any discussion about race. The following model outlines the CCAR process designed to "engage, sustain, and deepen interracial dialogue about race in order to examine schooling and improve student achievement" (Singleton, 2015, p. 26). We discuss each element of this protocol in detail at the opening of the next chapter, but the document in the following activity lists the steps and agreements, conditions, and suggestions at the heart of these conversations.

Activity

The Successful Urgent Conversation

Select a teacher from your willingness/capacity quadrant with whom you need to address an issue. Use the seven-step process for reaching clarity on the issue (write it out), and then create your opening statement according to the guidelines in the bottom half of Figure 5.5. An interactive version is available for download on this book's website at racialequityleadership .com (Chapter 5 section).

Figure 5.5 A Model for Direct and Clear Conversations

OBJECTIVES	AGREEMENTS, CONDITIONS, AND SUGGESTIONS
Think of an issue that needs to be addressed with a staff member perpetuating inequities in your school. Make sure that your partner fully understands and acknowledges your position and interests. Bring clarity to what is needed for resolutions and what next steps will be necessary to get there. Determine how you will hold each other responsible for keeping your agreements. In follow-up, reflect on how these agreements help strengthen the work of your P.R.E.P.	• Speak your truth • Stay engaged • Experience discomfort • Accept and expect nonclosure • Keep it personal, local, and immediate • Keep the spotlight on racial intersection • Engage multiple racial perspectives • Monitor the agreements • Establish working definitions of race and racism • Examine the presence and role of whiteness • Enter with courage • Practice humanity • Exit with empathy CCAR protocol is essential for the follow-up after your opening statement.

OBJECTIVES	AGREEMENTS, CONDITIONS, AND SUGGESTIONS
YOUR 60-SECOND OPENING STATEMENT	
• Name the issue:	
• Select a specific example that illustrates the behavior or situation I want to change:	
• Describe my emotions around the issue:	
• Clarify why this is important. What is at stake to gain or lose for me, others, the team, or the organization?	
• Identify my contribution(s) to this problem:	
• How I will state my wish to resolve this issue:	
• What I will say to invite my partner to respond:	

Source: Adapted from Scott (2004) and Singleton (2015).

Case Study for Examining a Racial Problem of Practice

The following brief case study invites you to apply what you have learned about racial beliefs and behavior and effective communication tools to examine how you would respond to a racial incident with your staff. The case takes place in a suburban elementary school district in the Midwest and involves the following individuals:

- A first-year female principal of color
- A white female assistant principal who has been in the building for several years
- A nontenured, third-grade white female teacher
- A Black nonlicensed female behavior specialist in charge of working with disruptive behavior in classrooms. She has been in this position for 15 years and is assigned to the white female teacher's classroom for behavioral support.

Background

The situation occurred midway through the school year. The white assistant principal came upon a loud and heated argument between the white classroom teacher and the Black behavior specialist during the school day. The white assistant principal intervened and stopped the argument. She reported the situation to the new female principal of color.

The argument began when the white teacher interrupted the Black female behavior specialist who was working with an upset Black female student in the hallway. The white teacher disagreed with how the behavior specialist was handling the situation. She told her to remove the student from the hallway and take her to the office for disruptive behavior. The behavior specialist was trying to de-escalate the student by redirecting her and coaching.

The principal asked the teacher and behavior specialist to meet in the morning in a restorative circle to see if the situation could be resolved. The meeting went poorly, and no relationships were restored. The following occurred during the meeting:

- The teacher used stereotypes in talking about the Black female behavior specialist, such as describing her as loud and aggressive.

- The teacher stated that she did not feel safe with the Black female behavior specialist.

- The teacher cried.

- The teacher wanted her union representative to join them.

- The behavior specialist remained silent.

As the meeting got progressively worse and it was getting close to school start time, the principal asked the two individuals what they could do to move forward and support students even though this situation had not been resolved. In response:

- The teacher stated that she did not want the behavior specialist to work with her or any of her students.

- The behavior specialist replied that she had to work with students in the teacher's room because it was her job, and she could not *not* do her job.

- The principal agreed that the behavior specialist did not have to work with students in the teacher's classroom until this situation was resolved.

The principal held follow-up meetings individually with both the teacher and the behavior specialist, yet the situation remained unresolved. The principal is unsure of the next steps but knows she needs to address the situation.

Questions for Examining the Case Study

1. What is the racial problem of practice?

2. What might be stopping the leader from addressing this problem/situation?

3. What are the possible actions to address this problem/situation short-term?

4. What are the possible actions to address this problem/situation long-term?

5. What resistance can be expected, and how might the leader move through the resistance?

Racist Ideas, Racist Policies

Leading your teachers to ignite change includes having critical conversations that will reverse negative trends and keep your school focused on expanding racial awareness. We have explored the facets of systemic racism that demand our willingness to transform our beliefs and behaviors and rewrite the culture of our schools, and understanding racist practices at an even deeper level can help us move ahead with more clarity. Ibram X. Kendi (2017a), for one, is broadening our awareness by breaking down the problem of inequity in our institutions, including education, from a new perspective.

Kendi (2017a) rejects the assumption that racist policies are the product of hateful, ignorant individuals who use their racist ideas to create these policies. Instead, his research concludes that the causal relationship goes in the opposite direction: Historically, those who practiced racial discrimination (e.g., through slavery, segregation policies) fostered racist ideas among white people that led to ignorance and hate and allowed the discrimination to continue. In other words, those in power who benefited from racist acts or policies like slavery, segregation, and mass incarceration created racist ideas of Black people so that others would consider Blacks deserving of slavery and other forms of oppression. This distraction worked its magic to suppress resistance to racial discrimination in all its forms, an outcome that Kendi (2017a) describes as "the principal function of racist ideas in American history" (p. 9).

As consumers of contrived racist ideas, whites blame Black people for problems that are actually created by those who hold the power and glean the benefits of oppression. Whites have been manipulated into feeling hatred for Blacks so that they will not be motivated to challenge racist practices against Blacks, as expressed in this causal relationship:

Racial discrimination > racist ideas > ignorance/hate
(Kendi, 2017a, p. 9).

"Racist ideas have done their job on us," Kendi writes (2017a, p. 9). "We have a hard time recognizing that racial discrimination is the sole cause of racial disparities in this country and the world at large." This view invites us to take another look at racial ignorance and hatred and its role in perpetuating the inequities in our schools. Which educational policies have been written by those who believe that students of color are unable to learn due to poverty or other family situations? Which policies have been written by leaders who believe that Black students are innately more aggressive and dangerous than white students and so more deserving of discipline? Why do those policymakers hold those beliefs? Who benefits? Consider the simple example of funding for public schools that is taken as the "norm." Property taxes collected in higher-income districts result in better-funded schools. Lower-income districts whose housing is valued less gather less in property taxes and have less to spend on schools. The issue involves a few more variables, but in general, the overarching policy of funding public education marginalizes people of color and benefits whites. On the federal funding level, Kendi (2017b) remarks that white people "have been led to believe that the problem is not Republican politicians who are steering money from public education to the military; the problem is women who are having more children because they want to have more welfare, and that's why the state has less money for them" (n.p.).

Kendi's (2017a) analysis of American history is part of the vanguard calling for education policy that acknowledges the role of systemic racism and does not blame students of color for inequities in test scores. This understanding states that when policymakers do not reflect on their implicit bias (shaped by the powers that be), their conscious or unconscious actions about discipline, testing, grade weighting, and other policies serve to promote white achievement at the expense of the achievement of students of color. The following reflection gives you an opportunity to examine your school policies in light of Kendi's (2017b) ideas as shared in a brief video.

Reflect on This
My School Process and Policy

After watching the 6-and-a-half-minute video of Ibram X. Kendi (2017b) found on the book's website at racialequityleadership.com (Chapter 5 section), think about a policy in your school that may be driven by a racist idea. Analyze that policy by

1) filling out the chart in Figure 5.6 and

2) using Kendi's (2017b) causal relationship to consider the policy's origins and development: racial discrimination > racist ideas > ignorance/hate.

Figure 5.6 Innovation and Equity Lens Policy Review

Is this review process relevant to the policy?   Yes   No   Notes: _____

Innovation and Equity Lens Policy Review   Policy # _____

Date _____

How does this policy impact our core values and mission?	Who benefits?	Whose voices are needed?	What needs to change?	How will the policy be monitored?
How does this policy deliver on our core values and vision?	Who benefits from the current policy? How?	Which internal and external voices will we ask for guidance on this policy?	What needs to change in the current policy to deliver equitable outcomes?	What are the changes in this policy meant to address or deliver?
Does this policy allow us to think differently?	Who is adversely impacted by the current policy?	What will we ask them?	Is the needed change within our circle of influence?	How will we measure or monitor the impact of the changes to this policy?
Does this policy allow us to innovate to achieve equitable outcomes?	What is the impact on them?		What data or other evidence indicates these changes will lead to more equitable outcomes?	

Desired Outcomes

Monitoring Process

Source: Minnesota Equity Alliance (2018). Reprinted with permission.

126

To apply these ideas further, let's look at one school's grade-weighting policy to examine the role of racist ideas in drafting the policy (see Figure 5.7). After reading the policy, which is posted on a district's public website, answer the questions that follow.

Figure 5.7 Sample School Grade-Weighting Policy

Sample School District Policy

School district (A district in the central United States)

File: IKC

Adopted: April 28, 1994

Revised: June 27, 2006

WEIGHTED GRADES

The Board of Education of the School District encourages students to challenge themselves academically and to pursue the most rigorous and challenging courses that best promote their academic achievement. It is the intention of the board to recognize and encourage additional effort and learning required in classes beyond the usual level of difficulty. To accomplish this, a weighted grade scale will be implemented and used externally for college admission and internally for determining high school grade point average and eligibility for school academic awards and honors.

Weighted grade point average will be displayed on student transcripts. All students taking high school courses may choose between a weighted or regular grade point average at the end of their eleventh-grade school year. The selected grade point average will be the only grade point average to appear on the student's transcript for his or her senior year of high school.

Beginning with the class of 2010, high schools will not include rank or rank their students in any way on transcripts.

High schools will consider the number of students desiring weighted grade classes when determining the number of sections offered.

The following grade scale will be used for weighted grades.

A = 5.0

B = 4.0

C = 3.0

D = 2.0

F = 0.0

Criteria for Determining Which Courses Are Weighted:

1. Only courses in the following departments may be weighted: language arts, math, science, social studies, and foreign language, with the exception that all advanced placement courses, pre-international baccalaureate and international baccalaureate courses, and fifth-year language courses are to be weighted.

2. Weighted courses must be other than those specifically required for graduation.

3. Weighted courses may be offered in Grades 9, 10, 11, or 12.

4. Weighted courses must include material of greater depth and breadth, be more rigorous, and be more academically challenging than other courses for the college bound. Instructors should expect that students in weighted courses are able to work independently.

5. The expected rate of learning in weighted courses must be much greater than in regular college-oriented courses.

6. Weighted courses include those comparable in intellectual challenge and student ability level to advanced placement courses.

End of File: IKC

1. What is the original racist idea in this policy?

2. What is racist about this policy?

3. Who benefits from this policy?

4. Does this type of policy exist in your school?

5. What would an antiracist policy on this topic look like?

In this chapter, you learned details about your school at a level you may not have observed previously and began to work with communication tools to integrate your knowledge into your leadership practice. As we move forward on the Theory of Action pathway from the first tier of "knowing," Part II begins with specific leadership strategies for creating change.

References

Jackson, R. R. (2013). *Never underestimate your teachers: Instructional leadership for excellence in every classroom.* Alexandria, VA: ASCD.

Kendi, I. X. (2017a). *Stamped from the beginning: The definitive history of racist ideas in America.* New York: Bold Type Books.

Kendi, I. X. (2017b). *How does self-interest shape today's narratives?* [Video file.] Retrieved from https://www.youtube.com/watch?v=f4Zt73MML5s.

Mayer, M., & Dufresne, D. (2009). *Willing and able: The commitment to excellence.* Retrieved from https://med.wmich.edu/sites/default/files/F3.pdf.

Minnesota Equity Alliance. (2018). Retrieved from https://www.equityalliancemn.org/.

Scott, S. (2004). *Fierce conversations: Achieving success at work & in life, one conversation at a time.* New York: Berkley.

Singleton, G. E. (2015). *Courageous conversations about race: A field guide for achieving equity in schools.* Thousand Oaks, CA: Corwin.

Vang, H. (2013). *Student shadowing notes example* [personal materials].

PART II

Integrating Knowledge Into Practice

Racism is an old idea. A tradition that harms children is not worth conserving or continuing. Life is wealth and relationships are wealth. Domination, subjugation, exploitation, and the luxury of looking away is a poverty of the soul. But we have choices. We can learn and grow.

—Sun Yung Shin (2016)

A Principal's Critical Duty

CHAPTER 6

Knowing and Understanding High-Return Instructional Strategies

My early successes in life were, I knew, a product of the consistent love and high expectations with which I was surrounded as a child, both at home and at school.

—Michelle Obama (2018)

Thirteen years ago, Minneapolis metro-area elementary principal Shelley Nielsen had an encounter with a parent that changed everything she understood about culturally relevant education. She and other principals in her district had already received years of training in equity and culturally relevant programs by Ruby Payne and Glenn Singleton, but her interaction that day with the father of a Black male student was pivotal. The situation revolved around her school's policy about lunch accounts, which at the time included stamping a child's hand when their account was out of funds. The school considered it a simple reminder for parents, figuring that children often forget to let them know that they need to put more money in the account. The father came to her office that day and said, "Do you have any idea what it feels like to walk around with a mark on your hand?" Shelley thought, *No, I don't.* She grew up in a poor white family and took reduced-price lunch, but her school used tickets back then.

"I don't have any idea," she said.

"Actually, you haven't walked in my shoes at all," he said.

"You're absolutely right. I have not, and I have so much to learn from you" (S. Nielsen, personal communication, April 5, 2020).

As she told us this story, Shelley said, "When I think back on it now I want to cry. Our district had been doing a lot of work to do better with our students of color, but my conversation with that father changed me. I realized that if you're really going to make your practices culturally relevant, you have to know your students and families. You have to start with that relationship. The journey is about authentically knowing somebody else, being vulnerable and fully open to hear another person's story and experience. Being culturally relevant means fully knowing our students, understanding their schema, their culture, the things that are important to them as part of their family."

Shelley tells her families at the start of every year that they are their children's first educators, and it is the school's privilege to join them in the journey. "We're not trading off," she says. "We authentically believe that what they bring to the table is as important as what we bring to the table. My staff constantly hears this from me—the school is joining the family."

In her role as principal of a school with a primarily white teaching staff, Shelley has developed a strategy for working with teachers who need to address their lack of success with their students of color and move toward culturally relevant teaching. With one teacher who lacked an authentic relationship with their Black students, for example, Shelley began on technical ground by sitting down with the teacher to look at 3 years of data. As typically happened, it took some time for the teacher to read the real story of the data. When Shelley asked the teacher what they saw, their first response was that they were "struggling more with reading than math." The teacher felt that some of their students didn't know how to read and, as a teacher, they didn't have the skill set to teach them at that level. Shelley then asked if the teacher saw any success stories in the data, and they said that their white students were doing very well. "I'm able to grow them more than a year, particularly my kids who come in at grade level at the beginning." When Shelley asked how their testing and grading looked for their students of color, the teacher got defensive and, as Shelley described it, moved into the feeling quadrant of the Courageous Conversation compass. She told the teacher to pause a minute and look into that feeling quadrant. To move them from feeling to thinking, she asked:

"What feedback are you getting from your students of color in your room? What are they saying to you?"

"I don't even know what they're saying to me," the teacher said.

"I need you to think about what messages they are giving to you, both unspoken and the spoken words they're saying in your class." They talked about the teacher's beliefs about their Black and Brown students, and they became vulnerable enough to eventually admit which group was "furthest" from them.

"Shelley, I realize right now that I struggle the most with my Black girls," the teacher said. "I'm intimidated by them, and they don't like me. I don't know what to say because I'm not relevant to them. I don't have Black girls at home; I've got a girl and a boy, and I even struggle with my own daughter." As Shelley helped the teacher see how they were bringing their socialized experience into the classroom, they moved into a new space about their responsibility to them and how to radically change their teaching.

"I need to read books on Black girls—this is what I need!" the teacher said. "I need to find out what Black girls are reading so I can be relevant in my classroom."

That meeting took place 3 years ago, Shelley said, "and right now they're a totally different teacher. We had to start with something technical, drill it down, and keep going around that compass. I try to make sure

I'm reading them correctly, because when people start to get into 'list and defend' about their behavior, they're angry and in the feeling quadrant. I need to help them move into a more productive zone."

Another way Shelley leads her teachers to create culturally relevant classrooms is to bring them together to collectively look at their data and create lessons. When they recently discovered that they were doing a good job teaching students how to sound out words but, as testing revealed, a poor job helping them to understand what they were reading, they put their focus on comprehension and created "a culturally relevant lesson through all the comprehension benchmarks." They used Jackson's (2011) and Hattie's (2012) work to determine how to "ignite" a lesson; chunk it into small, manageable pieces; and create spaces for students to give them feedback on how well they taught. "The teachers were going to make sure students could see what a finished project should look like and, at the end of the lesson, ask the students to tell them how they did as a teacher," Shelley said. "It's all about the teacher finding out from the students how she is showing up to be successful." Culturally relevant lessons allow students to not only see themselves in the material but also talk about what their family would do and what their perspective looked like. "That's student voice," Shelley said. "We spend a lot of time talking about the power of student voice and how it helps us in creating authentic lessons."

Related to Jackson's (2011) approach about identifying student strengths, Shelley said that "it's my job to identify teachers' strengths because I want them to know that I see them as valuable and that I know they're here for a reason. Regardless of the fact that there are opportunities for growth, there are always going to be strengths they bring to the table, and we have to recognize that."

Through her years of leadership, Shelley has come to believe that the hardest work for principals is continuing their own growth, such as in making adaptive changes—changes that challenge long-held beliefs and behaviors. This is evident in her recent work to transform her school's discipline methods from punitive to restorative by working out a solution with families. Rather than staying with the old approach of responding to a specific behavior with a specific action, regardless of the circumstances, Shelley puts together a restorative circle with staff and families. "That's adaptive," she said, "and it's uncomfortable." She will call a family and arrange a meeting in which she asks what they would like from her in order to work on the issue together. "When you open it up this way you have to be very willing to do something that is totally outside your comfort zone, something you've never done in the past. Being a partner means I'm truly asking for their input. I'm going to work with that parent on what they believe is the best thing, because they know their child better than I do."

Our conversation with Shelley took place shortly after Minnesota's governor ordered schools to close in March 2020 due to the coronavirus. The new challenges arising for her and principals across the country in that stressful environment included getting all students supplied for online instruction at home. She was confident that "whatever we're putting in place will work for those who look like me," she said, so her priority was to actively engage her Black and Brown families to help her organize instruction that would work for them. Some households did not have Internet or a computer, a fact brought clearly to light during the pandemic. Trying to supply these students with the computers and services they needed—instead of settling for the paper packets that their teachers had never even seen—was, for Shelley, one way to walk her talk about being here to take care of each other. Quoting Paul Wellstone, the late U.S. senator from Minnesota, who stated, "We all do better when we all do better," she said that the pandemic was forcing us to pause and take care of each other because we didn't have a choice. When it came to trying to give quality instruction to all students in the midst of a national crisis, she found it unfortunate that the country was making the attempt because it had no choice rather than because "it was the right thing to do all along."

Shelley sees herself as constantly making the rounds of the Theory of Action we introduced in this book (see Figure 6.1), which begins with knowing ourselves and our purpose and winds toward implementing best practices (covered in this chapter) that result in high achievement for all students. Even with those positive results, the process always takes us back to the beginning to continue mining and transforming ourselves. "I'm a work in progress," Shelley said. "I still have a lot to learn about becoming a racially conscious person and antiracist leader, and my journey is nowhere close to being finished. But I'm in it. For me, it's not just about work; this is my life. It's about who I am 100% of the time. It's not how I show up as a principal, it's how I show up as Shelley. I still have a lot of growing to do."

Figure 6.1 Theory of Action

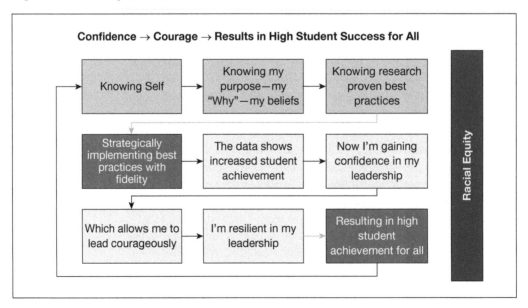

The practices Shelley described, such as integrating Hattie's (2012) visible learning approaches and Jackson's (2011) pedagogy of confidence to create equitable and culturally relevant classrooms, are discussed in detail in this chapter and the next. We also delve into the what and how of culturally relevant teaching and methods for assessing instructional methods.

Understanding successful instructional practices is absolutely critical for school leaders. Since the greatest impact on learning comes first from teachers and second from principals, principals are challenged to know and share what types of instruction work best (Seashore Louis et al., 2010). Because principals hire teachers and evaluate performance and teaching, our institute is dedicated to developing principals who value impactful mind-sets, beliefs, and instruction as they hire teachers.

In our experience as educators, principals, and district leaders, we have found that many principals come to the work without knowing about effective instruction. Principals enter a school still following old methods that are ineffective and sometimes harmful, and without understanding the high-return strategies promoted by Hattie (2012) and Jackson (2011), for example, they are not able to shift instruction to suit the students in our classrooms today. The beauty of Hattie's (2012) research, while it does not expressly address race, is that the high-impact methods he describes work for all children. Jackson's (2011) method, explored in depth in the next chapter, brings the high-quality practices typically reserved for gifted programs into all classrooms to benefit all children. Knowing Hattie's (2012) and Jackson's (2011) work empowers principals to upgrade the instruction in their schools that results in high achievement for every child.

The instructional strategies in this and the following chapter will dispel many myths principals may have about teaching. How many of us bought into the idea that small classes improve learning or that pulling kids out of a classroom and "fixing" them in another will benefit them? Research doesn't prove those practices work. While a smaller classroom is more convenient for the teacher, since she doesn't change her instruction when her class size is reduced from 28 to 20, her results are the same. Without changing her approach, her class size doesn't make a difference. Research also doesn't prove that putting students in categories and grouping some as low-achieving will allow them to catch up, because they never do. As we'll see, what *does* improve achievement are high expectations, relationship building, teachers getting feedback from students and vice versa, identifying student strengths, and other practices promoted in Hattie's (2012) and Jackson's (2011) research.

Before exploring the high-return instructional strategies Hattie (2012) identified in his analysis of 95,000 studies, let's return to the Courageous Conversation protocol introduced in the last chapter and described by Shelley as a tool she uses in every staff meeting and one-on-one interaction with teachers. Your work to integrate proven-effective instructional strategies in your school will include having conversations that tackle some deeply held beliefs about teaching. "Going around the compass," as Shelley calls it, can be a solid technique for productively navigating those difficult conversations.

Protocol for Singleton's Courageous Conversations

Talking productively about race and introducing change in our schools requires a thoughtful strategy. Each participant in a conversation about race is working within the larger system of a dominant white culture that perpetuates racial inequity in every layer of society. Only by being willing to acknowledge this power dynamic can we engage in conversations that will, piece by piece, disrupt the status quo. As Sue (2015) writes, "The invisibility of White racial superiority and minority inferiority is a well-kept secret as long as people are not allowed to talk about it" (p. 104).

We find Singleton's (2015) Courageous Conversation protocol an essential tool for holding discussions about race in our institute, and we train our principals to use it in their leadership. Honest dialogues about our school's barriers to achievement for students of color are "an educational necessity" (Singleton, 2015, p. 26) that can be achieved with this strategy. Singleton defines the Courageous Conversation as a dialogue that

- engages those who won't talk,

- sustains the conversation when it gets uncomfortable or diverted, and

- deepens the conversation to the point where authentic understanding and meaningful actions occur (p. 26).

The Courageous Conversation protocol consists of two elements, the *four agreements* that identify how the process is carried out and the *six conditions* that guide the content of the discussion. Since dialogues about race challenge comfort levels beyond those of "normal" discussions, the four agreements create a space in which discomfort can arise without participants shutting down through silence, anger, defiance, or judgment. This is achieved by participants agreeing to the following:

The Four Agreements

1. Stay engaged

2. Speak your truth

3. Experience discomfort

4. Expect and accept nonclosure

Source: Singleton (2015).

The protocol is designed to be carried out in a particular order that follows the Courageous Conversation goals of keeping participants engaged, sustaining the conversation, and finally deepening the discussion. The following description of the six conditions begins with Singleton's (2015) definition; then indicates the *engage, sustain,* or *deepen* role of the condition; and concludes with our shortcut phrase.

The Six Conditions

1. Establish a racial context that is personal, local, and immediate. *[Engage participants to consider their own racial experiences, awareness, etc.]* Short rule: Focus on the PERSONAL, local, and immediate.

2. Isolate race while acknowledging the broader scope of diversity and the variety of factors and conditions that contribute to a racialized problem. *[Engage participants to consider their own racial experiences, awareness, etc.]* Short rule: ISOLATE race.

3. Develop understanding of race as a social/political construction of knowledge, and engage multiple racial perspectives to surface critical understanding. *[Sustain the conversation, embracing multiple perspectives.]* Short rule: Normalize SOCIAL CONSTRUCTION and multiple perspectives.

4. Monitor the parameters of the conversation by being explicit and intentional about the number of participants; prompts for discussion; and time allotted for listening, speaking, and reflecting. Use the Courageous Conversation Compass [introduced below] to determine how each participant is displaying emotion—mind, body, and soul— to access a given racial topic. *[Sustain the conversation, embracing multiple perspectives.]* Short rule: Monitor agreements and conditions and ESTABLISH PARAMETERS.

5. Establish agreement around a contemporary working definition of race, one that is clearly differentiated from ethnicity and nationality. [Ethnicity = culture (language, customs, etc. shared by a group); nationality = location/citizenship; race = skin color and other physical characteristics. Race is a social and cultural "construct of human variability based on perceived differences in biology, physical appearance, and behavior" (Haynes & Smedley, 1999, p. 38).] *[Deepen the dialogue by advancing into difficult issues about race.]* Short rule: Use a "WORKING DEFINITION" for race.

6. Examine the presence and role of whiteness and its impact on the conversation and the problem being addressed. *[Deepen the dialogue by advancing into difficult issues about race.]* Short rule: Examine the presence and role of "WHITENESS." (p. 28, annotated by the authors)

Source: Adapted from Singleton (2015).

The fourth condition recommends using Singleton's (2015) compass (see Figure 6.2) as a personal check-in tool to navigate where we are during a conversation about race. At any given moment, a participant may be responding emotionally, intellectually, morally, or relationally, as Singleton (2015, pp. 29–30) describes:

- *Emotionally*, we respond to information through *feelings*, when a racial issue strikes us at a physical level and causes an internal sensation such as anger, sadness, joy, or embarrassment. This response is seated in the *heart*.

- *Intellectually*, our primary response to a racial issue or information may be characterized by personal disconnect with the subject or a steadfast search for more information or data. Our intellectual response is often verbal and based on our best *thinking*. This response is seated in the *mind*.

- *Morally*, we respond from a deep-seated *belief* that relates to the racial information or event. This belief has to do with the rightness or wrongness of a given racial issue. The justifications for one's moral views are often situated in the "gut" and may not be verbally articulated. This response is situated in the *soul*.

- *Relationally*, we connect and respond to racial information through our *acting* or what is most often characterized as specific behaviors and actions. This response is aligned with the *hands and feet*, our limbs for doing.

Figure 6.2 Courageous Conversation Compass

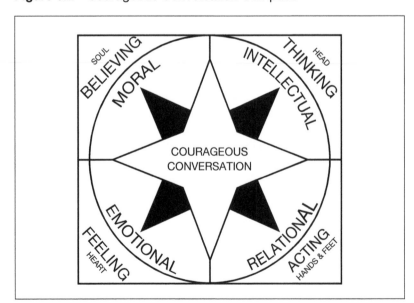

Source: Originally printed in Singleton, G. *Courageous Conversations About Race: A Field Guide to Achieving Equity in Schools, Second Edition* (2015). Corwin Press. Thousand Oaks, CA.

Guided by the compass, our conversations about race allow us to understand how we are personally engaged. In sharing where we are with the group, the compass "leads us to a mutual understanding of our varied beliefs and opinions" (Singleton, 2015, p. 29).

Each element of the Courageous Conversation protocol enhances participants' ability to grapple with uncomfortable issues by being aware of their own responses and moving through them rather than becoming paralyzed or acting out their anger or fear. The protocol promotes genuine, attentive listening to each other so that conversations about race in our schools can meet the ultimate goal of helping educators "improve education for *all* children" (Singleton, 2015, p. 31).

High-Return Instructional Strategies: John Hattie's Visible Learning, Part II

Guided by the Courageous Conversation protocol, principals can feel more confident about leading meetings and communicating with staff and the community about issues that can be uncomfortable and challenging for some. As you learn more about your school, including the specific needs of each of your teachers, and prioritize the steps that will move your school into your vision for equity, the evidence-based practices in this chapter and the next will help you turn your vision into reality. Specific strategies aligned with the approaches we introduced in Chapter 3 are developed here as a tool kit for implementation.

In Chapter 3 we discussed Hattie's (2012) concept of mind frames, or ways of thinking, that reflect how teachers and principals view their role as educators. We now turn to Hattie's ranking of teaching strategies and interventions to explore what delivers the lowest to highest results for students. As noted earlier, Hattie's research as of 2019 is based on an examination of more than 1,600 meta-analyses that report on the achievement of 300 million students around the world as published in more than 95,000 studies.

Hattie's (2012) rankings are effect sizes that show the magnitude of a teaching intervention, which is far more informative than simply stating that a strategy shows improvement. As Hattie (2012) explains, with a bar set at zero, 95% of what happens in education shows enhanced achievement; however, half of that "advancement" is of such low magnitude that it can be considered trivial. Looking at the normal distribution curve of educational intervention effect sizes in Figure 6.3, we should focus on those in the center that offer *at least an average gain in learning* and give serious consideration to every intervention above that average. The sweet spot, or average gain in progress, is measured as an effect size of 0.4, which marks the center point on Hattie's (2012) barometer of influence (see Figure 6.4). Hattie calls this measure the hinge point, where an intervention brings a year's worth of growth in a school year. Interventions above 0.4 are "above the norm and leading towards a more-than-expected growth over a year" (p. 272). The higher the effect size, the more impactful the strategy. Hattie's findings are startling at one level, showing us that highly touted improvement tactics such as reduced class sizes and elementary-grade homework actually have a lower than average impact on student progress. This research helps us steer away from weak practices and forge ahead with those that promise the most improvement in achievement for all students.

Items in the sampling of low-impact strategies listed in Figure 6.5 may look familiar, since they have a long tradition of use. Retention has a detrimental effect, resulting in lower reading scores when students reach middle school, yet approximately 2.4%, or 2 million students, continue to be held back each year, including 6.2% of first-graders (Hwang & Capella, 2018). In addition, retention rates are highest among students of color; for example, first-grade Black students are held back at twice the rate of white students (Warren, Hoffman, & Andrew, 2014). Repeating an early

Figure 6.3 Hattie's Distribution of Effect Sizes Across All Meta-Analyses

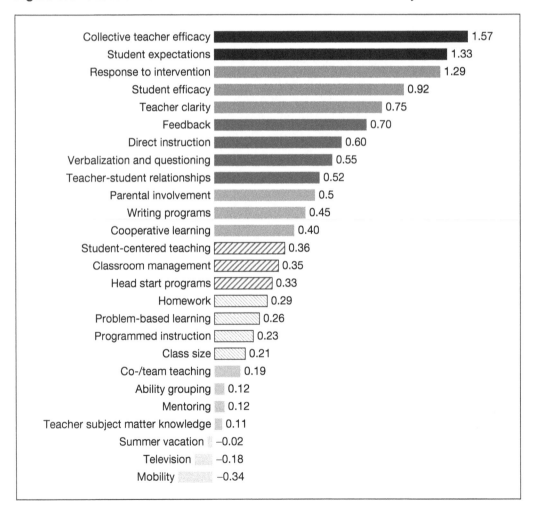

Figure 6.4   Hattie's Barometer of Influence

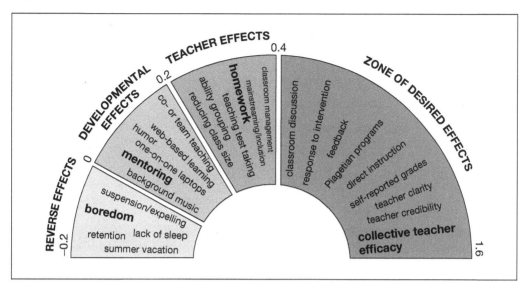

Figure 6.5   Selected Low-, Medium-, and High-Impact Strategies and Interventions From Hattie's (2012) Meta-Analysis

Low-Impact Strategies

RANK	INFLUENCE	EFFECT SIZE
148	Retention	–.13
144	Student control over learning	.04
140	Whole-language programs	.06
136	Teacher subject matter knowledge	.09
133	Gender	.12
131	Ability grouping	.12
125	Matching teaching and learning styles	.17
120	Within-class grouping	.18
113	Reducing class size	.21
109	Individualizing instruction	.22

Medium-Impact Strategies

RANK	INFLUENCE	EFFECT SIZE
86	Using simulations and gaming	.33
62	Teacher expectations of students	.43

(Continued)

Figure 6.5   (Continued)

RANK	INFLUENCE	EFFECT SIZE
44	Home environment	.52
41	Influence of peers	.53
36	Phonics instruction	.54
32	Providing worked examples	.57
29	Direct instruction	.59
28	Cooperative vs. individualistic learning	.59

High-Impact Strategies

RANK	INFLUENCE	EFFECT SIZE
27	Concept mapping	.60
26	Comprehension programs	.60
17	Vocabulary programs	.67
15	Acceleration	.68
14	Meta-cognitive strategy programs	.69
12	Teacher–student relationships	.72
11	Reciprocal teaching	.74
10	Feedback	.75
4	Formative teacher evaluation	.90
4	Teacher credibility in eyes of students	.90
1	Student expectations of self (teachers creating the conditions for students holding themselves to high levels)	1.44

Source: Hattie (2012).

grade does not provide the "gift of time" for students to advance, but rather "triggers a more 'negative cascade' and has a detrimental impact on subsequent reading achievement (Hwang & Capella, 2018, p. 578).

Another set of "tragedy strategies," ability grouping and tracking, remain in place. Despite extensive pushback against ability grouping (in-class elementary grouping) due to research about the inequities it fosters and other negative impacts, the practice "has attained a popularity unseen since the 1980s, used with over 70% of students" (Loveless, 2013, p. 18). Tracking (middle and high school grouping in distinct subjects) is also widespread, particularly in math classes. In the 1990s and 2000s, approximately 75% of students were enrolled in "distinct ability-level math classes" (Loveless, 2013, p. 18). Reducing class size, whose impact falls only halfway between the zero and the hinge point, remains a popular fix in the minds of many parents and educators, even though decades of studies have debunked its effectiveness (Filges, Sonne-Schmidt, & Nielsen, 2018). A poor teacher will not get better results with a smaller class size, but a good teacher will do well in any class size.

To replace these low-impact strategies with those that provide students with at least a year of growth, we now turn to some of Hattie's (2012) above-average practices. The number-one-rated strategy shows that teachers who help students develop high expectations for themselves promote extraordinary growth in learning. According to Hattie (2012), "Educating students to have high, challenging, appropriate expectations is among the most powerful influences in enhancing student achievement" (p. 60). This strategy includes getting students involved in predicting their performance, "making the learning intentions and success criteria transparent," and "providing feedback at the appropriate levels" (p. 60).

The second highest-rated strategy (not shown in the summary in Figure 6.5), "Piagetian programs," relates to using instruction backed by an understanding of how students think at any given stage of their development. The message of this influence, based on Piaget's renowned theories of cognitive development, is that "knowing the ways in which [students] think, and how this thinking may be constrained by their stages of development may be most important to how teachers choose material and tasks, how the concept of difficulty and challenge can be realized in different tasks, and the importance of developing successive and simultaneous thinking" (Hattie, 2009, p. 43). Briefly, Piaget's theory recognizes four stages:

1. Sensorimotor stage (birth to 2 years): Intelligence is seen in action as a child interacts with the environment.

2. Preoperational stage (2 to 7 years): Thinking is dominated by the child's own perception, believing everyone thinks the same way; learns to use symbols and language.

3. Concrete operational stage (7 to 12 years): Logical reasoning emerges, but only about objects that can be seen or are understood as real; exploration of concepts.

4. Formal operational stage (12 to adulthood): Logical thinking expands to abstract ideas, potential events, analogy, and metaphors.

Hattie (2012) draws on Piaget-inspired research to recommend that teachers 1) design lessons that appropriately challenge their students' cognitive levels, allowing them to practice thinking in the classroom, and 2) facilitate dialogue that sparks discussion among all voices and views, since learning is a collaborative process.

Establishing credibility in the eyes of students is another highly impactful strategy (ranked fourth) with an effective size of 0.90. Students find teachers credible when they believe they can learn from them because they are "believable, convincing, and capable of persuading students that they can be successful" (Fisher, Frey, & Smith, 2020, p. xiii). Visible learning defines teacher credibility as "students who regard their teacher as a credible authority based on their perceptions of competence, trustworthiness, and perceived caring. Is this teacher someone I can turn to for feedback, help, knowledge, and depth of understanding, and am I prepared to invest in her or his assigned tasks to enhance my learning?" (Corwin Visible Learning Meta^x, 2019).

Equally as influential as teacher credibility is formative evaluation (0.90), the teacher's act of guiding students with feedback and additional instruction throughout the lesson rather than at the end. Instead of a lot of uninterrupted teacher talk, formative evaluation meets students where they are from moment to moment. This strategy connects with Hattie's (2012) mind frame #1: "Teachers/leaders believe that their fundamental task is to evaluate the effect of their teaching on students' learning and achievement" (p. 182). Optimal teaching is not so much about perfecting a set of strategies as it is about the interaction between what the teacher and students are doing, whether that is during one lesson or over the course of a series of lessons. As Hattie (2012) explains,

> This means evaluating what we are doing and what the student is doing, and seeing learning through the eyes of students, as well as evaluating the effect of our actions on what the student does and the effect of what the student does on what we then need to do . . . together, this is the essence of excellent teaching. (p. 182)

Related to formative evaluation, feedback is among the top 10 influences for high achievement. When the teacher's sole focus is giving feedback to ensure students' growth and understanding, she is always considering three questions:

1. Where am I going? (What are my goals?) This question relates to learning intentions that are clearly presented by the teacher and just as clearly understood by students.

2. How am I going there? (What progress is being made toward the goal?) With this question, teachers consider their progress in achieving understanding based on an expected standard, prior performance, or the success or failure of some part of a task.

3. Where to next? (What activities need to be undertaken next to make better progress?) This question guides teachers into making the best decisions about future lessons, such as "choosing the next most appropriate challenges" (Hattie, 2012, p. 132).

In a productive classroom climate, students feel open to making errors rather than threatened by the possibility of being judged by the teacher or their peers. Feedback has its biggest impact in this environment because it thrives amid "the tension between what we *now* know and what we *could* know" (p. 139). In fact, feeling comfortable about making errors, which is the premise of the growth mind-set approach to teaching and learning, is at the core of visible learning.

The classroom environment also factors into mastery learning, another above-average influence. This practice is founded on the idea that all students can master difficult material, even though they learn at different speeds. Classroom conditions for achieving mastery include high levels of cooperation between students, frequent and focused teacher feedback, and variable time allowed to reach levels of attainment. Reciprocal teaching, which ranks number 11 in influence, is a reading comprehension strategy that calls for students and teachers and/or peers to have a conversation while reading a text. In these dialogues, students practice the literacy skills of summarizing, questioning, clarifying, and predicting.

Another high-level impact is the increasingly well-known action of creating positive teacher–student relationships. Hattie (2012) writes that the essence of a student-centered teacher's relationship with children is "the student seeing the warmth, feeling the encouragement and the teacher's high expectations, and knowing that the teacher understands him or her" (p. 158). Building this relationship "implies agency, efficacy, respect by the teacher for what the child brings to the class (from home, culture, peers), and allowing the experiences of the child to be recognized in the classroom" (Hattie, 2009, p. 118).

The importance of three factors—transparent goals/teaching intentions, "absolutely obvious" success criteria, and regular peer work (teachers working together)—sums up much of Hattie's (2011a, 2011b) advice about high-impact instruction. These practices, along with professional development that educates teachers about the most beneficial evidence-based strategies, can help principals blaze new trails for high achievement for students of color.

While Hattie's (2012) work rarely addresses strategies for racial equity specifically, the overall message of visible learning directly applies to educators committed to closing opportunity gaps. Noting one study, Hattie (2012) made this point by writing, "Across the grades, when instruction was challenging, relevant, and academically demanding, then all students had higher engagement and teachers talked less—and the greatest beneficiaries were at-risk students" (p. 80). He calls on principals to be courageous about discussing evidence-based impacts, stating that it is crucial for them to create "an atmosphere of trust and collegiality to allow the debates to turn to the evidence of the effect on student learning—on a regular basis." This action "requires strong 'learning leaders' to permit, encourage, and sustain the discussions on impact" (Hattie, 2012, p. 176).

Reflect on This

Instructional Methods at My School

Watch the following visible learning videos, provided through links on this book's website at racialequityleadership.com, Chapter 6 section, with your leadership team:

1. John Hattie: *Visible Learning Pt. 1: Disasters and Below-Average Methods*

2. John Hattie: *Visible Learning Pt. 2: Effective Methods*

After viewing the videos, think about the instructional methods used by teachers in your school.

Identify three to five disasters/below-average methods currently implemented in your school.

Identify three to five successful methods currently implemented in your school.

As a leadership team, select one of the disasters/below-average practices you identified and consider the following:

1. List the action steps needed to eliminate this practice in your school.

2. Identify what barriers might be in place.

3. What might be the political fallout?

4. Begin implementing the action steps.

As you move to eliminate a below-average instructional practice, journal your team's barriers, successes, and other outcomes. Use these reflections to move forward and continue to eliminate below-average practices in your school.

Learning From Mentors

Instruction That Supports Student Pride, Place, and Potential

Nasreen Fynewever

Fynewever is an assistant principal at a suburban middle and high school outside Minneapolis, Minnesota, who came to her position after serving 15 years as an educator, including as the school's dean of students. Born in Bangladesh, she identifies as a Brown educator who has learned firsthand that "high-yield instructional strategies remove barriers." Her reflections illustrate how some of the practices in this chapter, such as providing meaningful feedback, impact students' lives.

Reentering class after a racial wound was one of the most difficult steps to take as a student myself. I knew how to take notes, I knew how to study, and I knew how to keep phone calls to the front office or to my parents from happening. I knew how to "play the game" of school, and I found it to be a safe enough place from other circumstances in my life, so I nearly perfected it. However, one place it never let up was with the color of my skin being different from most of my peers and all (read: every single one) of my teachers. I taught myself how to reenter class while my heart was still aching and my young mind was confused about my human value. I assimilated and acted like nothing hurt because the sooner I was back in the rhythm, the sooner I could get back to what I knew how to do.

I now reflect on the number of students over my years in equity and leadership work whom I have seen hold the tension of school being both abrasive and yet a refuge from some swirling realities in their lives. This fuels the work I do when interacting with teachers and their growth. I am eager to see teachers interact with the lives of Black and Brown young people with an intentionality of creating space for students to claim power and purpose amid a society that has questioned and demeaned them. I believe that the value of the student's story and an urgency of spreading their success through celebration and recognition can be intertwined with content mastery. Students who sense they belong and will not be overlooked, overseen, and microassaulted against will delve into content for the explorers and freedom-seekers they are. A classroom space that holds inquiry and meaningful feedback for both adults and young people helps relationships form and students have a strong sense of belief in themselves. I ask teachers if they can name places where the positive relationships adults assume they have may be falsified by grades and assignments holding higher value than student stories, needs, and justice advocacy.

In discussions about instructional growth with these teachers, I often guide the conversation toward reflection on student use of self-assessment and student use of formative assessment over time. I am grateful for the number of teachers willing to consider that a student's identity as a learner is often demotivated by school-imposed grades, whereas the value and celebration of the young person's growth of skills and critical reflection that was not present or less formed at the start of the unit or semester fuels self-efficacy. Students implored to identify their own growth can gain a transferable skill to other areas of life and an ability to view themselves as valued contributors to groups around them. When students can see the scope and sequence of where they were and what they acquired/learned, they often quickly share other places in life where they have done this, and we see them revel in the affirmation and celebration. Our ability to employ meaningful formative assessments allows pride pathways for students to journey versus how the standardized assessments contribute to the oppressive parts of schooling. Let us start naming when practices deconstruct compliance-based education so that our young people's pride, place, and potential are forefront.

I have witnessed numerous times that the teachers who have student input on best methods for formative assessment have watched students see instruction

(Continued)

(Continued)

and content shift from nonimportant to being seen as a co-created community space for all people to have involvement in history, the present day, and the world we are building. Whether it is project-based learning, action research, or justice advocacy for students, the personhood of our students must be reinforced. In this, our raised consciousness as adults for the racial identity and learner identity of our students is shown to be valued higher than their basic mechanics of schooling compliance. High-yield instructional strategies remove barriers, and as a Brown student and educator myself, I am ready for these to be commonplace. We must have high expectations through both self- and formative assessments to authentically demonstrate our high value of each person. Students enter our classroom with a myriad of needs, wounds, and ever-evident brilliance; our classrooms must give space for such alongside the formal content. Our young people deserve this (N. Fynewever, personal communication, July 28, 2020).

Teaching gaps continue to beg the question: Why have we persisted, decade after decade, in using ineffective instructional strategies? The following chapter explores the role of white culture in shaping the beliefs, behavior, and policies that guide curriculums and practices, and how we can change the long-standing trajectory from disempowering students to empowering them through effective instruction. Hattie (2012) implores school leaders to prioritize discussions with teachers about the impact of evidence-based high-return instruction practices. We should create "an atmosphere of trust and collegiality to allow the debates to turn to the evidence of the effect on student learning—on a regular basis. It requires strong 'learner leaders' to permit, encourage, and sustain the discussions on impact" (p. 176).

References

Corwin Visible Learning Meta^x. (2019, July). *Meta^x influence glossary*. Retrieved from http://www.visiblelearningmetax.com/content/influence_glossary.pdf.

Filges, T., Sonne-Schmidt, C. S., & Nielsen, B. C. V. (2018). Small class sizes for improving student achievement in primary and secondary schools: A systematic review. *Campbell Systematic Reviews, 10*. doi:10.4073/csr.2018.10

Fisher, D., Frey, N., & Smith, D. (2020). *The teacher credibility and collective efficacy playbook, grades K–12*. Thousand Oaks, CA: Corwin.

Hattie, J. (2009). *Visible learning*. New York: Routledge.

Hattie, J. (2011a, December 1). *Visible learning. Pt1: Disasters and below-average methods* [Video file]. Retrieved from https://www.youtube.com/watch?v=sng4p3Vsu7Y

Hattie, J. (2011b, December 1). *Visible learning. Pt2: effective methods* [Video file]. Retrieved from https://www.youtube.comwatch/?v=3pD1DFTNQf4

Hattie, J. (2012). *Visible learning for teachers: Maximizing impact on learning*. New York: Routledge.

Haynes, M. A., & Smedley, B. D. (Eds.). (1999). *The unequal burden of cancer: An assessment of NIH research and programs for ethnic minorities and the medically underserved.* Washington, DC: The National Academies Press. Retrieved from https://www.nap.edu/catalog/6377/the-unequal-burden-of-cancer-an-assessment-of-nih-research.

Hwang, S., & Cappella, E. (2018). Rethinking early elementary grade retention: Examining long-term academic and psychosocial outcomes. *Journal of Research on Educational Effectiveness, 11*(4), 559–587. https://doi.org/10.1080/19345747.2018.1496500

Jackson, Y. (2011). *The pedagogy of confidence: Inspiring high intellectual performance in urban schools.* New York: Teachers College Press.

Loveless, T. (2013, March). How well are American students learning? *Brown Center Report on American Education, 3*(2). Retrieved from https://www.brookings.edu/wp-content/uploads/2016/06/2013-brown-center-report-web-3.pdf.

Obama, M. (2018). *Becoming.* New York: Crown.

Seashore Louis, K., Wahlstrom, K. L., Michelin, M., Gordon, M. Thomas, E., Leithwood . . . Moore, S. (2010). *Learning from leadership: Investigating the links to improved student learning* [PDF file]. Retrieved from https://d1wqtxts1xzle7.cloudfront.net/8530141/learning-from-leadership_final-report_march-2010.pdf?1328847508=&response-content-disposition=inline%3B+filename%3DLearning_from_leadership_Investigating_t.pdf&Expires=1597344927&Signature=akJjrqg6aO2UmwybOkk~lnoLpy3t fqC9q4mcJz0E4qcsnpVGZRqxwEXwNt9cACoYLoXKOHofuV72QiP8miz7 YUpV5D7lwG-fogmrWMaKn85~RMxm1nT8pcH-A1lYBQ3uqXCC3PCdVt KE2CrQfCov3Do~xKwaulUeKAL-6ADXosk2G7WZQjpXeiSydF3FjFwe3qL JQH~4khwT4lt9ZomP3i8EPd8JPsoTAXlvsDZrTEA49kQ5NVYVQTXqBy WVSVAv4RJgyCtRcloiX9y43GqD1tAwtMbGaJD9rUvNdHGWNJRysjWM sCSVGCz7Q3jifu4kXAwuTtA2umVVPlDeQYOulA___&Key-Pair-Id=APKAJ LOHF5GGSLRBV4ZA.

Singleton, G. E. (2015). *Courageous conversations about race: A field guide for achieving equity in schools.* Thousand Oaks, CA: Corwin.

Sue, D. W. (2015). *Race talk and the conspiracy of silence: Understanding and facilitating difficult dialogues on race.* Hoboken, NJ: John Wiley & Sons.

Yung Shin, S. (2016). *A good time for the truth: Race in Minnesota.* St. Paul: Minnesota Historical Society Press.

Ensuring Racially Conscious Pedagogy

CHAPTER 7

Our bold, audacious vision is to eliminate the crime of squandered potential.

—Veronica McDermott (Perkins-Gough, 2015)

María Graver, a native of Chicago, has held administrative positions as an equity coordinator and assistant principal in Minnesota following her years as an elementary teacher in Washington, DC; Tucson, Arizona; and Edina, Minnesota. Her expertise on racially conscious pedagogy developed alongside several years of work as a racial equity consultant to U.S. corporations and government sectors such as county employees and district judges. As a Latina, she said, racial equity work is different for her than for her white peers, because it is not just about work—it's about survival.

Graver's insights about leading teachers toward racially conscious practices began with a reminder that this work always begins with knowing ourselves. Not until we uncover our racialized socialization and beliefs can we begin to develop a racially conscious lens that will give us the perspective we need to get the most from equity training and to lead others:

> If an administrator doesn't have a well-developed and consistent racial justice lens, they are not ready to do any instructional supervision. Often, it is teachers who receive training, but not administrators. We administrators often think we know what's going on, but we don't; we think we've had all the training because we're in charge, but we don't. So the leader's equity lens must be developed first. Actually, we like to use the term "equity lasik," because you can't take that on and off like a lens.
>
> When working with teachers, I believe that quality instructional supervision is *the* thing that can change the racialized opportunity gap. Leaders must have the courage to analyze teachers' data when talking to them, to look at how their kids are scoring and see the trends that have been happening for years. After getting the message from their data, I've often had math teachers, in particular, ask how they can integrate racially conscious content into their classrooms. We talk about bringing in the history of a theorem or math strategy, since we know that most math originated in Egypt and East Africa. They can find pieces of history in which people of color applied

math, such as the story of the Black women NASA scientists in *Hidden Figures* and tales about the African American regiments in World War I and World War II who plotted aviation flights. Math teachers can surface the truth in that hidden history. Kids might become more interested or they might tune out, but it's a simple way to bring in cultural relevance. And in the endeavor of finding that information for students, you're finding it for yourself. A more complicated way is to ask kids how they might use the math theory or concept in their daily life.

When teachers ask, "How do I do it?," I always ask, "Whose story is being told? Whose math (or any other subject) are you teaching? Who benefits from the way the story is being told, and who is missing from the story?" We can start there with teachers as they make their lesson plans. It may sound simple, but this is also about reminding teachers that we are in education because we are lifelong learners. Not that the lesson plan you wrote last year wasn't great, but this year it could be better, and it needs to be based on the needs of our kids.

All the culturally relevant work we do is never going to be enough if we don't get to know individual students. We do a fairly good job of building relationships with our students and families in elementary, but then it falls off. We need to afford teachers the time to get to know their kids, who they are and where they're coming from. That's our job, knowing what they're bringing and what we can build on. Teachers should know their students' strengths so they can build on that to bust open that paradigm of deficit-based thinking. When you are formally observing a teacher, you've got to set clearly measurable goals and not overwhelm them. If you see seven things that could be better, choose three. Co-create the learning and pound on those, and tell the teacher when you'll be back to look for those things.

We have success with teachers building relationships instead of just putting kids out. Their data does change. People become aware of what they've been doing, and they don't want to be that person.

It's also important to get feedback from students. I've found that kids are really generous and honest about what's going on in class. They want people to like them; they don't want to misbehave. We need to help teachers understand that when a student is doing x, y, or z while they're teaching, they should have a conversation with that student to try to understand their behavior. "What's going on? What do you need right now?" When we have social capital with kids they will tell us when the instruction is not working, and we can get rid of the deficit-based approach.

One of the biggest jobs administrators have to do is create systems and structures to repair the wounding that public education has caused in communities of color. Desegregation was not integration. Think of all that was lost when Black, Brown, and Indigenous kids went into schools where teachers didn't love them like the teachers they had before. Consider what a parent's experience was in their school. It's very likely they didn't feel welcomed in their own schools or communities. Make sure when teachers reach out to families they are cognizant of that wound. Start to repair that relationship with schooling by inviting parents into the system. Parents need to feel safe and supported and open to telling you what they think you can do to help their child. Take every opportunity to model as an administrator that you are reaching out to families to invite them in, to find what's going to engage them in school communities.

Much of what racially conscious pedagogy comes down to is that kids are going to remember the material we teach them, but not all of it. So, what are we teaching them? To value their curiosity and love of learning. Even if they don't want to learn about this specific thing in physics, they're curious, and they'll stick with you because, number one, they like you, and number two, they like to learn. They value that relationship they have with education and with you. (M. Graver, personal communication, August 16, 2020)

Graver is also aware that students of color repeatedly get the message that they do not matter, that their well-being or happiness do not matter. This is especially prevalent in Minnesota, she said, a state where, one of her colleagues likes to say, "We're so white, you can see us from space." The impression of students that they do not matter is not a message coming from just one teacher "but is the message they get over and over," Graver said. "We must demonstrate to kids repeatedly, never *not* be demonstrating to them, that they matter." Since the majority-white teaching staff in Minnesota and elsewhere has internalized beliefs about white culture that impact their perceptions of students, the following section takes a closer look at the details of this culture and its effects.

The Impact of White Culture on Beliefs, Behavior, and Policy in Education

As discussed in Chapter 5, culture is the collective tradition and way of life of a group of people, "the behaviors, beliefs, values, and symbols that they accept, generally without thinking about them, and that are passed along by communication and imitation from one generation to the next" (Choudhury, n.d.). Culturally relevant pedagogy recognizes that our schools are embedded in a dominant white culture comprising of traits and assumptions that differ from the cultural norms of students of color who make up the majority of learners. For example, "rugged individualism," the first trait in Figure 7.1, contrasts with the collectivistic culture of Hispanic families, for whom "group activities are dominant, responsibility is shared, and accountability is collective" (Aud, Fox, & Kawal-Ramani, 2010). As such, Hispanic children are raised in a culture that emphasizes cooperation, harmony, and collectivity in contrast to white American children whose families and society emphasize self-reliance, autonomy, independence, and competition.

Figure 7.1 Aspects and Assumptions of White Culture in the United States That Impact School Beliefs, Behaviors, and Policies

RUGGED INDIVIDUALISM	EMPHASIS ON THE SCIENTIFIC WORK ETHIC
• Self-reliance • Individual is primary unit • Independence and autonomy highly valued and rewarded • Individuals assumed to be in control of their environment: "You get what you deserve"	• Objective, rational, linear thinking • Cause-and-effect relationships • Quantitative emphasis
COMPETITION	**STATUS, POWER, AND AUTHORITY**
• Be No. 1 • Win at all costs • Winner-loser dichotomy • Action orientation • Master and control nature • Must always "do something" about a situation • Aggressiveness and extroversion • Decision-making • Majority rules (when whites have power)	• Wealth = worth • Heavy value on ownership of goods, space, property • Your job defines you • Respect authority
JUSTICE	**TIME**
• Based on English common law • Protect property and entitlements • Intent counts	• Adherence to rigid time schedules • Time viewed as a commodity

COMMUNICATION	FUTURE ORIENTATION
• "The king's English" rules • Written tradition • Avoid conflict and intimacy • Don't show emotion • Don't discuss personal life • Be polite	• Plan for future • Delayed gratification • Progress is always best • "Tomorrow will be better"
HOLIDAYS	FAMILY STRUCTURE
• Based on Christian religions • Based on white history and male leaders	• Nuclear family (father, mother, 2.3 children is the ideal social unit) • Children should have own rooms, be independent
HISTORY	AESTHETICS
• Based on northern European immigrants' experience in the United States • Heavy focus on the British Empire • Primacy of Western (Greek, Roman) and Judeo-Christian tradition	• Based on European culture • Woman's beauty based on being blond, thin—"Barbie" • Man's attractiveness based on economic status, power, intellect
PROTESTANT WORK ETHIC	RELIGION
• Hard work is the key to success • Work before play • "If you didn't meet your goals, you didn't work hard enough"	• Christianity is the norm • Anything other than Judeo-Christian tradition is foreign • No tolerance for deviation from single god concept

Source: Adapted from Katz (1990).

Culture can also be described in terms of its external and internal elements, as envisioned by Hall (1989) in the image of the cultural iceberg. The external aspects that we can see, hear, and touch, such as food and language, make up only about 10% of a group's cultural identity. The internal elements pictured below the water line in Figure 7.2 are deep, unconscious beliefs, values, thought patterns, and myths that underlie how a culture communicates, perceives the world, and more. These aspects are unknown to those outside the culture until they explore it. As Hall (1989) explains, exploring another culture at the deep level is transforming: "Beneath the clearly perceived, highly explicit surface culture, there lies a whole other world, which when understood will ultimately radically change our view of human nature" (p. 15).

Figure 7.2 Hall's Cultural Iceberg

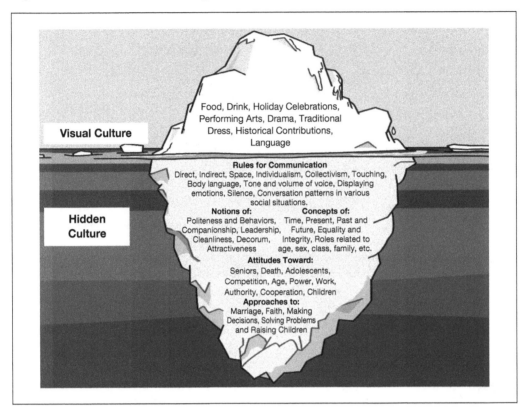

Source: Adapted from Hall (1989).
Image Source: pixabay.com/MoteOo

The iceberg analogy helps us understand why we make assumptions about other cultures based on superficial evidence, while missing the larger and more meaningful aspects of what makes the culture unique. This also explains why we can find resistance to the idea of culturally relevant teaching in our schools.

Culturally Relevant Teaching

As María Graver identified so well, elements of Jackson's (2011) and Hattie's (2012) models can be found in the theory and practice of culturally relevant (or culturally responsive) teaching. Geneva Gay (2002) defines culturally relevant teaching as "using the cultural characteristics, experiences, and perspectives of ethnically diverse students as conduits for teaching them more effectively" (p. 106). A professor of education at the University of Washington–Seattle, and one of the leading experts on multicultural education, Gay (2002) explains that the practice is "based on the assumption that when academic knowledge and skills are situated within the lived experiences and frames of reference of students, they are more personally meaningful, have higher interest appeal, and are learned more easily and thoroughly" (p. 106). Gloria Ladson-Billings (2004) of the University of Wisconsin–Madison, who pioneered the concept of culturally relevant pedagogy; Gay (2002); and others have documented the success of culturally relevant teaching for marginalized students given the opportunity to learn through these validating processes and environments.

White cultural norms, particularly ideas about white majority rule, linear thinking, and styles of communication, may underlie some of the common misconceptions about culturally relevant teaching that show up in conversations about equity. Irvine and Armento (2001) define these misconceptions as a set of myths:

> *Myth 1.* Culturally responsive pedagogy is a new and special type of pedagogy relevant only to low-income urban students of color.
>
> *Myth 2.* In schools with diverse student populations, only teachers of color are capable of demonstrating the essential elements of a culturally responsive pedagogy.
>
> *Myth 3.* Culturally responsive pedagogy is a "bag of tricks" that minimizes the difficulty of teaching some students of color.
>
> *Myth 4.* Culturally responsive pedagogy requires teachers to master the details of all the cultures of students represented in the classroom.
>
> *Myth 5.* Culturally responsive pedagogy reinforces stereotypes about children of color because this pedagogy categorizes and labels children based on their race and ethnicity.

In reality, culturally relevant teaching can be taught by teachers of any race and encompasses evidence-based, culturally validating content; learning experiences; and relationships. In her book *The Dreamkeepers*, Ladson-Billings (2009) chronicles how she initially developed the concept of culturally relevant teaching from her own successful teaching methods in an urban school. Her research then examined the practices of other teachers who fostered academic success for their Black students in urban districts. "Who are the teachers capable of transcending the labels and categories to support excellence among all students?" she wrote. "I call them dreamkeepers" (Ladson-Billings, 2009, p. 16). Examining the shared qualities of these teachers, Ladson-Billings (2009) identified their characteristics as a template to which teachers and leaders can aspire. In terms of teachers' conceptions of themselves and others, for example, teachers with culturally relevant practices share the following characteristics:

- *Have high self-esteem and a high regard for others.* They consider themselves professionals and conduct themselves accordingly, from dressing well to keeping their classrooms neat and organized, all of which sends a message to students that they care about their role and its impact on students.

- *See themselves as part of the community, see teaching as giving back to the community, and encourage their students to do the same.* They engage in community organizations and find ways to "build a sense of togetherness and team spirit" (p. 44) among their students through trips and/or group activities.

- *See teaching as an art and themselves as artists.* These teachers understand and use "scientific principles of pedagogy" (p. 45) but also expand on their technical skills with creative lessons and are willing to be spontaneous to engage students.

- *Believe all students can succeed.* Some teachers experiment with many projects to give students opportunities to find where they are most successful and then incorporate those projects into other subjects; others ask students to make goals for the day and reflect on how they did at the end of the day.

- *Help students make connections among their community, national, and global identities.* Local, national, and international news items and prompts about prominent figures spark dialogues that make meaningful connections.

- *See teaching as "digging knowledge out" of students.* They share "an overriding belief that students come to school with knowledge and that that knowledge must be explored and utilized in order for students to become achievers" (p. 56).

Ladson-Billings (2009) describes the stark differences between culturally relevant teaching practices and "assimilationist" teaching, which invalidates the cultures of students of color and seeks to "ensure that students fit into society" (p. 24). *Society* means, of course, the dominant white society and its culture. In addition to describing the contrasts between culturally relevant and assimilationist teaching in terms of teachers' conceptions of self and others, as discussed, Ladson-Billings (2009) compares these two styles of teaching through two other lenses. Looking at the social relations between teachers and students, one contrast shows that a fluid, "humanely equitable" (p. 60) teacher–student relationship is the opposite of a fixed, hierarchical conception of what that relationship should be. Another stark difference is teaching that develops a community-like learning environment in contrast to one that encourages "competitive achievement" (p. 60). Culturally relevant teaching also promotes collaborative learning rather than isolated, individual learning.

The final category, which compares teachers' conceptions of knowledge, describes culturally relevant perceptions of knowledge as continuously evolving and being shared by teachers and students. The opposite, assimilationist conception is that knowledge is unchanging, a static "thing" to be passed from the teacher to the student. The culturally relevant perspective views knowledge critically, while the contrasting outlook sees it as infallible. In terms of defining academic excellence, the culturally relevant teacher takes "student diversity and individual differences" (p. 60) into account for a more complex assessment, while an assimilationist point of view considers excellence unrelated to diversity or individuality.

Since the practices and perspectives in the assimilationist viewpoint resonate with some of the facets of white culture as depicted earlier, this section reminds us that many of the challenges confronting equity-minded school leaders are based on the systemic inequities of society, not on student deficits. Ladson-Billing's (2009) work also reveals that the nature of culturally relevant teaching runs parallel to aspects of visible learning and the pedagogy of confidence, from building strong student–teacher relationships and holding high expectations to offering enrichment based on student strengths. Her observations about successful culturally relevant teachers suggest a pathway for school leaders to guide their teachers into practices that can raise achievement for all students of color:

1. Nurture student competence by *treating students as competent* with intellectually challenging methods that reflect their experience and culture.

2. Create scaffolded classroom learning that *builds on students' own "experiences, knowledge, and skills"* (p. 135) to keep advancing to more difficult knowledge. Scaffolding gives students incremental, tapered-off assistance that helps them become independent learners.

3. Keep *instruction*, not off-task content or behavior, the focus of the classroom.

4. First *establish what students already know and do* in order to expand their thinking and abilities.

5. Take the time and initiative to *know your students well.*

These culturally relevant practices apply to science and math as much as they do to reading and history. While some have considered science and math too "high order" to be subject to diversity concerns, Gay believes they are just as appropriate for culturally relevant teaching as courses like reading because they are human endeavors—and human beings are *cultural* beings. At the very least, Gay contends, science [and math] classes should include content about the contributions of a racially and ethnically diverse group of people (Atwater, 2010).

Ladson-Billings (1995) has described culturally relevant teaching as "a pedagogy of opposition" committed to "collective, not merely individual, empowerment" (p. 160). The aims of this pedagogy to produce academic success, maintain students' cultural integrity and groundedness, and develop students' "critical consciousness through which they challenge the status quo of the current social order" (p. 160) is nothing less than a blueprint for transforming society. Her call for developing the integrity and empowerment of students of color can inspire principals as you lead for equity, reminding you of the broadest impact of your work.

Integrating culturally relevant practices will bring your building into the 21st century in what may be the most meaningful way—making it a learning environment that is a true reflection of your community and the nation at large. By 2027, the percentage of white students enrolled in public schools is projected to decrease from the current 49% to 45%, with the largest increase in other students being Hispanic children, whose percentage is expected to increase from 26% to 29% (National Center for Education Statistics, 2019). Teaching from old paradigms based solely on white culture has not served all our students and would certainly continue to marginalize the new majority of Hispanic, Black, Asian/Pacific Islander, Native American/Alaska Native, and two-or-more-race students. Together, culturally relevant teaching, the approaches of visual learning and the pedagogy of confidence, and critical protocols like Courageous Conversations form a model for creating academic success for every student in our increasingly diverse communities. As Gay reflects, multicultural education "evokes one of the most fundamental issues of the human condition. . . . We are incredibly diverse. [The human family] is deep and it is complex; it is profound and it is incredibly beautiful" (Atwater, 2010, p. 161). As school leaders, we play a fundamental role in building communities that recognize and celebrate that beauty.

High Operational Practices: Yvette Jackson's *The Pedagogy of Confidence,* Part II

Guided by the Courageous Conversation protocol, principals can feel more confident about leading meetings and communicating with staff and the community about issues that can be uncomfortable and challenging for some. As you learn more about your school, including the specific needs of each of your teachers, and prioritize the steps that will move your school into your vision for equity, the evidence-based practices in this chapter will help you turn your vision into reality. Specific strategies aligned with the approaches we introduced in Chapter 3 are developed here as a tool kit for implementation.

As introduced in Chapter 3, Jackson's (2011) pedagogy of confidence is a science-based approach founded on three fundamental beliefs: 1) intelligence is modifiable; 2) all students benefit from a focus on high intellectual performance (HIP); and 3) learning is influenced by the interaction of culture, language, and cognition. Children achieve and thrive, she states, when their learning is nurtured by a collaborative "belief in the capacity and gifts of the students, the staff, and the community" and practices that come from those beliefs (Perkins-Gough, 2015).

Before delving into the practices, let's take another look at the science behind Jackson's (2011) method for eliciting high intellectual performance in all students. Neuroscience has documented the power of "gifted" programs to reverse underachievement, stimulate motivation, and activate the self-determination that leads to lifetime learning. Gifted pedagogies "enhance how students construct meaning and comprehend the world, resulting in strengthened competence, confidence, resilience and high intellectual performances" (Jackson, n.d.). Summarizing the neuroscience pathway of this high-level learning, Jackson explains that the process begins with the positive impact of feeling competent. When students and teachers recognize students' strengths and successes, their sense of competence leads to confidence and more:

> *Confidence acquired from competence* causes an individual to become intensely stimulated. This stimulation causes a burning of glucose, which results in the brain being energized, making an individual feel stronger, increasing the sense of confidence. The sense of competence and confidence activates neurotransmitters of pleasure: The endorphin release that helps students enjoy learning more focuses their attention more deeply and motivates a desire for self-directed learning. When feelings of competence are increased, the sense of possible achievement catalyzes the quest for self-actualization, while decreasing the release of catecholamines, the body's natural chemical response to stress. (Jackson, 2011, p. 9)

Teachers experience the same positive neurological pathway when their competence is affirmed by students' improvement and success:

> This feedback is a great asset to teachers, for it catalyzes positive relationships with students, generating enjoyment in work and a deep sense of competence and being valued. These responses activate the release of endorphins, dopamine and oxytocin, which increase creativity in the pursuit and design of effective teaching strategies and inspire greater collaborative relationships with students and staff. (Jackson, n.d.)

This science forms the rationale for practices that can counteract the debilitating effects of stress faced by students of color and other marginalized children in our schools. Students who experience "prejudice, degradation, stereotype threat . . . feelings of failure, inability to succeed, positional or marginalizing language, and feelings of low self-esteem" are inhibited by the neurological impacts of that stress (Jackson, 2011, p. 49). Stress weakens the prefrontal cortex, the most recently evolved region of the brain where creativity and high-order thinking takes place. Cortisol and neurotransmitters activated by stress cause the prefrontal cortex to "shrivel" (Jackson, 2011, p. 49), or go "off-line," as Datta and Arnsten (2019) describe:

> These newly evolved circuits are especially vulnerable to uncontrollable stress, with built-in mechanisms to rapidly take the PFC "off-line" and switch the brain from a reflective to reflexive state. . . . Thus, high levels of catecholamine released during uncontrollable stress switch the brain from a slow, thoughtful, reflective PFC-regulated state to a more reactive, reflexive state that may be advantageous during danger, but would be detrimental when more thoughtful solutions are needed. (pp. 2, 6)

At the same time, stress-induced brain chemistry boosts the brain's ability to form habits such as responding with self-sabotaging behavior and poor performance (Jackson, 2011, p. 49). Therefore, when stress increases, cognitive ability goes down and negative habits go up. Without an outlet for their frustration or a sense of control or social support, disenfranchised students are caught in a stress-induced cycle that fuels underachievement.

Jackson (n.d.) also discusses the damaging impact of "otherizing" labels attached to marginalized students that create stress and thus promote the cascade of neurological activity just described. "Language associated with prejudice, degradation or stereotype threat incite high levels of stress . . . that causes the emission of cortisol, which inhibits comprehension" (Jackson, n.d.). Old labels, Jackson (2011) suggests, should be replaced by those that reflect an equity-driven practice and belief in student potential:

"Otherizing" labels	Equity-driven labels
• Minority	• Students of color
• Disadvantaged	• School dependent (enrichment provided solely in school)
• Low achiever	• Underachiever
• Disability/disabled	• Variable learners
• [Also:] English Language Learners	• Multilingual learners

Using "gifted" pedagogy such as activating student strengths and providing intellectual enrichment transforms the stress-induced neurological cycle into the competence > confidence > motivation > self-actualization pathway of the pedagogy of confidence.

Jackson's (2011) model is built on seven high operational practices that affirm students' potential, activate thinking through specific cognitive skills, and make learning engaging by connecting it to students' lives.

The High Operational Practices of the Pedagogy of Confidence

- Identifying and activating student strengths
- Building relationships
- Eliciting high intellectual performance
- Providing enrichment
- Integrating prerequisites for academic learning
- Situating learning in the lives of students
- Amplifying student voice

(Jackson, 2011, p. 89)

The high operational practices replace status-quo approaches based on deficit thinking about student potential. Decades of that disbelief have produced an all-too-familiar set of policies that negatively impact students of color such as the following:

- Static, narrow testing
- Remedial education
- Tracking across all disciplines based on standardized test scores
- Unsubstantiated referrals to special education
- Inequitable suspension practices (Jackson, n.d.)

Jackson's (2011) work gives leaders a framework for transforming their schools from these deficit-thinking environments to energized, connected spaces for high achievement for all students. The methods that work don't cost a dime. Successful strategies like building teacher–student relationships, teaching from strengths, and creating a back-and-forth feedback loop between teachers and students don't require a multimillion dollar teacher training program. What's needed for high achievement for all students are teachers who see every student as brilliant, who have a passion for culturally relevant practices, and who strive to know their impact as evaluators of their own work. Those qualities, built on a commitment to developing racial awareness, are the recipe for success.

Following are Jackson's descriptions of the high operational practices that create high intellectual performance.

1. **Identifying and activating student strengths.** Teaching that encourages students to recognize and apply their strengths releases neurotransmitters of pleasure, motivating students to actively participate and invest in a learning experience, set goals for their learning, and follow through with their learning for meaningful application and deeper development of strengths for personal agency.

2. **Building relationships.** Students fare best cognitively, socially, and emotionally when they know they are liked, appreciated, and valued as part of a vibrant, caring community. Positive relationships stimulate oxytocin, positively impacting both the motivation and the memory capacity critical for learning.

3. **Eliciting high intellectual performance.** Students crave challenges. Their intelligence flourishes when asked to think at high levels about complex issues, demonstrate what they know in creative ways, and develop useful habits of mind such as reflection, raising substantive questions for deeper understanding, and thinking flexibly and innovatively.

4. **Providing enrichment.** Enrichment taps students' interests, generates strengths, expands their cognitive capacity, and guides them to apply what they know in novel situations for self-actualization.

5. **Integrating prerequisites for academic learning.** Foundation schema building activities are critical so that students have the right foundations for learning new information and acquiring new skills. This foundation heightens students' understanding, competence, confidence, and motivation.

6. **Situating learning in the lives of students.** Students perform most effectively when they can connect new learnings to what is relevant and meaningful to them. These connections validate their lived experiences activating the focusing of the brain through its reticular activating system (RAS). Without such personal connections, the new learnings are not likely to be retained and used effectively.

7. **Amplifying student voice.** Encouraging students to voice their interests, perspectives, reflections, and opinions and enabling them to make personal contributions is not only motivating but also builds the confidence, agency, academic language, investment, and skill students need to join wider communities of learners and doers in the world outside of school.

Jackson (2011) sums up the cooperative nature of successful teaching as a matter of confidence and competence: "Student motivation to learn is directly affected by teachers' confidence in their students' potential, concomitant with their own competence to nurture this potential" (pp. 4–5). To become confident that every student can achieve, teachers must first be aware of the systemic issues that have blocked achievement for students of color for decades. McKenzie and Skrla (2011) define this knowledge as *equity consciousness*, "a person's awareness of the level of equity and inequity present in behaviors, policies, settings, organizations and outcomes" (p. 12). The first half of this book addressed the ways every educator can explore their attitudes, assumptions, biases, and beliefs and where they came from, which is essentially each person's story of growing up in a society embedded in racist beliefs and the behaviors, laws, and policies that spring from them. When teachers develop equity consciousness, they raise their awareness of the level of fair and equitable treatment others around them are receiving and become more willing to help solve those inequities (McKenzie & Skrla, 2011, p. 12).

Raising the equity consciousness of teachers and other staff drives the second of Jackson's (2011) two-step action plan for principals—building what she calls a meditative learning community, a school in which "staff and communities share a passion for what they are collaboratively constructing and facilitating, and they get better at it as they interact regularly" (p. 159). A meditative learning community addresses obstacles to learning such as poverty, feelings of failure, the stigma that comes with marginalizing labels, lack of enrichment, and stereotype threats that cause students of color to feel they may be viewed through the lens of a negative stereotype or do something that confirms the stereotype. This community is committed to mediating the environment to overcome those barriers and make a positive impact on students' "intellectual development, self-directed learning, and self-actualization" (p. 158).

In a mediative learning community, students are empowered to have a voice in every aspect of their schooling, from curriculum to discipline policies to how the school is governed. This bold turnaround from viewing students as passive players in an adult-constructed and adult-controlled system changes the lives of school-dependent students, giving them an environment that mitigates "the effects of the potentially debilitating challenges they live through outside school" (Jackson, 2011, p. 160).

Leaders and staff within a mediative learning culture are committed to the following:

- Providing an environment that meets a child's fundamental need to feel emotionally and physically safe

- Based on the understanding that reading and learning are codependent, empowering students through an emphasis on literacy—teachers in all disciplines must teach text comprehension so all students can learn

- Focusing on "the impact of culture on language and cognition" (Jackson, 2011, p. 158)

- Building an environment that reflects all cultures and in which everyone understands and has a sense of ownership of this inclusive, respectful cultural norm

- Recognizing the cognitive plasticity of the brain and focusing attention on nurturing student development through high operational practices

- Acknowledging that a sense of belonging and self-esteem creates social fulfillment, therefore making social development an important part of implementing the pedagogy of confidence

- Offering academic content and opportunities that "develop the students' strengths, interests, passions, high intellectual performance, and drive for autonomy" (p. 159)

- Developing a shared culture of "positive reciprocal relationships" (p. 159) that include students as integral members of the community

In a meditative culture that incorporates the previous actions, teachers make sure students feel they are co-partners in their own learning, working with their teachers to build on their strengths. This sense of value ushers in a feeling of belonging that makes students feel more confident, and this confidence stimulates changes in the brain and body that optimize cognitive functioning. To create this environment of a mediative culture and optimal learning, therefore, school leaders must address two critical needs: 1) creating a mediative environment in which the awareness, attitudes, and perceptions of all staff, members of the school board, and members of the community inside and outside the school are recultured to express "fearless expectation and support for all students to demonstrate high intellectual performance" (Jackson, 2011, p. 13) and 2) building support and structures that will allow all instructors to deliver high-level pedagogy.

As such, principals are challenged to do the following:

Cultivate a Mediative Learning Community
- Recognize each teacher's needs in terms of raising racial awareness and expectations, recognizing that everyone may be on a different point of readiness along the path
- Address resistance by mastering the successful urgent conversation

Enable Professional Development to Ensure Teachers' Understand
- Intelligence is modifiable.

- Every student benefits from a focus on high intellectual performance.

- Culture, language, and cognition interact to influence learning.

- Student–teacher relationships are key.

- Student voices must be brought to the table to discover their motivation and how the learning environment impacts them.

- Students must have opportunities to dialogue with teachers and benefit from the cultural bridge between them.

- Engaging in discourse allows students to practice language and share their ideas and perspectives in a guided way.

- When teachers shift their frame of reference to that of the student, students engage in guided dialogical thinking, in which they learn problem-solving, decision-making, and taking a position.

Embracing the science-backed methods of the pedagogy of confidence creates an environment in which the *inherent intellectual capacities of all students* are recognized, developed, and given voice. In this relationship-driven culture, students mediate teachers' teaching by sharing their frames of reference, and teachers mediate students' learning by engaging in practices reshaped by those student perspectives. The following reflection invites you to consider what a meditative learning community, or culture, would look like in your school.

Reflect on This

My School's Meditative Culture

Answer the following in your journal:

1. What interferes with creating a mediated culture?

2. What are your first steps as a leader in ensuring a mediated culture is in place?

The pedagogy of confidence that evolved out of Jackson's (2011) successful work with urban students is a reciprocal, collaborative process that reflects the social nature of learning. It empowers students to pursue their futures with high-level thinking and social skills, all bound together with confidence in their unique strengths that can serve them throughout their lives.

Learning From Mentors

Transforming Instruction

Silvy Un Lafayette, Ph.D.
District Administrator

Jessica Busse
Assistant Principal

> *The following stories of practice from two leaders show what it looks like to focus on student voice, relationships, diverse perspectives, culturally relevant pedagogy, feedback, a solid vision, and courageous conversations—all with the goal of disrupting the status quo to improve learning for students of color.*

Born in a refugee camp in Thailand, Dr. Silvy Un Lafayette grew up in a suburb of Minneapolis after her Cambodian family moved to the United States when she was young. Her parents had been successful professionals in Cambodia, but in the United States they left their careers behind to find work available to non-native English speakers and pursue the American Dream of seeing all six of their children go to college. She and her siblings were the only Cambodians in her high school, and other than a few families of color, the school was predominantly white. Watching how her parents had been treated as immigrants and the low expectations directed at her siblings in school, she came to her career as a middle-school math teacher, assistant principal, and district administrator with firsthand knowledge of the impact of race in society, education in particular. "Because of my experiences," she said, "I constantly think about the faces within the data, relating them to my parents, siblings, and my son who is half Cambodian and half Black. Seeing who is being served and who is not is personal" (S. Un Lafayette, personal communication, May 27, 2020).

In her current work as the director of assessment, research, and evaluation in a suburban district of Minneapolis, Un Lafayette draws on her experience to help interpret school data as she collaborates with principals to develop racially equitable curricula and policies in their schools. She stays consciously aware of her racial autobiography and how it sheds light on the issues facing the 47% students of color and majority-white leadership and teaching staff in her district. "I always try to lead authentically with my identity as a Southeast Asian Brown woman who grew up in Rosemount, Minnesota," she said.

Un Lafayette recently worked with Jessica Busse, whose 4 years as an assistant principal in suburban Minnesota districts follow 8 years as a high school math teacher in Arizona, to explore solutions for the opportunity gap revealed in the school's math scores. "The narrative about math data at Busse's high school was that state testing wasn't giving us good data because of the high opt-out rate," she said. "That is true, but it is only part of the issue. When I think about standardized testing and see disaggregated data that shows who is being successful and who is not, I see it as a reflection of our system, but not of students.

Jessica and I talked about related data in her school, such as discipline and attendance, and the fact that grades are determined by teachers, to see what else is impacting those math scores. These factors continued to build the case that Black and Brown kids are not being served."

Un Lafayette finds it easier to work with principals who have a vision for what they want their departments to look like. As a principal who had clearly articulated an equitable vision, Busse had processed a survey, for example, to find out where her math teachers stood on testing and instruction. Busse's survey revealed that the department was divided into two camps regarding instruction. The first believed that if students don't pass a test the first time, they shouldn't be able to take it again. *That's too easy*, they thought. These teachers did not see poor test results as an opportunity to ask what those scores said about their teaching. The second camp held the opposite view, stating that it was their responsibility to ensure students learn material they didn't get the first time around. They were focused on giving students an opportunity to learn rather than on the first-time test grade.

For the first group of teachers, the survey revealed, "feedback" looks like projecting the answers to a homework assignment on the board the next day, and if some students have trouble, they will raise their hands and the teacher will explain. If a student doesn't raise her hand, no explanations. The other group of teachers saw the value in taking the time to understand how each student communicated and responded to difficult material so they could get the feedback they needed to teach them successfully. Whatever decision the math department leader made would make her unpopular with one of those groups.

"What bubbled up for Jessica and me in our discussion about that survey was how those practices reflected the beliefs of the adults in that department," Un Lafayette said, adding, "Jessica and the math department head would find it easier to talk to teachers about the data, but a dialogue about the data as a reflection of their beliefs would be the harder conversation. There were math teachers who reached out to us and to the department head to say, 'We need to have this conversation. There are people who don't believe the data is telling the bigger story, but we believe it is, and we want to do something about it, and we need leadership to come in and tell us what to do.'"

Even as a newbie to her current district, Un Lafayette knows that principals feel they have 100% permission from her and the rest of the district administration to help lead that conversation. Many of them, like Busse, act on it. "Jessica is one of our more courageous principals," she said. "She is willing to step into that space and wants to dig into the beliefs of the math department, even if people will continue to be uncomfortable."

Transforming math instruction, Busse said, has involved changing teachers' minds about teaching subjects in isolation. She believes in bringing together standards such as geometry and algebra to show how to build a deck, for example. In terms of math, real-world functionality makes the subject culturally relevant. "Look at all the standards of math I've used to build the deck," she said, "and building it also has value because it saved me x amount of money. If I just talked about the angles of the wood, or what a right angle was, the lesson would have no value" (J. Busse, personal communication, May 27, 2020).

(Continued)

(Continued)

Busse also uses her "math mind" to begin potentially difficult conversations about any issues with teachers. "Facts and numbers are hard to argue," she said, "so I find that when I use data to demonstrate a point about grading practices or another situation we need to address, the conversation goes better. That's the entry point. When the discussion gets emotional, I ask the teacher to consider the feelings and emotions of the students who are not being served well rather than dwell on their own emotions, after they identify them. At the end of the day, I remind them, it's not about us adults; it's about the students we teach. This is one of the benefits of having great relationships with students, especially the ones in trouble. When they are able to tell you how they feel about their schooling, you can use that as a tool in conversations with teachers to find a method that works."

Busse believes that being an equity leader also means bringing in student voices to transform instruction and programming. "More and more I believe it's about listening to our students and talking to them about what we can do to make a learning environment more friendly and learner focused," she said. "One thing we've been intentional about this year is how we cluster our students of color. Over and over again we've heard our students of color say, 'I want to go into this advanced placement class, but I don't want to be the only Black/Latino,' or 'When I walk into an AP class, I don't feel like I belong.'"

"So how do we create an environment in which our students of color feel accepted and comfortable? It takes a lot of conversations with these students to find out what a class looks like where they feel welcome. We had those conversations, and we also worked with teachers to create a new model that dismantles the typically all-white honors and IB curriculum. Now, we no longer have honors civics and regular civics. We have ninth-grade civics, where every student is taught the same content but can choose their level of assessment. Students get to decide the depth they want to go, such as delving into the challenge of synthesizing the information or staying with the who, what, where, and why. We offer the same for physics. It's a choose-your-own adventure way of learning."

Un Lafayette appreciates that she can take data to her principals and talk about her vision and what it says about their school system. "I try to humanize it," she said, "telling them that it's not about the quantitative data; it's about the families who put their kids in our system because they believe it's going to help their loved ones achieve their hopes and dreams. I show principals how to use the data to help their teachers improve instruction. Our kids are giving us the gift of data in the form of test scores and progress, so how are we looking at that data? Who needs to be challenged more, and what do we need to reteach? I talk to school leaders about how to let math scores direct us to creating culturally relevant lesson instruction."

Culturally relevant instruction, Un Lafayette noted, does not necessarily show up in lesson plans but in how the classroom is run. She shared the example of a second-grade class in one of the district's two Title I schools, which is also a targeted support school because of its historically larger opportunity gaps and high number of free or reduced-lunch students. "All these demographics would typically tell us that student growth in math and reading would be below average, but their growth is exceptional and their math scores blow away all the other districts in the state. When I looked at how they have been growing their students in math over the last 3 years, I wondered what was happening there and made a visit with my team.

"Walking into those second-grade classrooms, we couldn't see the teachers at first. Everyone was on the floor, working in groups, and we would find the teacher in one group working with an individual student. We stepped into other classrooms and saw the same thing, a space in which the teacher was not the giver of knowledge but the facilitator of knowledge. This was very clear. Students were allowed to collaborate and encouraged to work with each other without a teacher hovering— this was not a silent classroom. We also learned that two of the teachers helped run a program called Bring It Home designed to support multilingual families. They created an afterschool space to build community by bringing parents and students together to work on concept-based math and literacy activities. After these sessions, the parents take more activities home to engage in with their children. Since that visit we've been evaluating the program and found from survey feedback that the families appreciate being in affinity with teachers and other parents who experience school in similar ways. The teachers in this school are not only killing it in the classroom but also leading the way in terms of making the family connection."

Un Lafayette is pleasantly surprised about responses from some white teachers and parents about the work. "When I enter into conversations about data or just talk about education in other spaces, I always bring in my lens as a person of color, a refugee kid," she said. "Sometimes I expect my white colleagues to stay neutral in conversations where it's easier to maintain the status quo, but I underestimate them. For example, in a recent gifted/talented team meeting, I was heartened when the white teacher consultants looked at the data and said, 'How can we say we're about racial equity and continue to run this program the way it is?' These teachers and others in our system believe in identifying all students as gifted and talented, regardless of race, while others are protective of that space and unintentionally uphold whiteness as property.

"Change happens when teachers, who have the most political power, say we need to change the system. We also have an awesome school board and parents in the district, not just people of color but also white families. I believe the foundation for change in our district is there, and we need to be honest and talk about what gets in the way. Addressing our gifted/talented program in terms of equity is not about getting rid of it but redefining what it means and how it plays into how we can offer more for all our students. If we can just name the problems with instruction and programs, get through them, and do it in collaboration, I see movement. I see hope."

Our mentors' stories bring a real-world dimension to many of the practices discussed in this chapter and Chapter 6. Their experiences add to your knowledge of research-proven strategies, from the Courageous Conversation protocol and Jackson's (2011) high operational practices to Hattie's (2012) influences and the elements of culturally relevant pedagogy, each expanding your capacity to lead for equity. Your journey on the Theory of Action has now moved into implementing these practices, which leads to the potential for improved data that will build your confidence and resilience as a courageous leader. In the next chapter, we delve into more real-life stories, this time on a national scale, as well as the school and life realities of students of color.

References

Atwater, M. M. (2010). Dr. Geneva Gay: Multicultural education for all disciplines. *Science Activities, 47*(4), 160–162. doi:0.1080/00368121003753902

Aud, S., Fox, M. A., & KewalRamani, A. (2010, July). *Status and trends in the education of racial and ethnic groups.* U.S. Department of Education. Retrieved from https://nces.ed.gov/pubs2010/2010015.pdf.

Choudhury, I. (n.d.). *Culture.* Retrieved from http://people.tamu.edu/~i-choudhury/culture.html.

Datta, D., & Arnsten, A. (2019). Loss of prefrontal cortical higher cognition with uncontrollable stress: Molecular mechanisms, changes with age, and relevance to treatment. *Brain Sciences, 9*(5), 113. Retrieved from https://doi.org/10.3390/brainsci9050113.

Gay, G. (2002). Preparing for culturally responsive teaching. *Journal of Teacher Education, 53*(2), 106–116.

Hall, E. T. (1989). *Beyond culture.* New York: Anchor.

Hattie, J. (2012). *Visible learning for teachers: Maximizing impact on learning.* New York: Routledge.

Irvine, J. J., & Armento, B. J. (2001). *Culturally responsive teaching: Lesson planning for elementary and middle grades.* New York: McGraw-Hill.

Jackson, Y. (n.d.). *Transformational pedagogy: Cashing the promissory note of equity for all students—especially those who are marginalized.* Retrieved from https://capacitybuildingnetwork.org/article8/.

Jackson, Y. (2011). *The pedagogy of confidence: Inspiring high intellectual performance in urban schools.* New York: Teachers College Press.

Jackson, Y. (2020). *7 high operational practices.* Retrieved from https://www.learningpersonalized.com/wp-content/uploads/2019/03/High-Operational-Practices-.pdf.

Katz, J. H. (1990). *Some aspects and assumptions of white culture in the United States* [Slide]. Retrieved from http://www.cascadia.edu/discover/about/diversity/documents/Some%20Aspects%20and%20Assumptions%20of%20White%20Culture%20in%20the%20United%20States.pdf.

Ladson-Billings, G. (1995). But that's just good teaching! The case for culturally relevant pedagogy. *Theory Into Practice, 34*(3), 159–165. Retrieved from https://www.jstor.org/stable/1476635.

Ladson-Billings, G. (2004). *Crossing over to Canaan: The journey of new teachers in diverse classrooms.* San Francisco: John Wiley & Sons.

Ladson-Billings, G. (2009). *The dreamkeepers: Successful teachers of African American children* (2nd ed.). San Francisco: John Wiley & Sons.

McKenzie, K. B., & Skrla, L. (2011). *Using equity audits in the classroom to reach and teach all students.* Thousand Oaks, CA: Corwin.

National Center for Education Statistics. (2019). *Elementary and secondary enrollment.* https://nces.ed.gov/programs/raceindicators/indicator_rbb.asp.

Perkins-Gough, D. (2015, June). Rewriting the script in urban schools: A conversation with Yvette Jackson and Veronica McDermott. *Educational Leadership, 72*, 14–21. Retrieved from http://www.ascd.org/publications/educational-leadership/summer15/vol72/num09/Rewriting-the-Script-in-Urban-Schools.aspx.

The State of Things

CHAPTER
8

Black people in the United States differ from all other modern people owing to the unprecedented levels of unregulated and unrestrained violence directed at them.

—**Cornel West (2001)**

Early into this new decade, our schools face both long-held and new challenges. The Covid-19 pandemic is uprooting traditional practices and demanding innovation at every level. Teaching gaps are still wide and unacceptable. Students of color continue to be disciplined with more severity than white students for the same conduct, and Black girls face discriminatory treatment based on deeply held stereotypes. Children of color hear racist statements on talk shows and from the leader of the country and live in fear of the escalating racial bullying that these words ignite. While grappling with these issues, principals can strengthen their practice by reflecting on and analyzing current events and facts about today's educational dilemmas. This chapter is designed to help you do just that.

Bias in the News: Strengthening Practice by Analyzing Leadership Actions in Current Events

This Changes Everything

In the spring of 2020, even the Covid-19 pandemic that had isolated people and nations, shut down economies, and killed more than 160,000 Americans seemed to be no match for the disruption of society that would follow the police killing of George Floyd in Minneapolis. Floyd's death on May 25 launched an eruption of anguish and anger over the culture of police brutality that time and again ended in death for unarmed Black men. Peaceful and in some places disrupted Black Lives Matter (BLM) protests sprang up in big cities and small towns across the country and world, and people demanded structural change in policing. The number of protesters expanded until BLM far surpassed any other social protest movement in U.S. history, with up to 26 million people taking to the streets (Buchanan, Bul, & Patel, 2020). In the nation's timeline, there may well now be a pre–George Floyd and post–George Floyd America. This time, there may be no turning back from a moment that has shifted policing policies (bans on chokeholds), brought down statues of Confederate generals and removed Confederate flags, seen a surge of truth telling by people of color that has expanded racial awareness, and changed the behavior of leaders in business, politics, and sports. As African American studies scholar Charles Ross commented, "You cannot sit around now in this post–George Floyd period we're in and say, 'We're going to continue to take this safe position.' No. Either you have an issue with racism or you do not" (Branch, 2020).

While Covid-19 was exposing the racial disparities in health care and other institutions that put people of color more at risk, the post–George Floyd era took the country's pent-up anxiety to the breaking point. Reports of white supremacists agitating peaceful protests, the militarization of police and use of federal troops to attack protesters, the rise of overt white nationalism, and the communications of the president of the United States whose social media posts were given warning labels or removed for their incendiary content all came together to fuel the protests. Floyd's death beneath the knee of a police officer who ignored his pleas that he could not breathe, captured on video, brought the brutality of racism into everyone's consciousness. Along with headlines about Floyd's death, the protests, and dozens of cities revamping their policing policies, we've seen other changes take place on a national scale. The post-Floyd period has not only made BLM the largest movement in U.S. history but also forced organizations like the NFL, for example, to rethink its stance on taking a knee as a peaceful protest. This story of leadership during crisis is a transparent example of interest convergence in action, in which a white-dominated leadership group resisted Black interests until it was in their interest to do so.

The act of bending a knee during the national anthem at NFL games as a way of protesting police shootings of unarmed Blacks and systemic racism in general began with San Francisco 49ers player Colin Kaepernick in 2016. Rather than support the players' right to free speech and peaceful demonstration, white team owners enacted an NFL policy in 2018 that directed players to stay in the locker room if they didn't want to stand during the anthem. If they failed to follow the rule, their team would be fined, and the team could also fine the player. Although 70% of NFL players are Black, 94% of NFL team owners and 75% of head coaches are white (Harper, 2018).

The debate about kneeling during the anthem wore on until the killing of George Floyd and the subsequent mass protests. In June 2020, NFL commissioner Roger Goodell released a video statement apologizing for the league's actions. "We, the National Football League, admit we were wrong for not listening to N.F.L. players earlier and encourage all to speak out and peacefully protest" (Belson, 2020). In this new era, in which two-thirds of Americans support BLM protests (Behrmann, 2020), *standing up* during the national anthem has become the exception for professional athletes, with each team member taking a knee as they line up on the field. As owners of the most profitable U.S. professional sports league, NFL leaders could not ignore the shift in public sentiment. This highly visible controversy showed how Black efforts for racial equity are blocked until whites find a benefit for themselves in promoting the cause.

Another example of what happens when a high-profile person's lack of racial awareness clashes with the public takes us to a New York City TV studio in the recent past.

Still Dealing With Blackface

In 2018, Megyn Kelly was on the air five mornings a week with *Megyn Kelly Today*, a talk show that directly followed NBC's *Today Show*. She hosted with a studio audience and reached about 2.4 million viewers, not a stellar following in the world of network TV but a big reach nevertheless. On October 23, Kelly brought in three celebrity guests to talk about Halloween costumes, creating an all-white panel. She introduced the segment this way:

> I have to give you a fair warning—I'm a little fired up over Halloween costumes this morning. I mean, truly, political correctness has gone amok. There are strict rules on what you may and may not wear issued by someone who thinks they're the boss of you. . . . You can't wear anything Mexican based, no sombrero, no maracas; that's cultural. . . . You cannot dress as a Native American; that's apparently been some rule up [*sic*] for a long time. (*Megyn Kelly Today*, 2018, October 23)

As the show got rolling, Megyn brought up the controversy over blackface costumes and shared her opinion.

> What is racist? Because you do get in trouble if you are a white person who puts on blackface on Halloween, or a black person who puts on whiteface for Halloween. Back when I was a kid that was okay, as long as you were dressing up as, like, a character. (*Megyn Kelly Today*, 2018, October 23)

While the studio audience applauded most of Kelly and her panel's people-are-just-too-dang-sensitive-today comments, others at NBC were not amused. Her defense of blackface ignited a public and media backlash that compelled her to write an apology to her network colleagues expressing what she had apparently learned over the course of the day: "I realize now that such behavior is indeed wrong, and I am sorry" (Johnson, 2018). She stated that blackface was an "abhorrent" part of our cultural history and concluded, "I've never been a 'pc' kind of person—but I understand that we do need to be more sensitive in this day and agree" (Johnson, 2018). The next morning, Al Roker, cohost of *Today*, said on air that Kelly's apology to the network was not enough and that she owed "a bigger apology to folks of color around the country" (Fang, 2018). Later that morning Kelly began her show with an apology directed at her audience in general: "I was wrong and I am sorry" (Miller, 2018). She then introduced two Black guests to further the discussion, Roland Martin of the show *Roland Martin Unfiltered* and Amy Holmes, cohost of PBS's *In Principle*.

Martin and Holmes offered a succinct history of blackface as a caricature of Black people, and Holmes explained, "What people don't understand is that Black people in America . . . for 399 years [have had] this constant assault, this degradation and demeaning of how we look and how we act" (*Megyn Kelly Today*, 2018, October 24). The two guests' remarks may have enlightened some white viewers, but Kelly's efforts did not prevent NBC from canceling her show. She left the network with her multimillion-dollar contract paid in full, an amount, incidentally, twice as much as the combined salaries of the previous stars of that morning show spot, Black hosts Tamron Hall and Al Roker (Michaels, 2018).

Kelly's instinct to reject the idea of blackface as racist revealed the "normalness" of bias among whites of any age, educational background, or class. Before starting a career in TV news, Kelly had spent 10 years as an attorney, and her high-ratings tenure as a Fox News anchor prior to joining NBC put her on *Time* magazine's list of the 100 Most Influential People in the World. Despite her extensive education and media career, she did not encounter a challenge to her racial bias until that October morning of 2018. Her comfort level in publicly mocking those who found fault in blackface and appropriating Native American and other cultures revealed how thoroughly matters of race are ignored in our culture. Kelly was called out for her lack of understanding, but her behavior reflects the prevalence of bias passed down from generation to generation. Recent events show that students can be equally bold in accepting blackface as an appropriate costume.

During that same lead-up to Halloween in 2018, headlines in the Rochester, Minnesota, media covered the story of three male high school students who had uploaded a photo of themselves in KKK costumes and blackface. The two teenagers in KKK hoods posed on either side of their blackface classmate with arms raised in the KKK salute (Med City Beat, 2018). The district superintendent sent a letter to parents stating that the incident was being investigated, and the following Monday the high school's student diversity council held a "Stronger Together" event to give presentations and provide a space for dialogue (Molseed & Cutts, 2018). In April 2019, four white male students from a high school in Flossmoor, Illinois, posted a Snapchat video of themselves in blackface at a fast-food drive-up window making, as one report stated, "disparaging remarks about African-American girls" (Justich, 2019). A week later, three white teenagers from another suburban Chicago school district posed in blackface in their car at a gas station for photos they posted on social media (Koeske, 2019).

The slate of blackface incidents and dressing in KKK hoods and garb occurring in schools and colleges across the country, as well as cases of racial bullying, factor into the rising number of hate crimes reported each year. Hate crimes increased by 17% in 2017, with 7,175 incidents compared to 6,121 in 2016. The 2016 number was also an increase over 2015's 5,850 cases. The 2017 count was the first consecutive 3-year annual increase and the largest single-year increase since the aftermath of 9/11, which drew an uptick in anti-Arab and anti-Muslim incidents (Berry & Wiggins, 2018).

Reflect on This

A Lesson on Blackface

Using the Pyramid of Hate to Analyze Biased Behaviors

Analyzing blackface and KKK-impersonation incidents on the Pyramid of Hate, we regard these acts as examples of bias-motivated violence. Portraying Blacks as caricature figures rather than human beings and impersonating the KKK, "America's first terrorist organization" (Southern Poverty Law Center, 2011), are assaults and threats that represent the history of violence against African Americans. Those who make these offenses normalize this form of violence and dismiss its history that has not only brought lasting harm to African Americans but also contributes to systemic racism.

Watch Megyn Kelly's 13-minute segment, "Amy Holmes, Roland Martin Talk to Megyn Kelly About Blackface Comments," linked on this book's website, racialequityleadership.com (Chapter 8 section). Reflect on the following in your journal:

1. What did you learn?

2. If you did not know the history or insights that Martin and Holmes provided, how could you have educated yourself and others?

3. How would you respond to those who argue that blackface and KKK impersonations are not violent?

4. As an educational leader, what is your work with this kind of experience?

Racial Bullying in Schools, in the News, and by the Numbers

Data show that bullying around racial lines in our schools grew more frequent and severe during the 2016 presidential election season and continued to increase. Concerns about these experiences prompted the

Teaching Tolerance project at the Southern Poverty Law Center (SPLC) to administer a survey to more than 10,000 school administrators, teachers, counselors, and other staff shortly after the election of Donald Trump as president in November 2016 (Costello, 2016). As a candidate, Trump had produced a racially charged climate with divisive rhetoric targeting people of color, such as describing Mexican immigrants as criminals and rapists (Gass, 2015); calling for a shutdown of Muslims entering the United States (Taylor, 2015); referring to "the Blacks," a phrase that linguists describe as labeling African Americans as "other" (Desmond-Harris, 2016); and identifying Blacks as living in poverty with bad schools and no jobs and therefore with nothing to lose by voting for him (LoBianco & Killough, 2016).

In a summary of the survey, the SPLC reported that "the increase in targeting and harassment that began in the spring has, according to the teachers we surveyed, skyrocketed. It was most frequently reported by educators in schools with a majority of white students" (Costello, 2016). In addition to the data reported in Figure 8.1, 90% of respondents remarked that they had seen a negative impact on students' mood and behavior following the election, and 80% stated that their marginalized students (including Blacks, Muslims, immigrants) suffered from heightened anxiety. Forty percent had witnessed derogatory language directed at students of color, and 2,500 of the educators provided narratives about specific incidents that were "directly traced to election rhetoric" (Costello, 2016). Due to that correlation,

Figure 8.1   Southern Poverty Law Center Survey on Racial Incidents in Schools After the 2016 Presidential Election

WORDS/SLURS/IMAGES USED IN BULLYING	NUMBER OF RESPONDENT MENTIONS
Swastikas	54
Confederate flags	31
The KKK	40
"Build the wall"	476
Deportation	672
The n-word	117
Lynching	7
Noose	5
Africa (send back to)	89
Slavery (return to)	20

Source: Costello (2016).

the researchers referred to the survey findings as "the Trump effect." Educators' stories included a high school counselor from Arizona who described an assembly in which a group of white students held up a Confederate flag, and a middle school teacher in Indiana who observed white students making remarks to Latinx students such as "We can't wait until you and the other brownies are gone." A high school teacher in Michigan heard a student say, "Bet those Black people are really scared now." An Illinois high school teacher wrote that whites yelled "Terrorist," "Pack your bags," and "Go back to where you came from" to immigrants on the school bus, and "We'll burn you" to a Jewish student. While teaching a unit about world religions, a middle school teacher in Washington was interrupted by a student who blurted out, "I hate Muslims."

In Virginia, a sixth-grade white student waited for a Black student to come out of the boys' restroom and tried to provoke a fight by calling him "n----r." In Washington, a high school student walked down the hall chanting "White power!" A high school teacher in Oregon found vandalism in the boys' bathroom that targeted a specific Black student with mentions of the KKK and use of the n-word. Teachers saw swastikas carved and written on walls for the first time in their careers, and a middle school counselor in Florida recalled writing up two suicide assessments and two threat-of-violence assessments for students in a 24-hour period. Black students were "without hope," the counselor wrote, after all the violence threatened against them. A high school teacher from Tennessee found

> "Kill the n*****s" etched in school bathroom. Paper with n-word left in my classroom. . . . Students have told me they no longer need Spanish (the subject I teach) since Trump is sending all the Mexicans back. A Black student was blocked from entering his classroom by two white students chanting, "Trump, Trump." (Costello, 2016)

Another study suggesting a connection between racial bullying in schools and the divisive political climate studied Virginia's statewide 2013, 2015, and 2017 school climate surveys that had been taken by 155,000 seventh- and eighth-grade students (Huang & Cornell, 2019). The researchers found that in regions that favored the Republican candidate, 18% of students reported experiencing bullying in the past year (2016), and 9% affirmed that students in their school experienced racial bullying. These responses contrasted with the survey data from years prior to the election, which revealed no meaningful differences.

Annual FBI data also suggest a connection between school bullying and the national climate impacted by the president's racial rhetoric. The agency reported that crimes at K–12 schools and colleges escalated by 25% in 2017, which marked the second year in a row in which these racial assaults increased by about one quarter (Keierleber, 2018).

Stories in the media put human faces on the vocabulary of bullying listed in Figure 8.1, such as the April 2019 report about a white sixth-grader in New York City who walked up behind a Black classmate, wrapped a noose he had made out of yarn around his neck, and said, "This is what your ancestors went through" (Edelman, 2019). Even the youngest students of color continue to endure these assaults: In May 2019, Black scholar Michael Eric Dyson told the media that his 6-year-old grandson had been bullied and threatened in the lunch line at his school in Washington, DC: "The student called my grandson the B word, the MF word and the N-word, then told him that he was going to take his father's gun and shoot him," Dyson said (Aviles, 2019).

Reflect on This

"The Only Way to Fight Hate"

Shortly after a string of three deadly hate crimes that occurred within 72 hours in October 2018, Nancy Gibbs (2018) published an essay about the state of hatred in the United States. Gibbs, the visiting Edward R. Murrow Professor at the Harvard Kennedy School of Government and former editor in chief of *Time* magazine, wrote that these violent times—11 worshippers killed at a Pittsburgh synagogue, mail bombs sent to people critical of the president, and the fatal shooting of two Blacks in a Kentucky grocery store—thrust us into a "master class on hate." Hate, she wrote, "slipped its bonds and runs loose, through our politics, platforms, press, and private encounters."

The solution, she contended, lies in engagement, from teachers staying after school to tutor and employees demanding a humane culture at work to raising money for environmental projects and volunteering to help get out the vote. Leadership to heal the culture of hate will be about modeling kindness and fighting alienation, she wrote. Everyone must do the work.

Read Gibbs's short essay "The Only Way to Fight Hate," linked on this book's website at racialequityleadership.com (Chapter 8 Section), and consider her message and the classifications of the Pyramid of Hate in Figure 8.2. Ask yourself the following:

1. Where do you see adults perpetuating the pyramid of hate within your schools?

2. Where do you see students perpetuating the pyramid of hate within your schools?

3. What acts of kindness, love, and decisions to fight hate have you witnessed?

4. What are you doing, as a leader, to provide space, education, and actions to fight hate within your schools?

Figure 8.2   The Anti-Defamation League's Pyramid of Hate

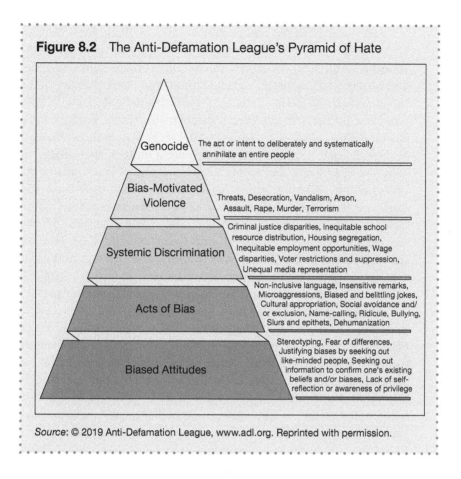

Source: © 2019 Anti-Defamation League, www.adl.org. Reprinted with permission.

Black Male Achievement: The Minneapolis Strategy

One of the starkest dilemmas in education has been the focus of innovative programs at the state, city, and school district levels. Oakland, California, and Minneapolis, Minnesota, school districts have been at the vanguard of addressing this issue—the learning of our most at-risk group of students, Black males. Nationwide, the Black male graduation rate is 59% compared with the white male rate of 80%, and large gaps exist between Black and white males in reading, math, and science scores (Schott Foundation, 2015; National Center for Education Statistics, 2018). Oakland opened its Office of African American Male Achievement (AAMA) in 2010, spearheaded by founding executive director Christopher Chatmon, and created an elective course called the Manhood Development Program. Taught by Black male teachers, the class consists of a curriculum about Black history and culture, leadership and character development, college and career guidance, family engagement for college readiness, field trips to museums and colleges, and a commitment to recruiting and developing Black male teachers.

Five years later, by founding the Office of Black Male Student Achievement (OBMSA), Superintendent Bernadeia Johnson made Minneapolis the second district in the country (Hawkins, 2014) to designate what is called "a specific structure to support the achievement of the lowest-performing group of students" in the district—Black males, who also make up the district's largest demographic (Office of Black Male Student Achievement, n.d.). Director Michael Walker designed the curriculum, B.L.A.C.K. (Building Lives Acquiring Cultural Knowledge), to cover the history and themes of "the lived reality of black men in the United States" (OBMSA, n.d.). Classes address Black male labor and employment; how Black masculinity is portrayed in popular culture; issues in education, law, incarceration, and criminal justice; and traditional and nontraditional family structures (OBMSA, n.d.). Like the Oakland program, the Minneapolis program refers to B.L.A.C.K. students as kings to develop positive identities and, as Walker explained, "awaken the greatness that is already inside of them" (Johnson, 2017).

Walker's program combines the coursework with mentorship, leadership development, and service learning. Kings have full access to Black male mentors from the community and in turn serve as mentors themselves: High school kings mentor middle school students, and those students mentor Black males in elementary school. Kings gain leadership experience through opportunities to make decisions together on how OBMSA should be run and in projects that require them to work, plan, and organize. The service learning element, designed to reverse the sense of inferiority that often comes from being the recipient of services, involves volunteer projects that engage the kings in understanding and helping alleviate social problems. According to OBMSA, this active learning brings a validation from the community and gives kings "a voice in improving others' lives while at the same time improving their own" (OBMSA, n.d.).

The B.L.A.C.K. curriculum and other OBMSA components embody a journey in which Black male students grapple with the following questions: Who am I? Who are we? What is our current state? Where am I going, and how do I get there? Once I am there, how do I stay and advance?

Unlike the Oakland program, the Minneapolis model also includes professional development for school staff. Principals who commit to the B.L.A.C.K. program must also agree to enroll the entire team in their buildings to a selection of workshops (nine are available) that concentrate on, for example, strategies for engaging Black males, addressing unconscious bias, linking Black families and communities to schools, and interpreting individual results of the Intercultural Development Inventory (IDI). Walker regards this long-term adult component, designed to change the mind-sets and beliefs of educators, as perhaps the most important work of the program (M. Walker, personal communication, May 13, 2019). When educators believe in their kings, young Black men are motivated to learn, as shown in Walker's belief framework (see Figure 8.3).

Figure 8.3 Michael Walker's Belief Framework

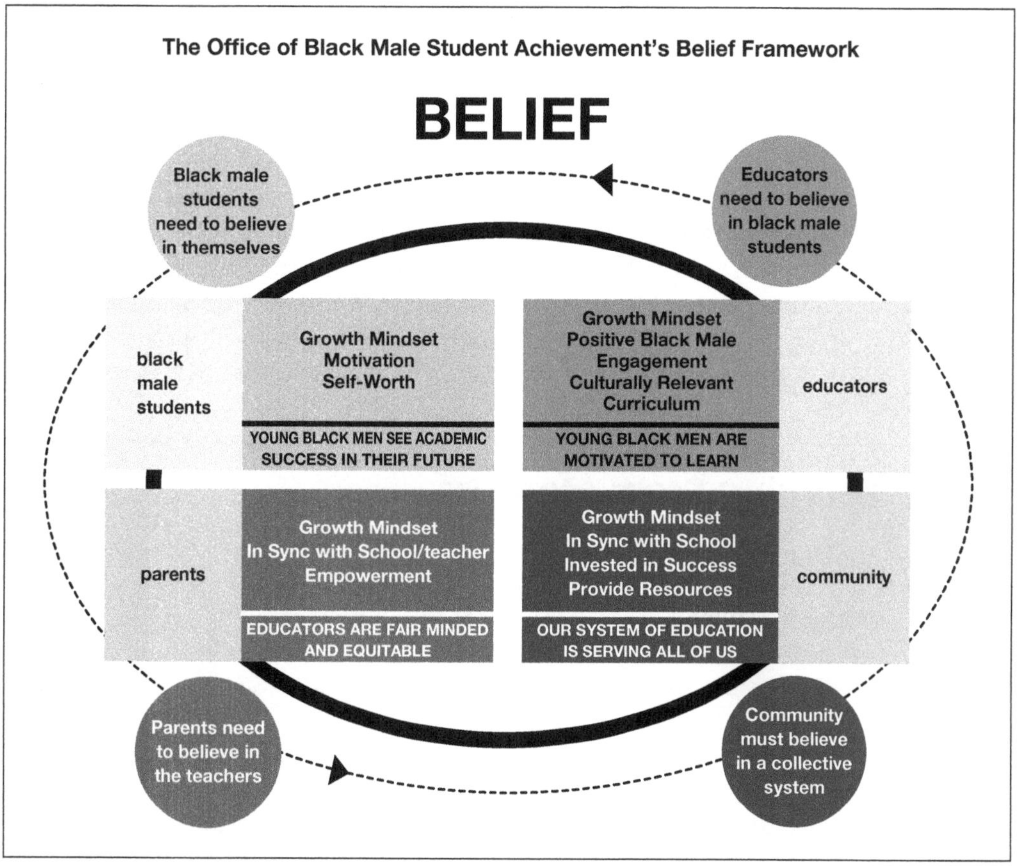

Source: Created by Michael Walker for the Minneapolis School District Office of Black Male Student Achievement. Reprinted with permission.

The overall effect of the Minneapolis program has had a positive impact on academic outcomes, according to a study conducted by the school district (Walker, Vanden Berk, & Zumbusch, 2017). The study reported that participation in B.L.A.C.K. increased kings' GPA and high school credit readiness. Compared to the 130-student control group, which shared a set of baseline characteristics with the 77 selected B.L.A.C.K. participants in the study, the B.L.A.C.K. kings gained a statistically significant annual GPA increase of 0.125 points if they attended the program for 1 year and 0.171 if they participated for 2 years. Translating this over the entire course of high school, the Minneapolis School District's kings could see their GPA increasing to a range from 2.78 to 2.96, which vaults them into the opportunity to apply to more competitive colleges (Walker et al., 2017). Credit readiness, which indicates a high school student's on-track status for graduating in 4 years, also improved to a statistically significant degree, according to the study. B.L.A.C.K. participants rated an 87% readiness, while students in the control group averaged a 71% readiness (Walker et al., 2017). A more recent summary of the program's impact reported that 54% of kings graduated in 2018 compared to 47% of nonprogram Black male students. Office of Black Male Student Achievement data are always based on comparisons of Black males to Black males, a decision, Walker explained, based on the students' input:

> We are getting students whose outcomes are traditionally lower than the district averages, even for black males. Our kings shared with me early on when I was doing my one hundred days of listening that they were tired of being compared to white students. "Compare us to ourselves," they told me. "Let us figure that out." I respect and value that. We are very big on being true to student voice, so they are at the tables with all our big decisions. (M. Walker, personal communication, May 13, 2019)

Learning From Mentors

Looking in the Mirror

Michael Walker

The Minneapolis School District's Office of Black Male Student Achievement (OBMSA) is one of only two school district programs in the country set up to develop Black male achievement. In addition to the special curriculum, the Minneapolis model, led by its founding director Michael Walker, incorporates a professional development program for adults to help them address their racial bias and learn strategies for engaging Black students and their families and communities. More than 1,200 faculty and staff members receive professional development per year in the Minneapolis program (Office of Black Male Student Achievement, n.d.).

One thing I keep saying is that this is not something you can just do in your day-to-day job. It's got to be something you're committed to throughout your life. So if you're just going to do this work from 8:00 to 4:00, it's going to be tough for you. If you're not thinking about this, if you're not changing how you interact in your normal life, then when you get to school you might play a part for a little while, but eventually that stuff comes out.

How are you changing your mind and beliefs all the time? How are you putting yourself in situations to learn and grow and do better and challenge your thinking? A lot of times we look at this—myself included—as window work, saying, "Look at what they're doing." We've got to look in the mirror in this work and ask, "What am I doing? How am I helping or hurting this situation? What do I believe? What do I think?" It's easy to look out the window and see what everybody else is doing, but looking in the mirror is the hardest part, and it's the real work (M. Walker, personal communication, May 13, 2019).

The Racial Discipline Gap

Despite federal law that prohibits schools from discriminating in how they discipline students based on race, racial discrimination in school discipline has increased over the past five decades. In 1974 and 1975, the Children's Defense Fund issued the first studies about the racial disparities in school discipline (Edelman, Beck, & Smith, 1975). The researchers' remarks about racial discrimination in school suspensions could have been written today to describe the common assumptions and behaviors that persist nearly 45 years later:

> Some will claim that disproportionate suspension of black children simply reflects their disproportionate misbehavior. We reject this view. All the evidence we have seen . . . makes plain that disproportionate suspension of blacks reflects a pervasive school intolerance for children who are *different.* . . . The fact is that many school districts treat black children differently from white children. Some black children are suspended for offenses for which white children are not suspended, or receive different treatment for similar offenses. (Edelman et al., 1975, p. 13)

What *has* changed since those groundbreaking studies is the suspension rate of Black students. In the 1970s, Black students were suspended at twice the rate of white students (Edelman et al., 1975), and today, at 16%, they are suspended at more than 3 times the rate (U.S. Department of Education Department for Civil Rights, 2014).

In 2014, the U.S. Department of Education Department for Civil Rights reported that "Black students were three times more likely to be suspended or expelled than white students despite any evidence that suggested Black students as being more likely to misbehave." This suspension rate gap is illustrated in Figure 8.4. The Department for Civil Rights also found cases where "African-American students were disciplined more harshly and more frequently because of their race than similarly situated white students."

Black boys and young men experience, by far, the most suspensions, expulsions, and arrests in our schools. The most recent data from the U.S. Department of Education Department for Civil Rights (2018) reported that while Black male students represented 8% of students in the 2015–2016 school year, they accounted for 25% of students who received an out-of-school (OOS) suspension and 23% of students who were expelled.

Zero-tolerance discipline policies that inflict out-of-school suspensions and expulsions regardless of circumstances are large factors in the school-to-prison pipeline that pushes students out of school and into the criminal justice system. Severe discipline like long-term suspension or expulsion given for even minor infractions puts students of color at risk

Figure 8.4 K–12 School Suspension Rates by Race/Ethnicity, 1972–2012

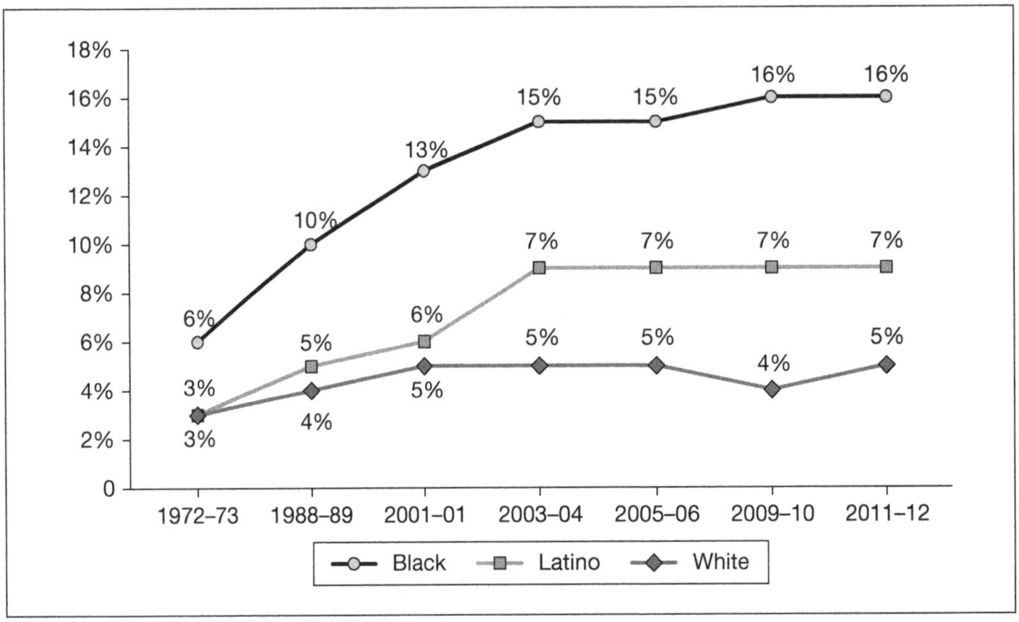

Source: Losen, Hodson, Keith II, Morrison, & Belway (2015). Reprinted with permission.

by often leaving them unsupervised and easily falling behind in their classes, all of which increases the chance that they will disengage and drop out. Having a criminal record sets up a young person for roadblocks and disadvantages that can last a lifetime.

The 20-year trend in zero-tolerance policies aligns with a larger police and security presence in schools that has come in the wake of school shootings. The racial discrimination found in school discipline and policing in schools has led to Black students being 2 times as likely as white students to be referred to law enforcement or arrested—another "key touchpoint along the school-to-prison pipeline" (Rafa, 2019).

Since the evidence is clear that Black students are disciplined and arrested at an alarmingly higher rate than white students who commit the same infractions, we believe a significant part of the solution lies in transforming the racial attitudes of school principals, the central decision makers regarding discipline. Young and Laible (2000) concluded that "white principals do not have a thorough understanding of racism in its many manifestations—for example, individual, institutional, societal—nor do they comprehend the ways in which they are perpetuating white racism in their schools, even though most are well-meaning individuals" (p. 377). A recent study of white, Black, and Latinx male and female principals in Texas built on this point to investigate principals' perspectives on the racial discipline gap (DeMatthews, Carey, Olivarez, & Saeedi, 2017). The study categorized the principals' attitudes into three categories that reflected their "beliefs about race, neutrality, antecedents to misconduct, and appropriate discipline in response to misconduct" (p. 12).

Principals described as *overt racial justifiers* viewed Black culture as adverse to the institution of education, blamed poor parenting for student misbehavior, and considered Black families "deviant and problematic." They made overtly racist statements about Black families, such as "they don't raise their children or share the same values as most White people" (DeMatthews et al., 2017, p. 13).

Rigid rule enforcers made their final decisions about discipline based on policy alone without regard to circumstances. While not making overtly racist remarks like the overt racial justifiers, these principals followed rigid codes, even if they recognized that "students had difficult home lives, or if suspension would aid a student in learning from their poor choice or correcting their behavior" (DeMatthews et al., 2017, p. 14). *Flexible and cognizant disciplinarians* considered the context of situations and believed in a case-by-case, individualized approach to discipline. They thought about the outcomes of their decisions and viewed misconduct as a result of multiple variables in the school, the student's life, and the community.

In order of severity, overt racial justifiers made decisions about discipline based on rigid attachments to policy and, as reflected in the racist remarks they made about Black families, on their discriminatory perspectives about Blacks and Black culture. Rigid rule enforcers also believed in staying exclusively with code to guide their discipline, even though they showed more awareness of the elements that may be involved in student behavior and did not express overtly racist views. Flexible and cognizant disciplinarians were the reverse of both other categories, putting a priority on individual circumstances with an understanding of the contextual elements of an issue.

As the call for school discipline reform rings louder, research is underway to explore the impact of more flexible views of discipline district-wide. A 2018 study of Chicago Public Schools (Hinze-Piper & Sartain, 2018), for example, found that revised policies to reduce suspensions led to a small but statistically significant rise in test scores and improved attendance (beyond the number of fewer suspension days). In addition, the changes in policy, including fewer suspensions for severe infractions, did not make any students feel less safe in their schools except in schools serving predominantly Latinx students. Looking specifically at the schools that serve predominantly Black students, the study found "large significant differences" (p. 240) in students' perception of school climate when fewer suspensions for severe infractions were made. Students increasingly felt that teachers supported their learning, that they had good relationships with their teachers, and that they felt connected to their school. The positive impacts found in this study, which analyzed 7 years of data, support advocates of discipline reform who point out the lack of evidence for the claim that lowering suspension rates has a negative impact on learning and other student experiences.

Reflect on This

Comparing My Leadership Experiences With the 2017 Texas Study

Based on the study, the following barriers were identified by principals:

- Limited time
- Reliance on rigid policies
- Struggling/overwhelmed teachers
- Teacher race
- Teacher experience
- Administrator feels powerless

***

1. How does your experience support or challenge these barriers?
2. What in the study surprised you or made you uncomfortable?
3. What personal connections and/or assumptions were made within the category descriptors? Where do you fit?
4. How do your experiences (personal and with administration) support or challenge these categories?
5. Do your current policies perpetuate or interrupt racial inequities?

Investigating the Troubling Data About Black Girls' Discipline and Achievement: Who Is to Blame?

Like Black boys, Black girls face high suspension rates and wide teaching gaps, but they also encounter distinct social pressures and biases. "Girlhood Interrupted: The Erasure of Black Girls' Childhood," a study released by Georgetown Law Center's Center on Poverty and Inequality (Epstein, Blake, & González, 2017), reports that society's perception of Black girls leads to "adultification," a debilitating stereotype. The center's survey of 325 adults across the country showed that American adults believe that Black girls, from the age of 5,

- need less nurturing,
- need less protection,
- need to be supported less,
- need to be comforted less,
- are more independent,

- know more about adult topics, and

- know more about sex.

Adultification, in which adults perceive Black girls as adult-like and biologically older than they are, is dehumanizing, robbing Black girls of their childhood innocence. The lens of adultification perceives that "Black youths' transgressions are intentional and malicious, instead of the result of immature decision-making—a key characteristic of childhood" (Epstein et al., 2017, p. 6). Not given the opportunity to make mistakes and benefit from adult guidance about those mistakes in the same manner that white children are guided puts Black girls at a disadvantage. As a stereotype, adultification is a form of bias that may form the foundation for more complex types of prejudice and discrimination.

In a single school district in Kentucky, Epstein et al. (2017) also reported that Black girls

- made up only 8% of enrollment but 13% of students suspended;

- were 2 times more likely to be disciplined for minor violations (e.g., dress code violations, inappropriate cell phone use, loitering) than white girls;

- were 2.5 times more likely to be disciplined for disobedience than white girls;

- were 3 times more likely to be disciplined for disruptive behavior than white girls;

- were 3 times more likely to be disciplined for fighting than white girls; and

- were 3 times more likely to be disciplined for bullying or harassment than white girls.

Epstein et al. (2017) also reported national data about Black girls' experience and found that Black girls are

- 2.7 times more likely than white girls to be referred to juvenile justice,

- 0.8 times less likely than white girls to have their cases diverted, and

- 1.2 times more likely than white girls to be detained.

In light of the fact that Black girls receive a disproportionate amount of discipline in schools and more severe outcomes in the juvenile justice system than white girls, the Georgetown Law study (Epstein et al., 2017) suggests that adult perspectives of Black girls may be the cause of this differential treatment. Where do these perspectives come from? The Georgetown study addresses this by presenting an overview of three Black feminine stereotypes that have persisted since their origins in the South during slavery, stereotypes embedded in the American psyche and evident in films and other forms of popular culture. The "Sapphire" stereotype depicts Black women as loud, angry, emasculating, unfeminine, and aggressive, while the "Jezebel" stereotype is characterized by seduction and hypersexuality. The "Mammy" stereotype portrays Black women as loving, nurturing, self-sacrificing, and asexual. Educators may unconsciously refer to these images when interpreting Black girls' behavior and respond with harsher discipline.

These images conflict with traditional white perceptions of ideal femininity as "docile, diffident, and selfless" (Epstein et al., 2017, p. 5), which may account for the harsher discipline inflicted on Black girls by white school leaders. By this theory, white ideas of femininity, assumed by whites to be universal standards, become the benchmark upon which Black girls are compared and perceived to be inferior. Could this be why white principals discipline Black girls more harshly than white girls, to try to teach them to be more "acceptable"? And why teaching gaps between Black and white girls are exceptionally large (see Figure 8.5)?

In *Pushout: The Criminalization of Black Girls in Schools*, Morris (2016) writes about the current memes that also create misperceptions of Black girls—prevalent labels of the "loud" Black girl who talks back to teachers and "ghetto" Black girl who fights in the halls (p. 12). These memes, along with stereotyped representations of Black women, are part of a "prevailing consciousness that accepts an inferior quality of Black femininity" (p. 12), which underlies the criminalization of Black girls that pushes them out of schools "and often render[s] them vulnerable to further victimization and delinquency" (p. 4). To more accurately describe the impact of this criminalization, Morris (2016) broadens the term "school-to-prison pipeline" to "school-to-confinement pathways" when discussing Black girls' punitive treatment in schools. In addition to jail or prison, forms of social exclusion facing Black girls include house arrest, electronic monitoring, and detention centers. The lasting effects of these treatments and jail time involves not only Black girls' own adult lives but also those of "future generations of girls and boys, who are more susceptible to being involved with the judicial system as a result of their mother's incarceration" (Morris, 2016, p. 11). Society's debilitating, harmful consciousness about Black girls casts them "as social deviants rather than critical respondents to oppression—perceived and concrete" (Morris, 2016, p. 11).

A study of girls of color in Oakland, California, (Ohlson, Bedrossian, & Ortega, 2016) illustrates the impact of stereotyping and sexualization discussed earlier. Participants voiced their disappointment in society's low expectations for them and strong pressure to conform their behavior and presentation due to being judged and stereotyped on how they look and speak. They received mixed messages about being girls and women, on the one hand facing pressure to conform to family expectations of proper behavior and on the other feeling society's expectations that as

Figure 8.5 Minnesota State High School Graduates Accountability Test Results for Black and White Girls' Achievement

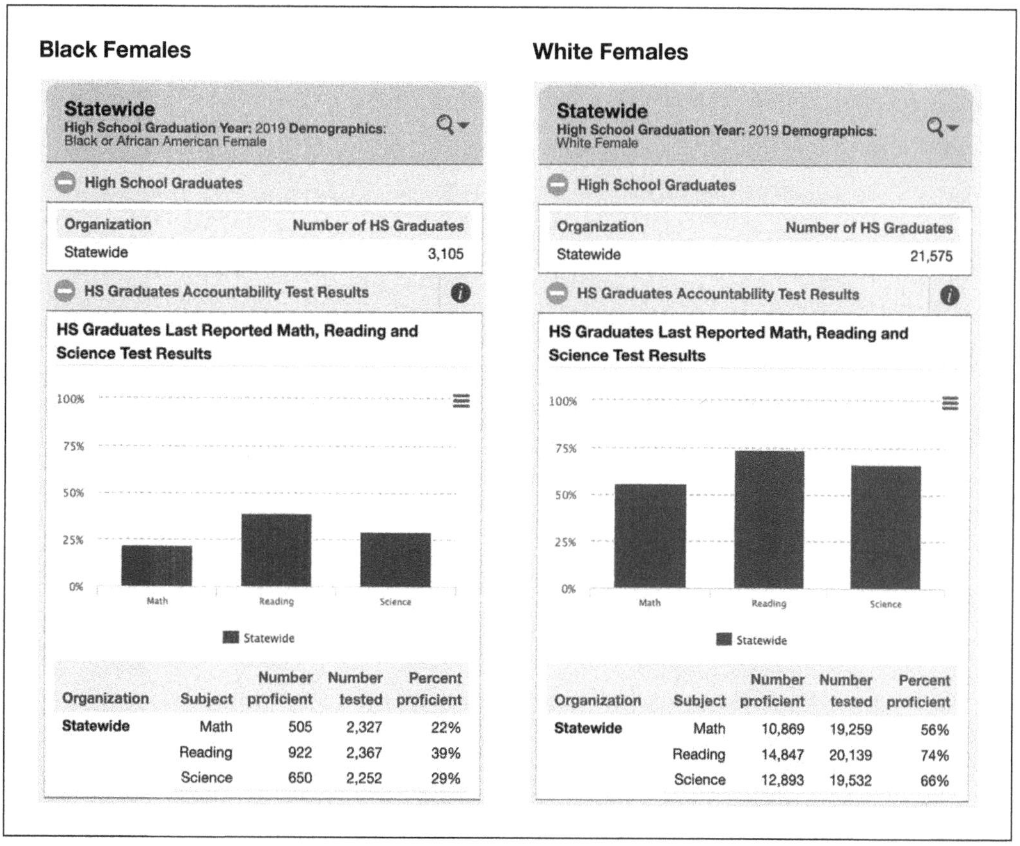
Black Females
Statewide
High School Graduation Year: 2019 Demographics: Black or African American Female
High School Graduates
Organization Number of HS Graduates
Statewide 3,105
HS Graduates Accountability Test Results
HS Graduates Last Reported Math, Reading and Science Test Results
100%
75%
50%
25%
0%
Math
Reading
Science
Statewide
Organization Subject Number proficient Number tested Percent proficient
Statewide Math 505 2,327 22%
Reading 922 2,367 39%
Science 650 2,252 29%
White Females
Statewide
High School Graduation Year: 2019 Demographics: White Female
High School Graduates
Organization Number of HS Graduates
Statewide 21,575
HS Graduates Accountability Test Results
HS Graduates Last Reported Math, Reading and Science Test Results
100%
75%
50%
25%
0%
Math
Reading
Science
Statewide
Organization Subject Number proficient Number tested Percent proficient
Statewide Math 10,869 19,259 56%
Reading 14,847 20,139 74%
Science 12,893 19,532 66%

Source: Minnesota Statewide Longitudinal Data System, 2020. Reprinted with permission.

girls they will fail by dropping out of school or, for Latina girls in particular, become teen moms. They feared becoming victims of violence and felt sexualized by boys and men. One girl described living with the prevalent stereotype of hypersexuality:

> We are all hyper-sexualized by society in general. Every male that you have some type of relationship with will think that they are entitled to you because society sexualizes you. You are here as a girl of color for that reason: to be sexual. That's the worst stereotype. (Ohlson et al., 2016, p. 9)

While the girls in this study felt that their families could be overprotective, they viewed their families as sources of protection, strength, and safety. They longed for opportunities to learn from positive female role models of color and for more public spaces to safely have fun with their friends. Overall, they felt that in their city, "white girls enjoy privilege and freedom from the types of concerns facing girls of color and African American communities in particular" (Ohlson et al., 2016, p. 4).

Reflect on This

A Conversation With Black Women on Race

Watch the 6-minute *New York Times* video, *A Conversation with Black Women on Race*, linked on this book's website at racialequityleadership .com (Chapter 8 section), and list the biases and microaggressions the women describe.

Biases	Microaggressions
_____	_____
_____	_____
_____	_____
_____	_____
_____	_____
_____	_____
_____	_____

Next, ask yourself the following questions:

1. Have you held any of these biases?

2. Have you committed any of the microaggressions?

3. Have you witnessed any of these biases or microaggressions in others? If so, how did you respond? How would you respond now?

• • •

REFLECTION INTO PRACTICE: BLACK GIRLS IN YOUR SCHOOL

Think about a situation in which there was an issue with a Black girl in your school.

1. How was it dealt with?

2. What were the possible antecedents that led to the girl's issue?

3. How were the parents addressed?

4. How might you model this at a staff meeting?

Reflecting on Current Black Memoirs to Understand Race and Personal Experience and Develop Tools for Speaking to Parents

The current state of racial bias expressed in full view by media figures and national leaders, acts of bias-motivated violence on the rise, and troubling realities about school discipline come at a time when voices of color are being heard in greater numbers. New Black memoirs such as Clyde W. Ford's (2019) *Think Black*, Anthony Ray Hinton's (2018) *The Sun Does Shine: How I Found Life and Freedom on Death Row*, Michelle Obama's (2018) *Becoming*, Gabriel Union's (2017) *We're Going to Need More Wine*, Chimamanda Ngozi Adichie's (2015) *We Should All Be Feminists*, and Ta-Nehisi Coates's (2015) *Between the World and Me* reveal Black lives and inspire personal reflection.

In our institute, we read Coates's book and invite Black male principals from the community into one of our sessions to share how the book affected them.

Learning From Mentors

As Fathers and Sons, Black Principals Share the Value of Reading and Discussing Ta-Nehisi Coates's *Between the World and Me*

Gene L. Ward, Jr. and Marcus Freeman

Gene L. Ward, Jr., an assistant principal at a middle school in the St. Paul, Minnesota, Public School District, reflected on his discussion of Ta Nehisi Coates's *Between the World and Me* with fellow Black males as well as others enrolled in our Institute for Principal Leadership. The book reinforced his thinking about helping white teachers and administrators understand that even though they don't have the same lived experiences as their students of color, they can learn about their students' thoughts and how they show up when they come into school. He knows they can do this and develop the empathy that goes along with it because he had to do the same thing. He shared this story in our institute's session on *Between the World and Me*.

"As a classroom teacher, one of my white administrators said, 'I want you to work with this African American student.' I pushed back and said, 'I'm fine working with him, but I want to know why.' I asked, is it because I'm Black and the student is Black? I grew up in a small rural town in Wisconsin with maybe a couple hundred people. We were the only Black family there until I moved to

(Continued)

(Continued)

Madison, Wisconsin, in seventh grade, which is when I noticed that many of my experiences were similar to my white colleagues and counterparts. I may not have the same background as students who look like me, but I have to be empathetic to their situation" (G. Ward, Jr., personal communication, June 4, 2019).

Like many white educators, Gene's administrator assumed that because he was Black he would be more impactful with Black students. But Gene felt more aligned with the privileges of the white middle class and had to made a conscious effort to learn about his students' lives and perspectives—just as white educators must do.

"I want principals to understand that you don't need to live the experiences, but you do need to know how students of color show up, which is more about your own understanding than about having the Black man teach Black children," Gene said. "My Blackness helps open the door, starts the conversation, but it's up to me to find some way to find some commonality."

For Gene, reading Coates's advice to his son launched his thinking about the types of advice and feedback he'd been given. Coates's discussion about white oppression of the Black body also gave him a bigger context for reflecting on his decision a few years earlier to grow out his hair. Coates writes (to his son) that the invention that is the "belief in being white" was designed, "first and foremost, to deny you and me the right to secure and govern our own bodies."

Gene considers growing his hair long as a "spiritual journey of getting connected to my roots and my authentic self," and by living that in his building he is an example of Black authenticity for his students and everyone else. "Right before I became a principal," Gene said, "I was thinking about cutting it, and a friend said, 'Don't cut your hair. At least wait until you get an administrative position so people won't think you had to sell out to get the job.' Having my long hair as an administrator validates my beliefs that I bring to the workplace," he said. "If I decide to cut it now, the message to students and staff will be that it's my own determination. This connects to the Coates book, where he talks about me, as a Black male, protecting my body, and the burden it is to be a Black male in society."

Marcus Freeman, the assistant principal of another middle school in St. Paul, shared his reflections about the impact of Coates's book on his personal and professional life. "I have Black daughters," he said, "and as I'm reading Coates's letter to his son I'm thinking of my own experience as a Black man, the conversations I had with my dad, my brother, and my grandparents around race and how to present myself in public" (M. Freeman, personal communication, June 3, 2019). This applies to the way he talks to his three daughters, determining the language he uses about what Blackness is and "how they are beautiful Black young girls who are trying to grow and become the best Black young women. I know that I have to build their armor because the world doesn't perceive them the way I do."

Marcus said that Coates's book really hit home in terms of describing the Black psyche. Blacks, he said, are always having these mental gymnastics going on in their brains, wondering *What is this about?* As an educator, it becomes tiresome. "My frustration with education is that the urgency and the ownership around Black kids failing is minimal," he said. "When you look at those who get promoted in the systems, folks who come from other places, this issue should be front and center—we should hear them ask, 'How are your Black students achieving?' But the urgency is not there, and if we continue to just perpetuate the failing kids, what is the point?

"These are conversations I have with other administrators in a group I coach. For white folks, race is rarely talked about. They don't know how to have the conversation with other white folks or people of color. Maybe coded language is being used, like when parents ask, during a tour of the school, what we're doing about behavior. My school is on one of the wealthiest blocks in St. Paul, and it's an interesting environment with a rich dichotomy of kids. We have students walking across the street who live in multimillion-dollar homes and some who are homeless. When white parents ask about behavior, I reframe it and talk about the supports we have in place. I tell them that we have to love these kids as they come to us; they're 11 to 13 years old, coming into puberty, and everybody grows at different rates. I try to illuminate the humanity in our young people and explain that this is a community for working together."

Marcus's school changed its tour policy so that he did not have to keep defending and justifying the students of color. Now he has students, Black and white, giving the school tours. "To me that is a lot more authentic," Marcus said. "They're going to keep it real and give it to you from a student's perspective, and I feel adults are a little more appropriate with young people, especially those who are touring them. They respect the scholar. Our administrative team came up with this policy together.

"I think people really do mean well. But there's always a wait and see, let's slow down the ideology when we talk about race and achievements. If it was flipped—if white kids were not achieving at an alarming rate—that wouldn't be acceptable. Things would be dismantled to make sure white kids were being successful. That's why I'm really thinking about doing something radically different on my own moving forward. It's not a one-size-fits-all; there has to be an intentional effort to make sure that young Black boys and girls are successful by creating a space and a school that is promoting and affirming that ideology and making sure that it happens."

Marcus emphasized Coates's discussion in the book about his education, in which some teachers seemed to have had good intentions but were part of a system in which the American Dream—the great myth of prosperity and upward mobility that comes at the expense of Black people—holds sway. He pointed out Coates's (2015) words in one section, where he tells his son:

> It does not matter that the "intentions" of individual educators were noble. Forget about intentions. What any institution, or its agents, "intend" for you is secondary. . . . Very few Americans will directly proclaim that they are in favor of Black people being left to the streets. But a very large number of Americans will do all they can to preserve the Dream. (p. 33)

Coates continues that white language of "intention" and "personal responsibility" was code for exonerating them from their treatment of Blacks. "Mistakes were made. Bodies were broken. People were enslaved. We meant well. We tried our best. 'Good intention' is a hall pass through history, a sleeping pill that ensures the Dream" (Coates, 2015, p. 33).

(Continued)

(Continued)

Marcus relates this to the resistance he finds in education. "It takes a long time to change biases," he said, "and many times, in my experience, with most of our teachers here and around the nation white women, they specifically struggle to deal with their own piece around racism. Many times they deflect and jump to their experience around being oppressed as a woman, and that gets in the way of dealing with their own privilege as white women and their biases against Black folks, and that shows up in the classroom or around leadership."

Tools for Practice
A Script to Talk to Parents of Color

Hello, this is (name).

How are you doing?

I am calling about (name).

First I want to tell (something positive) about (name).

He or she brings (something positive) to our classroom.

I am calling to partner with you about (what the issue is).

Thank you, and I look forward to connecting again about (name) and how well they are doing.

References

Adichie, C. N. (2015). *We should all be feminists*. New York: Anchor/Random House.

Anti-Defamation League. (n.d.). *Pyramid of hate*. Retrieved from https://www.adl.org/.

Aviles, G. (2019, May 2). *Michael Eric Dyson says grandson was threatened, called n-word at school*. Retrieved from https://www.nbcnews.com/news/nbcblk/michael-eric-dyson-says-grandson-was-threatened-called-n-word-n1000756.

Behrmann, S. (2020, July 28). Poll: Nearly two-thirds of Americans support protests against racial injustice. *USA Today*. Retrieved from https://www.usatoday.com/story/news/politics/2020/07/28/poll-most-americans-support-black-lives-matter-protests/5532345002.

Belson, K. (2020, June 5). As Trump rekindles N.F.L. fight, Goodell sides with players. *New York Times*. Retrieved from https://www.nytimes.com/2020/06/05/sports/football/trump-anthem-kneeling-kaepernick.html.

Berry, M., & Wiggins, K. (2018, November 14). *FBI stats on hate crimes are scary. So is what's missing.* Retrieved from https://www.cnn.com/2018/11/14/opinions/fbi-hate-crimes-data-whats-missing-berry-wiggins/index.html.

Branch, J. (2020, July 4). The anthem debate is back. But now it's standing that's polarizing. *New York Times.* Retrieved from https://www.nytimes.com/2020/07/04/sports/football/anthem-kneeling-sports.html#:~:text=The%20N.F.L.%2C%20which%20found%20itself,Players%20Association.

Buchanan, L., Bul, Q., & Patel, J. K. (2020, July 3). Black lives matter may be the largest movement in U.S. history. *New York Times.* Retrieved from https://www.nytimes.com/interactive/2020/07/03/us/george-floyd-protests-crowd-size.html.

Coates, T. (2015). *Between the world and me.* New York: Spiegel & Grau.

Costello, M. B. (2016, November 28). *The Trump effect: The impact of the 2016 presidential election on our nation's schools.* Retrieved from https://www.splcenter.org/20161128/trump-effect-impact-2016-presidential-election-our-nations-schools.

DeMatthews, D. E., Carey, R. L., Olivarez, A., & Saeedi, K. M. (2017). Guilty as charged? Principals' perspectives on disciplinary practices and the racial discipline gap. *Educational Administration Quarterly, 53*(4), 519–555. https://doi.org/10.1177/0013161x17714844

Desmond-Harris, J. (2016, November 9). *"All the black and brown people have to leave": Trump's scary impact on how kids think.* Retrieved from https://www.vox.com/identities/2016/10/20/13319366/donald-trump-racism-bigotry-children-bullying-muslim-mexican-black-immigrant.

Edelman, M. W., Beck, R., & Smith, P. V. (1975). *School suspensions: Are they helping children? A report.* Retrieved from https://files.eric.ed.gov/fulltext/ED113797.pdf.

Edelman, S. (2019, March 16). Upper East Side school ignored racist bullying of sixth-grade son, says mom. *New York Post.* Retrieved from https://nypost.com/2019/03/16/upper-east-side-school-ignored-racist-bullying-of-sixth-grade-son-says-mom/.

Epstein, R., Blake, J. J., & González, T. (2017). *Girlhood interrupted: The erasure of black girls' childhood.* Retrieved from https://www.law.georgetown.edu/poverty-inequality-center/wp-content/uploads/sites/14/2017/08/girlhood-interrupted.pdf.

Fang, M. (2018, October 24). Al Roker calls out NBC colleague Megyn Kelly for blackface defense. *Huffpost.* Retrieved from https://www.huffpost.com/entry/al-roker-megyn-kelly-nbc-blackface-segment_n_5bd05f57e4b0d38b587e53db.

Ford, C. W. (2019). *Think black: A memoir.* New York: Amistad.

Gass, N. (2015, December 8). *The 15 most offensive things that have come out of Trump's mouth.* Retrieved from https://www.politico.eu/article/15-most-offensive-things-trump-campaign-feminism-migration-racism/.

Gibbs, N. (2018, November 1). The only way to fight hate. *Time.* Retrieved from http://time.com/5441420/gibbs-beyond-hate.

Harper, S. R. (2018, May 24). There would be no NFL without black players. They can resist the anthem policy. *Washington Post.* Retrieved from https://www.washingtonpost.com/news/posteverything/wp/2018/05/24/there-would-be-no-nfl-without-black-players-they-can-resist-the-anthem-policy/.

Hawkins, B. (2014, July 25). Michael Walker might have the toughest job in Minneapolis. *Minneapolis Post*. Retrieved from https://www.minnpost .com/learning-curve/2014/07/michael-walker-might-have-toughest-job-minneapolis/.

Hinton, A. R. (2018). *The sun does shine: How I found life and freedom on death row*. New York: St. Martin's Press.

Hinze-Pifer, R., & Sartain, L. (2018). Rethinking universal suspension for severe student behavior. *Peabody Journal of Education, 93*(2), 228–243. https:// doi.org/10.1080/0161956X.2018.1435051

Huang, F. L., & Cornell, D. G. (2019). School teasing and the bullying after the presidential election. *Educational Researcher, 48*(2), 69–83. Retrieved from https://doi.org/10.3102/0013189X18820291.

Johnson, K. (2017, January 11). *Excellent educator: Black male student achievement program's king Walker*. Retrieved from https://minnesota.cbslocal .com/2017/01/11/excellent-educator-black-male-student-achievement-programs-king-walker/.

Johnson, T. (2018, October 23). *Megyn Kelly apologizes for questioning why wearing blackface is considered racist*. Retrieved from https://www.nbcnews .com/news/nbcblk/megyn-kelly-apologizes-questioning-why-wearing-blackface-considered-racist-n923521.

Justich, K. (2019, April 30). *High schoolers stage walkout after photos of classmates in blackface surface: "We want justice."* Retrieved from https:// www.yahoo.com/lifestyle/high-schoolers-walkout-photos-classmates-blackface-210815742.html.

Keierleber, M. (2018, November 14). *New FBI data: School-based hate crimes jumped 25 percent last year—for the second year in a row*. Retrieved from https://www.the74million.org/new-fbi-data-school-based-hate-crimes-jumped-25-percent-last-year-for-the-second-year-in-a-row/.

Koeske, Z. (2019, May 6). Mokena police received complaint about white Lincoln-Way students dressed in blackface, chief says. *Chicago Tribune*. Retrieved from https://www.chicagotribune.com/suburbs/daily-southtown/ news/ct-sta-lincoln-way-blackface-complaint-st-0507-story.html.

LoBianco, T., & Killough, A. (2016, August 19). *Trump pitches black voters: "What the hell do you have to lose?"* CNN. Retrieved from https://www.cnn .com/2016/08/19/politics/donald-trump-african-american-voters/index.html.

Losen, D. J., Hodson, C. L., Keith II, M. A., Morrison, K., & Belway, S. (2015, February 23). *Are we closing the school discipline gap?* University of California Los Angeles. Retrieved from https://civilrightsproject.ucla.edu/ resources/projects/center-for-civil-rights-remedies/school-to-prison-folder/federal-reports/are-we-closing-the-school-discipline-gap/AreWe ClosingTheSchoolDisciplineGap_FINAL221.pdf.

Med City Beat. (2018). *Racist Halloween display prompts backlash*. Retrieved from https://www.medcitybeat.com/news-blog/2018/john-marshall-students-kkk-display-prompt-condemnation.

Megyn Kelly Today. (2018, October 23). Are these Halloween costumes too controversial to wear? [Video file]. Retrieved from https://www.youtube .com/watch?v=VY1Hf2taOPY.

Megyn Kelly Today. (2018, October 24). Amy Holmes, Roland Martin talk to Megyn Kelly about blackface comments. [Video file]. Retrieved from https://www.youtube.com/watch?v=XppMrfnkcDY.

Michaels, M. (2018, April 25). *NBC's $69 million bet on Megyn Kelly is turning into a disaster*. Retrieved from https://www.businessinsider.com/megyn-kelly-salary-nbc-low-ratings-2018-4.

Miller, H. (2018, October 24). Megyn Kelly issues on-air apology for blackface defense: "I was wrong." *Huffpost*. Retrieved from https://www.huffpost.com/entry/megyn-kelly-apologizes-on-air-blackface_n_5bd06a13e4b055bc9486e2a6.

Minnesota Statewide Longitudinal Data System. (2019). Retrieved from http://sleds.mn.gov/#highSchoolAcademics/orgId--999999000__groupType--state__ECODEVREGION--FOC_NONE__COHORTID--2019__categories--race_6%7Cgender_F__p--33/orgId--999999000__groupType--state__ECODEVREGION--FOC_NONE__COHORTID--2019__categories--race_3%7Cgender_F__p--1

Molseed, J., & Cutts, E. (2018, November 1). *Update: Rochester schools investigate "racially charged" costumes*. Retrieved from https://www.postbulletin.com/news/education/update-rochester-schools-investigate-racially-charged-costumes/article_6dc6635c-ddf3-11e8-9f97-33a5557680e0.html.

Morris, M. W. (2016). *Pushout: The criminalization of black girls in schools*. New York: New Press.

National Center for Education Statistics. (2018, May). *The condition of education 2018*. Retrieved from https://nces.ed.gov/pubsearch/pubsinfo.asp?pubid=2018144.

Obama, M. (2018). *Becoming*. New York: Crown.

Office of Black Male Achievement. (n.d.) *Forms & documents*. Retrieved from https://blackmales.mpls.k12.mn.us/forms_documents.

Ohlson, B., Bedrossian, K., & Ortega, J. (2016). *Growing up in Oakland: A study of girls' experiences*. Alliance for Girls. Retrieved from https://www.alliance4girls.org/wp.../08/growing-up-in-oakland-report-dec-2016.pdf.

Rafa, A. (2019, January). *The status of school discipline in state policy*. Education Commission of the States. Retrieved from https://www.ecs.org/wp-content/.../The-Status-of-School-Discipline-in-State-Policy.pdf.

Schott Foundation. (2015, February 11). *Report: Gap between black and white male high school graduation rates still widening*. Retrieved from http://schottfoundation.org/about/press-releases/report-gap-between-black-and-white-male-high-school-graduation-rates-still.

Southern Poverty Law Center. (2011, March 1). *Ku Klux Klan: A history of racism*. Retrieved from https://www.splcenter.org/20110228/ku-klux-klan-history-racism.

Taylor, J. (2015, December 7). *Trump calls for "total and complete shutdown of Muslims entering" U.S*. Retrieved from https://www.npr.org/2015/12/07/458836388/trump-calls-for-total-and-complete-shutdown-of-muslims-entering-u-s.

Union, G. (2017). *We're going to need more wine: Stories that are funny, complicated, and true*. New York: Dey Street/HarperCollins.

U.S. Department of Education Department for Civil Rights. (2014, March). *Civil rights data collection: Data snapshot: School discipline, issue brief No. 1*. Retrieved from https://ocrdata.ed.gov/downloads/crdc-school-discipline-snapshot.pdf.

U.S. Department of Education Department for Civil Rights. (2018). *Civil rights data collection (CRDC) for the 2015–16 school year*. Retrieved from https://www2.ed.gov/about/offices/list/ocr/docs/crdc-2015-16.html.

Walker, M., Vanden Berk, E., & Zumbusch, J. (2017). *Office of black male student achievement—B.L.A.C.K. course impact study, internal draft*. Retrieved from https://blackmales.mpls.k12.mn.us/uploads/obmsa_impact_study_2017.pdf.

West, C. (2001). *Race matters*. New York: Vintage.

Young, M. D., & Laible, J. (2000). White racism, antiracism, and school leadership preparation. *Journal of School Leadership, 10*(5), 374–415.

Good Trouble

CHAPTER

9

Staying Engaged and Leading Through Resistance and Ruination

Do not get lost in a sea of despair. Be hopeful, be optimistic. Our struggle is not the struggle of a day, a week, a month, or a year, it is the struggle of a lifetime. Never, ever be afraid to make some noise and get in good trouble, necessary trouble.

—U.S. Rep. John Lewis (2018)

An immigrant from Chile, Valeria Silva came to Minnesota at age 23 and began her education career as an elementary teacher in St. Paul. When she moved into administrative roles, she consistently focused on creating equity, such as launching the state's first Spanish immersion program. As St. Paul's director of ELL programs and chief academic officer she created transitional learning centers that transformed the experiences and achievement of refugee and immigrant students. She became the superintendent of St. Paul Public Schools in 2009 after serving 25 years in the district, and during her 7 years in that role, racial equity was at the core of her Strong Schools, Strong Communities strategic plan. Her work, as described by the American School Superintendents Association, "resulted in achievement scores that were dramatically above state averages" (Griffin, 2018).

Currently consulting for the Puerto Rico Education Foundation, Silva is a mentor to the island's seven school superintendents. Since she began working in Puerto Rico in 2017, the island has been hit by Hurricane Maria, the subsequent collapse of the economy, an unprecedented number of earthquakes, and the coronavirus. Silva became familiar with the impact of crises and disasters early in life, living through the violent coup that installed military dictator Augusto Pinochet. At that time, she and her family slept on the floor to avoid bullet fire, and later, as a college student, she endured bombings and other violence on her campus in Santiago. Her story of leading through resistance and disasters is largely one of being part of an educational system that creates social and emotional crises for students of color, including refugee and immigrant children:

> After Puerto Rico's largest earthquakes in January [5.8 and 6.4 magnitude], we had to assess every school building because the construction was not designed to withstand multiple

201

earthquakes. We took all the kids out of school in January and put them back into schools in parts of the island farthest from the epicenter. The *pandemia* came a month later. In March the island went into lockdown. I don't know what else could possibly happen here, maybe a tsunami will be next. But the resiliency of staff and families is unbelievable.

In the mainland United States, American students of color and immigrant/refugee students face some similar challenges but also have unique differences. First, they have all experienced trauma that can never be erased from their minds. Little chips have entered their systems that tell them they need to be in survival mode because things are going to happen.

One thing that American teachers often fail to understand is that there is a difference between a refugee and an immigrant. Refugee children come from a traumatic environment such as a war zone and are here to avoid death or persecution. Immigrant families come here by choice to pursue a better life. Most refugee children have been living in poverty and camps, while immigrant children may come from middle-class families. These differences were never in the minds of teachers when I was directing the English Language Learners (ELL) program for the St. Paul District. They just saw a student to whom America was giving the chance to be free and be educated. The attitude was, "You need to adjust to us because we're providing you with an education you would never have had in your life." They saw dark skin and considered them all one group, with no understanding of their backgrounds.

A common element between African American students and refugees is their sense that they are second-class citizens. I have been to refugee camps, and you can see their low status in society and how they have internalized it. When they come into our schools, they have the trauma and the additional burden of learning a new language and culture. African American students also feel that they are second-class citizens. By the age of 3 they probably sense that there is a difference. African American students who do not seem to conform to our teaching practices and are diagnosed with emotional behavior disorder are often put in special education classes, while refugee and immigrant students are put in isolated English Language Learner (ELL) programs that separate them from English-speaking peers and the mainstream curriculum. I daresay that if you asked a teacher if she wanted this special ed kid—who most likely is an African American—in her class or this ELL kid, she would jump to have the ELL kid.

I created a plan for taking ELL students out of isolation when I was still a principal who was also put in charge of a school's ELL program. Seeing how things were done, I couldn't wrap my brain around why these students were not learning any content and being separated from the rest of the school. I started digging into the budget and wondered where the money from the state was going that belonged to those kids. I remember walking into the superintendent's office and asking, "Do you want a leader or do you want a bimbo?"

The guy looked at me and said, "What do you mean?"

"What we're doing is wrong for kids. So if you put me in this job that I'm killing myself over, I propose this model." Boom, I set my plan down on his desk. I was in my early 30s, and he looked at me like, who is this lady? Then he said, "Do what you need to do."

I got started and apparently sold it well enough to people that we went into the first year training ELL teachers on how to teach language through content, and it kept moving. It became the model for the state and then the nation.

When I was superintendent we did tremendous work with these inclusions, closing down schools-within-schools and literally removing walls and doors to absorb those students into the school. We created five transitional learning centers where refugee and immigrant children could find support and feel welcome and learn English while being challenged academically. This involved training all our ELL teachers at the Readers and Writers Workshop, the best system for teaching reading and writing, because they needed to know how to bring academic content into their language instruction. We got mainstream teachers and ELL teachers together for training in teaching reading, writing, and math to ELL students, which gave the ELL teachers tools about teaching that they didn't get in college. And we worked to move special ed students—more than 90% of them were African American—into mainstream classes.

The majority of our teachers are white and don't understand African American culture. African American students are survivors, and they have a different way of communicating, which I see as similar to my culture. Teachers will say that African American students are rebellious, don't follow directions, don't sit still, don't play well with others, and are rough and aggressive. Most of that is not aggressive behavior but a cultural way of being and communicating. In the Latino culture people talk over each other, and that is perceived by others as aggressive and rebellious and intimidating. I'm married to a white man, and at times when I say something in my way, he says, "Don't talk to me like that!" I say, "What do you mean?" At work here in Puerto Rico

I am able to be more direct and to the point in how I say things, because the culture is more like the one I grew up in.

I would sum up the key piece of my leadership in one word: courage. I can't believe the stuff I had the courage to push as a superintendent. I did have a load of fear, but I didn't project it and I was willing to lose my job rather than consent to do something that didn't work. I was very determined on the implementation of the strategic plan, so I pushed, pushed, pushed a ton of things in the first 5 years. At the time I knew I was pushing it, but as a leader there was no time to wait. If you waited, you sacrificed the kids having the benefit of that reform. Now that I'm a coach, I see the same reluctance to take action among leaders. I sometimes want to shake the superintendents by the shoulders and say, "Why do you not want to do what we're telling you to do? Don't you believe your kids will do better? That your teachers will do better?" Our students need courageous leaders who are not afraid of changing the status quo of the education system that was not built to ensure that they have a chance to be successful. (V. Silva, personal communication, August 7, 2020)

Leading Through Resistance

As school leaders, we have worked with white educators along many points of the spectrum of equity work. We understand that this is the work of a lifetime and that each goal has its own timing, depending on the commitment and training and one-on-one guidance teachers and staff receive. Too often, as Valeria Silva and the mentors you will hear from later in this chapter also share, we recognize that well-intentioned principals, teachers, and staff develop the vocabulary of this work but, when push comes to shove, resist taking action. Leaders must continuously assess their staff, as discussed in Chapter 5, to determine who needs to be challenged to the next level, stimulated, coached, or removed. Since such guidance, along with an unwavering commitment to your mission, is almost guaranteed to brew up what John Lewis (2018) called "good trouble, necessary trouble," being ready for resistance can help turn brick walls into windows. Part of that readiness is understanding white privilege and fragility, as we explored in Chapter 3. Patton and Haynes (2020) offer a few guiding questions to white educators about the genuineness of their commitment to equity that remind us of the prevalence of white privilege and fragility and may help leaders navigate resistance:

Can you resist dominant standards of Whiteness that insist on White leadership and White ways of knowing in favor of a reimagined White identity that listens to and partners with minoritized communities? Can you grapple with the

disappointment and mistakes that accompany racial justice
work? Can you apologize when you are wrong or make a
mistake without making an entire situation about you? . . . Can
you commit demonstrably useful acts for racial justice without
expecting a pat on the back? Can you resolve to do this work
because it does not nearly require the level of risk and harm
minoritized people encounter? (p. 44)

School leaders can remind themselves of these questions as one more
tool for preparing for pushback. A principal's courageous conversation
can point out that the teacher is relating to her students of color based on
her assumptions rather than a genuine understanding of them, focusing
on herself instead of the student's issue, looking for praise for work done
instead of addressing the matter at hand, or forgetting the realities her students of color face in and outside school.

The resistance we see in our schools is a microcosm of the national
scale of resistance that manifests in both discriminatory policies and the
condoning of racism through silence. One example of the latter came
after the U.S. Supreme Court's *Brown v. Board of Education* decision
that declared school segregation unconstitutional in 1954. Backlash in
the southern states included intensifying already rampant voter suppression methods and committing unchecked violence such as the lynching
of 14-year-old Emmett Till and angry mobs surrounding Black children
entering schools. That response, Anderson (2016) writes in her history
of American racism, would not have run as deep and deadly had gover-
nors, state and federal legislators, and other white authority figures "not
condoned the complete defiance of and contempt for" the Court's ruling
through their silence and inaction (pp. 75–76).

In 2020, the condoning of structures of systemic racism such as
police violence against unarmed Black men and women continues. In
the wake of the killing of George Floyd in Minneapolis in May, protesters throughout the country began calling out this form of racial injustice
and demanding changes in policing policies. Another form of resistance,
voter suppression, also continues, with President Donald Trump (2020)
claiming that mail-in ballots, propelled by the coronavirus' limitations
on large gatherings like voting places, will result in a fraudulent presidential election in November and suggesting that the election should
be delayed. Anderson (2016) reminds us that southern states "had been
vigilant in eviscerating black access to the ballot box" (p. 76) since the
Jim Crow era, and milestones such as the *Brown* decision and election of Barack Obama as the first Black president ignited new forms of
voter suppression. The 2008 election brought out a record number of
new Black, Hispanic, and Asian voters who supported a stronger federal role in policies such as raising the minimum wage and improving
education (Anderson, 2016), and the majority of them voted for Obama.
Rather than address those interests, Anderson writes, which would have

disrupted the hard-right-leaning movement of the Republican Party, the party resisted:

> Once it became clear that the voter turnout rate of blacks had nearly equaled that of whites . . . conservatives . . . hid [their] anger and determination behind a legitimate-sounding, noteworthy concern: protecting the integrity of the ballot box from voter fraud. . . . Paul Weyrich, a conservative activist and the founder of the American Legislative Exchange Council (ALEC), was explicit early on: "I don't want everybody to vote," he said, noting that the GOP's "leverage in the elections quite candidly goes up as the voting populace goes down." . . . ALEC stepped in to draft "model voter-ID legislation [that] . . . require[s], among other things, particular types of identification that . . . make it difficult for African Americans and others to vote." (pp. 140–141)

One of the primary goals of this book has been to support principals with strategies for dealing with resistance in your buildings and communities as you take action to create equity. As you have now discovered, several levels of work can come together to empower you to stay the course through challenging events and encounters, starting with understanding the implicit bias beneath resistance. You can then assess and guide teachers wherever they are along the racial awareness spectrum, using a specific protocol for courageous conversations, and help them implement effective instructional practices that bring achievement to all students and ignite pride in teachers that keeps the positive cycle going. This final chapter brings you more real-world stories of principals and administrators designed to remind you that the resistance you experience is not unique and that you are not alone. We hope you are inspired by the voices throughout this book that reveal what persistence, resilience, hope, effective strategies, and a genuine commitment to students look like. Following are three more stories from leaders who discuss how they grapple with resistance in their districts.

Learning From Mentors

Responding to Resistance

Dr. Aldo Sicoli and Dr. Michael Favor

Dr. Aldo Sicoli, the superintendent of a suburban district near Minneapolis, has served as a principal, assistant superintendent, and superintendent in the Minneapolis–St. Paul metropolitan area for 27 years. A white leader, he has known and worked with his current assistant superintendent, Dr. Michael Favor, for many years. Favor, a Black educator, has spent 26 years as a principal, dean of students, assistant superintendent, and superintendent primarily in the Minneapolis school district and its suburban districts. As their stories reveal, the two leaders have developed a close alliance. Working for equity in a district in which 52% of the students are children of color, they rely on each other's support daily. The following is part of a dialogue between them about dealing with resistance.

Coded Language, Distractions, and Opting Out

DR. FAVOR: Aldo and I often sit in meetings and give each other a glimpse when coded language comes up. We often hear it in hiring meetings—questions about qualifications and even the candidate's style of responding. We were in one interview where the Black male candidate not only answered the questions but also told a story with each one. That's part of the culture. The stories were brilliant and spot-on in terms of the questions, but because he didn't use the key words some of the interviewers were looking for, his credentials were questioned. His credentials were, in fact, far greater than those of the other candidate, who was a white woman. We see and hear these codes, and as racially conscious leaders we anticipate how to respond. The fragility comes, and you have to respond in a way that keeps people engaging in the conversation so we can work toward a result but also help them navigate their own fragility. Sometimes that means simply holding up a mirror up to what they're saying: "I'm going to say this out loud just so you can hear how it sounds."

DR. SICOLI: A few years ago the middle school was hiring an assistant principal. The head principal was an African American gentleman, a great leader. I wasn't involved in the AP interviews, but they were having them in the conference room right next to my office. I recognized five out of nine names on the interviewee list as African American administrators I had worked with in the previous district Mike and I were in. *This should be interesting,* I thought. At the end of the day I asked the assistant superintendent at the time, a white gentleman, how it turned out.

"Well, we're inviting a few back."

"Oh, who?" And he named all these white folks. I said, "Oh, really? How'd you land on that?"

"Well, you know, the principal said he really wanted an instructional leader."

Then I saw the principal afterward, and I asked him, "Are you comfortable where you landed?"

"Mmm."

"What do you mean? Tell me more."

"I thought these other candidates were really good, but others weren't as crazy about them. They wanted an instructional leader."

"But I happen to know some of the people you're bringing back have zero middle school experience; does that not matter?"

"Well, it didn't to them."

(Continued)

(Continued)

"You do what you want, but if I were you I'd trust my gut. You're saying you want to bring back a couple of these folks." He thought about it and called a white principal in the district and asked if he thought they could handle two African Americans at this school in administrative positions. After that talk he brought back a couple of the African American candidates and hired one of them. We see that sort of pressure and culture and code speak and all the rest. I've seen it in elementary hiring, where someone says, "I'm a primary grade teacher; I want someone with primary school experience. That African American candidate doesn't have it. Can't hire her."

DR. FAVOR: That principal was willing to make some change, but the leader above her did not commit to that tough conversation or making sure that it happened. Some people have privilege that allows them to opt out of the conversation, and sometimes they just ignore what Aldo and I ask them to do. Or they appear to be ready to jump in, but use people of color in a way that postures for them and makes them look better. That mentality of using people of color, especially when you're in leadership, is demoralizing. People use people of color as if they're pawns in a system that affirms them, the white leaders, instead of doing what's best for kids. Being a big old Black man, I've often had to deliver bad news while the other person sits back. People don't see them delivering the bad news. I don't deliver it in an angry way but hold people accountable to the work and the expectations while they sit back and let you do that and then take all the praise. But not Aldo. He isn't afraid to speak out, especially on controversial issues.

A prime example is what he said during recent internal Zoom meetings about the issue of student resource officers (SROs), the police officers who work as liaisons in our schools. Some are calling for an end to SROs in schools, but we've done work with our SROs that is different, and it's been working well. We've prepared our SROs so they're not involved in behavior issues but in prevention. They don't engage with students like SROs from other communities in the Twin Cities. Dr. Sicoli and I were really vocal about being on the right side of this, and as a white man leading the district, that puts him in the crosshairs. Although he has the support of communities of color, they may not support him on this, and he thinks it may cost him his job. I don't. I think once people see the information, they're going to be even more supportive because he's made sure so many things are done in prevention that are really different than what other districts do. As for me, I could be seen as upholding structural whiteness, basically an Uncle Tom, while others opt to remain silent with this. Many administrators never once put themselves out there on camera to the community. That silence is another example of people having the choice to opt out.

DR. SICOLI: Mike watches my back like you wouldn't believe. In these sensitive situations he knows how to talk with folks, he connects with Black community, he talks with individuals who are on a certain side of an issue and gives them information so they're not surprised, and he really helps us get through. Like on this issue, yes, I could lose my job. Things like that happen, but we're going to do the right thing. The right thing for our district and our students is, at least right now, to keep the officer who's working well in our high school, and the one that works part-time at the middle school. That's what our administrators and two head principals who are African American want. We surveyed our Black students, and they're evenly split on the issue. When George Floyd was murdered, we received about three dozen e-mails from students who had graduated in the past four to five years. They were almost all white students saying this is awful, you need to pull your liaison officer from the high school. Just because people want to take action and say this is a thing I can do right now, get rid of liaison officers, we shouldn't bend to that pressure because it's the thing of the day.

We're having these community conversations about race and healing around the murder of George Floyd. In the next one, which will be devoted to the issue of SROs, our high school principal will explain what the SRO does at the school and use data and other information. We'll continue conversations with the community via Zoom, and anyone, whether they're in the community or not, can sign up for them.

Mutual Support

DR. FAVOR: I have a tremendous amount of respect for Aldo, not just because of him as a leader and a friend but because we practice. We have conversations where he gets to know my fears of failing and I know his about not getting this right for children, not correcting the system or eliminating the gaps. We talk about this openly so as we're navigating our work together I can intensely support him around his fears and he can intensely support me. That's the kind of relationship principals should have with their assistant principals. I always shared my fears with my APs and teaching staff. They understood not only what drives me, the moral imperative, but also that that imperative is the reason we're here. This is what I understand when I come to Aldo. He's made it clear to me: "Mike, I'm not interested in you reducing gaps; we're going to eliminate these gaps. That is your job." And I respect that.

DR. SICOLI: I'm very fortunate to work with Mike. He is amazingly gracious because he navigates these situations in a way that's respectful of people, and that makes them think. Mike doesn't shut people down; he makes them feel valued, even when he sometimes can't understand their reasoning. The candidates we had in the interview he mentioned—one of whom was a Black male who illustrated his answers with stories—were both qualified to be a successful principal, but there was no comparison. One person had much more experience, had accomplished much more, and had given, in my view, one of the best interviews I'd ever heard. It was inspiring. I felt that I wanted to work with and for that person. His delivery was really reflective and thoughtful, so our colleagues' feedback after the candidates left was . . . weird. There were seven of us—three people of color, me, and three other white folks. The three white folks spoke up first, and I waited until the end. It was incredible. Their opinion and interpretation of who answered a specific question better was totally flipped from mine, and I thought, *were you not listening?* This person said this, this, and this, and you didn't hear it? It was beyond belief to listen to this. Finally, when Mike and the three colleagues of color started speaking up they gave a different viewpoint, and then I chimed in and we landed in a good place.

(Continued)

(Continued)

DR. FAVOR: Driving to work every day, I'm scared. I just turned 54, thank God, because there was a police shooting in this community. Philando Castile was shot here in 2016 during a traffic stop. I shared with Aldo that if I get stopped on my way to work, he's my first call. If the police stop me, I want him to know where I am, and I know he'll come to me. I'm wearing a shirt and tie every day; I'm doing things right. He knows my fears. That affirms, I believe, who he is, and it settles me to work harder for this community because I know he not only has my back as a leader, but he cares about me. I can't opt out when I get in the car to go home. I can't opt out when I'm in a meeting. People use race as a weapon, bringing up "equity" in a meeting when they don't get what they want, saying, "This isn't equitable. How is this equity?" Let's talk about equity all the time, not just when it's going to benefit you.

Student-Centered Action

DR. SICOLI: Resistance takes a lot of forms and can be subtle or very overt, depending on who is doing it—staff, parents, or others in the community. For example, in one district that Mike and I were working in we had a wonderful middle school principal who wanted to change the honors system. It was set up to require that students be enrolled in all three or four honors courses, and the principal wanted to open it up so that a student could be in just one. The idea was to get more kids involved and more staff teaching in and outside the honors level. We thought this would create more rigor for everyone.

We went through the process of changing the system, and you wouldn't think something like that would be controversial. But it was. A group of white privileged parents simply were not going to have it. They wrote letters to the editor of the local newspaper saying that the school was awful and out of control, and the newspaper wrote an opinion piece stating the same thing. The principal was a classy person through it all, even when we asked some of our "most supportive" parents, who happened to be white, if they would be interested in writing a rebuttal letter to the editor, and most of them said no. We did find one who would do it. That was pretty hard to believe. In situations like that, you find out who your allies are and who are not.

We went ahead with the plan anyway, and it went very well. The parent who spearheaded the movement against this was in the school's parent group, and when I asked her how it was going, she sounded as if her what-an-awful-school campaign had never happened, or at least was no big deal.

Another example of keeping students at the forefront of our decisions took place after the police killing of Philando Castile in 2016. About four months later, we had some high school students walk out of the building to the nearby Minnesota Department of Education (MDE) office with a list of demands. Seven of those 10 or 11 demands were about a more inclusive curriculum. When they returned to the high school they presented their demands to me. Later, I met with the district lead team and said, "They're right. Like every other school district, our curriculum isn't inclusive. We need to make this a priority—what do you think?" They agreed, so that's been the main focus of our professional development these past four years. We go about it differently within the district; elementary focuses on social studies because that was the easiest place to start, but the high school has created a more inclusive curriculum in every area. They have fairs where they showcase what they've done. Even those who don't have a full curriculum area, such as special education and ELL teachers, are using inclusive materials. That's really great. We just responded to what the students said, and we've made some good progress, but we still have a long way to go in so many areas.

Keeping it Real

DR. SICOLI: In my administrative career, I've seen that sometimes a school or district's reputation for equity is better than its record on action. As you get more administrators of color, the conversations about racial equity get more real. There will still be people who aren't comfortable with that, but we have to keep our focus on the students. We have to get the job done, and the pace has been way too slow.

DR. FAVOR: We share the same perspective on this. I think part of the slow pace is the culture that says we're not going to talk around race. You call it out, and much more intensely than I call it out. Sometimes I'll talk around it to get people to get there, but you just flat-out name it. I love that. We talk about *what you permit, you promote*. He doesn't permit avoiding or ignoring or just paying lip service to these things, and I appreciate that. That's what makes him a strong ally and leader, helping people in the room work together toward where we should be.

DR. SICOLI: Getting more leaders of color in the room helps, but dealing with resistance is part of the work. Often when I hire administrators of color they have difficulties with certain individuals who have been with a district for a long time, so I need to stay aware of how everyone is doing and help these relationships get better.

DR. FAVOR: To hear your frustration with navigating that is not only affirming for me, but it also helps me understand that I need to work with you and support you in that navigation because I've always had to do that. From being that middle school kid who was always kicked out of class for asking questions to going to college in Fargo, North Dakota, and having to steer through those systems— that's my experience. You see the system for what it is, you're trying to dismantle it, and it's disheartening for you because you want to change it right now.

DR. SICOLI: It's frustrating to the point that you do at times say, why am I doing this? Do I need to do this any longer?

DR. FAVOR: The system makes you feel that way. You understand this is a system in which people have been oppressed, and you feel it. You get that far better than many of the administrators—Black, white, it doesn't matter.

DR. SICOLI: If I feel some of that and I don't have racism and discrimination against me, I can't imagine what people of color feel as they try to make positive change for students of color.

(Continued)

(Continued)

Know Your Why

DR. FAVOR: For me, our work is incredibly gratifying when you see how our students are benefiting from a lens and a framework. Their ability to ask questions and question the status quo is really gratifying for me. I see the hope we provide them.

My message to principals is that you are a lighthouse for students. In a storm, you are that light. That light always has to bring people home and represent hope. Being that lighthouse weathers you. It wears on you, so I encourage you to have somebody to talk to. There are times I come into Aldo's office and just talk. A week ago I was talking to him and I broke down in tears. I said, "Man, Aldo, I just feel like I try to do things right, but I can't catch a break." Having somebody you can do that with is extremely important because when you're representing hope as you dismantle some of these systems, that's a heavy burden. Just know that hope is there. Hope will guide you and our children, but you have to be that lighthouse for this work.

DR. SICOLI: I'm honored he shares with me, and I learn so much from him. Mike is genuine. When he says it's about students, it's about students. He had already turned around a high school I came to later as a superintendent, and everybody in the community knew he had turned around that school. He was a much more effective principal than I had ever been. It was like magic. Every day on the announcements he'd tell kids he loved them. Every day he talked to kids as they got off the bus and he knew all about them and their families and their jobs. Kids, parents, and grandparents had his cell phone number. If something happened in the community, it didn't have to be in our district boundaries, it might happen in Minneapolis where a lot of the students also resided, he was the first to know, even in the middle of the night. It was powerful to watch him in action, and luckily years later he came here. He cares about people and he cares about kids.

What keeps you going is knowing that it's about kids. That's my advice for principals. Keep your focus there. Find ways to connect because they'll keep you going (A. Sicoli and M. Favor, personal communication, August 4, 2020).

Leading With a Racial Response to Local and Global Ruination

As we write this final chapter, the coronavirus continues to rage across the country, and school districts are grappling with decisions about opening schools in the fall of 2020. Leaders for racial equity have faced dramatic new challenges as they try to implement distance learning and continue school lunch programs while some of their low-income students and students of color are unable to participate or communicate due to lack of devices or online access. Leading for racial equity takes even more courage, confidence, and skill during crises like these. Wherever you are in your journey along the Theory of Action pathway to racially conscious leadership, you are better prepared to understand and address the unique challenges that fall on students of color during such crises. The Theory of Action pathway is a continuous loop of self-reflection, knowledge of proven best practices, and increasing confidence in our actions that leads to high achievement for all students. In times of crisis, the "knowing" element of this pathway expands to understanding the facts about how these events disproportionately affect families of color. With this awareness, we know what to look for as systems break down.

The data show us that when economic and natural disasters strike, people of color and those with low incomes, such as families whose children qualify for free and reduced lunch in school, are hit the hardest. During the Great Recession of 2007–2009, for example, families of color suffered a dramatically worse loss of wealth than white households. While white families' wealth fell 26.2%, the wealth of Black and Latinx families decreased by 47.6% and 44.3%, respectively (McKernan, Ratcliffe, Steuerle, & Zhang, 2014). Race also factored into the ability of people of color to recover after the recession, since criteria for qualifying for mortgages became stricter. As a result of this and prerecession issues such as race-based obstacles to financing, fewer Black and Latinx families own homes or have retirement accounts than whites. One year after the economy began to improve, three quarters of white families owned homes, while fewer than half of Black and Latinx families did. Without these "traditionally powerful wealthbuilding vehicles" (McKernan et al., 2014, p. 18), people of color have not had the same opportunities as white families to bounce back from the recession.

Race and income also create disparities in how people are impacted by natural disasters. As Hurricane Katrina approached New Orleans in August 2005, Black residents and those with less than a high school education were less likely than others to evacuate "because of lack of money, transportation, a place to go, or job requirements" (SAMHSA, 2017). Low-income people around the world are more vulnerable to disaster damage due to living in low-quality-construction homes and in areas of cities that are more exposed to flooding. In addition, a study about the Midwest United States reported that low-income people die more often from heat waves, even if free fans are distributed, in which case they do not use the fans "because of worries about high utility bills" (SAMHSA, 2017).

Transportation issues, work schedules, and discomfort dealing with government agencies make families with economic hardships less likely to navigate systems for receiving disaster aid, as we continue to see during the coronavirus epidemic. Low-income and low-socioeconomic-status families also experience more disaster-related stress and depression and may be more vulnerable to illness due to chronic health issues (SAMHSA, 2017).

The coronavirus epidemic that reached the United States in early 2020 has shown "deep racialized disparities" in cases and deaths, with a disproportionate number of people of color dying from the disease (Carpenter, 2020, para. 2). The racial impact of the virus soon became clear in media reports about essential workers—predominantly people of color—risking contamination by taking public transportation to work, working in crowded kitchens and meat packing plants, and returning home to their households. By July 2020, when the national coronavirus death toll reached 160,000, data exposed the wide racial divide in these deaths. Black Americans were dying at 3.7 times the rate of whites, Indigenous at 3.5 times, Pacific Islanders at 2.8 times, Latinxs at 2.5 times, and Asians at 1.4 times the rate (APM Research Lab, 2020).

If anything like a silver lining can be found in the country's tragic experience of the pandemic, it may be an increased awareness of systemic racism. Word has spread about the long-standing racial health and social inequities behind the coronavirus data, such as the following:

- **Discrimination.** Racial discrimination in health care, finance, housing, education, and criminal justice contribute to chronic stress that puts people of color at greater risk of contracting Covid-19 (Centers for Disease Control and Prevention, 2020, July 24).

- **Health care.** Lack of insurance, flexible work hours, childcare, or transportation can prevent some people of color from getting the health care they need. Language barriers and a fear of being checked for immigrant status also keep people away from clinics and hospitals (Centers for Disease Control, 2020, July 24).

- **Occupations.** People of color are disproportionately employed in essential work such as service or production jobs that cannot be done from home. Forty-three percent of Black and Latinx workers make up this workforce, while only 25% of whites are employed in these areas (Oppel, Gebeloff, Lai, Wright, & Smith, 2020). In Friedline's (2020) study of bank tellers during Covid-19, for example, 68% of her interviewees were women and 73% were Black, Latinx, and Asian. Half of these frontline workers worked directly with customers and weren't "paid nearly enough to risk their health for performing essential labor . . . about 75 percent of bank tellers earn less than $15 per hour and 31 percent receive public welfare." Friedline, a sociologist who researches racial discrimination in the finance industry, further described the experiences of the predominantly Black and Brown women bank tellers during the epidemic:

    [They] felt like they were expendable—especially early on when the death toll was low, and personal protective equipment was scarce. . . . A teller expressed resentment that her bank wasn't doing more to protect employees, especially "when . . . [the] higher-ups, they say, 'You're essential and we're here for you,'" from the comfort of their home offices. At one branch, employees drove from store to store during lunch breaks trying to find gloves and disinfectant after the meager supplies sent by corporate headquarters ran out.

- **Income and education gaps.** The economic insecurity of Black families due to lower wages, less savings, and higher unemployment rates than white Americans makes them less able to stay home from work, even if they're sick. Historic pay gaps remain wide, with Black men paid only 71 cents on the white male dollar and Black women paid 64 cents on the white male dollar (Gould & Wilson, 2020). As we've discussed in this book, education inequities ranging from disproportionate discipline practices to student silencing and ineffective instructional methods lead to achievement gaps, higher dropout rates, and obstacles to enrolling in college.

- **Housing.** Because they are more likely to live in apartments or condos, where residents are in closer proximity to neighbors and share hallways, laundry rooms, lobbies, and so on, people of color have been at a greater risk of exposure to the coronavirus. While 14% of white households live in multiunit housing, more than twice as many—29.2%—Black households live in these buildings (Gould & Wilson, 2020). Additional data reveal that Latinx families are twice as likely as white families to live in a crowded home of less than 500 square feet per person (Oppel et al., 2020).

These realities have harsh consequences for children of color during a pandemic. The Centers for Disease Control and Prevention (2020, August 7) reported that Hispanic children were 8 times more likely and Black children 5 times more likely to be hospitalized with the coronavirus than white children.

In a U.S. Senate committee hearing about Covid-19 and education, Dr. John B. King, Jr. (2020), CEO of the Education Trust, spoke about schooling issues stemming from some of the systemic problems listed earlier. Distance learning, for example, is difficult to roll out for every student when only 66% of Black families and 61% of Latinx families have access to broadband, compared with 79% of white families. In terms of food security, he added, the pandemic has crippled the school system that 20 million students depend on for access to meals.

Students of color whose parents work in essential jobs face higher risks of contracting the coronavirus and without Internet access or cell phones can be completely cut off from their schools. Students may need to care for younger siblings while their parents work extra jobs or longer hours, and if their parents lose their jobs they may need to go to work themselves and lose study time, if they are actually connected to online learning. One of our doctoral students, an associate principal in Minneapolis, has been struggling with these challenges and more, as she shares in the following section.

Learning From Mentors

Responding to Disaster

Isabel Rodriguez

Isabel Rodriguez, an associate principal in a Minneapolis District high school, faced ever-deepening challenges when Covid-19 school closings intersected with social unrest following the police killing of George Floyd in her city on May 25, 2020. As a Latina born in Puerto Rico who has been an educator in the United States for 23 years, Rodriguez believes that her person-of-color lens has helped her raise concerns about students that many of her other colleagues have missed. Students of color are the largest demographic in her high school (Black, 34.7%; Hispanic, 17.3%; American Indian or Alaska Native, 6.8%; Asian, 3%; two or more races, 1.7%; white, 36.3%) (Minnesota Report Card, 2020).

Since 3:10 p.m. on March 16, 2020, nearly 5 months ago, when we were officially told to leave our building for the coronavirus shutdown, we have been in a world of uncertainty. Our students of color were suddenly detached from the place they felt safe and basically told they were now on their own. That's when everything went down, when my work turned into trying to reach out to our families and make sure that our students' voices and families were heard, and when the exhaustion I felt as a leader set in. Communication was and is my biggest challenge. Before Covid-19, some of our families already had a fear of sharing where they live and their phone numbers. Some of them didn't even open a lunch account because that would mean having an e-mail account, and they feared that would risk them being tracked because of their immigration or legal status. All of this got augmented with Covid-19.

I felt that I was abandoning these students and their families because we couldn't reach out to them and they couldn't reach out to us. We learned how much of our student contact data was missing or out of date, so that's one of things we need to do moving forward. We need to get accurate information and create an environment in which families are not afraid to share that information with us and know that our schools in Minneapolis are a safe space for them. We need to teach them self-advocacy, that it is OK to reach out and tell us where they are, so if something like this happens again—another epidemic, a natural disaster, an emergency, or a snowstorm that lasts for more than 3 days—we can connect with them.

Some of our students, especially newcomers, did not have computers to check the school website or engage in distance learning or, if they did get a device, lacked the technical skills to use it. Disrupted communication systems made it difficult to ensure they had the devices they needed. A family would say they were told a device was being delivered, but it had been 2 days and they didn't have it yet. Or yes, we got the device, but not the charger.

By the time the district started to say we have to go to distance learning, many students didn't have devices. Some students who didn't have computers or tablets were working on their phones, and that wasn't fair. A phone is not an effective tool for writing an essay or a poem, but some students were trying. Although our district arduously tried its very best to serve families equitably and fairly, the process hit many obstacles. I don't think any school district in the nation was prepared for this pandemic, which is why we should be documenting these stories so we can learn from our mistakes, capitalize on opportunities to propel change, and be better prepared moving forward.

Another disastrous ramification of the coronavirus has been the social and emotional aspect, not only of our students and families but also our staff. By the end of the day, when we were doing distance learning, most of our teachers were overworked, sad, and depressed because students were sharing their personal stories. They were sharing this moment in their lives when their parents had lost their jobs and students had to take part-time jobs to help the family or take care of their younger siblings. They talked about their fear of not having food or knowing where to get it, of losing their jobs that were now lifelines to their families. I was sad for my students, some of my families, and some of our staff who lived alone and didn't have any social contact. That's why we created a daily coffee talk with teachers so we could just connect.

I heard these stories from our low-income and families of color too. One student reached out to me, saying, in Spanish, "My dad just got Covid and can't work; my mom just got Covid; there are seven of us living here, some are cousins, and we're so afraid." I reached out to social workers to get them some money and gift cards to get them through the week, but the social workers don't have the language skills to keep in touch and follow up with the family. That's where our multilingual support staff is supposed to come in, but they are also lost because they don't have a device provided by the district or don't want to use one—or their own phone—because of privacy issues. So you have less people to help your families when it comes to multilingual support.

Who do those families call? I don't know how many families I contacted up to 8:00 and 9:00 at night. The days got longer as the weeks went by, but they were so grateful when they heard a voice they could connect with. When I asked what they needed, it was like the sky opened up for them. I was just appalled by their situations. I told them where they could get food, where they could go to talk to a social worker if they weren't feeling well physically or emotionally. As a leader, I felt it was my responsibility to help families in this way and to address their needs, such as multilingual support, when decisions were being made. The work was exhausting, physically and emotionally. I was in full contact with my family liaisons, Somali and Hispanic, to support our families, and they were also exhausted. Teachers were tired. Families were tired. With the language barrier, how do you support your kid in writing or math if you don't understand English? How do you support your kid if you have to go to work?

Then, to top it off, George Floyd was murdered. That happened on a Monday. On Tuesday morning, our students' neighborhoods were literally and metaphorically on fire. Our school is just blocks away from the Minneapolis Police Department's Third Precinct, which was burned to the ground. So more jobs are lost; students and families are feeling the pain of another Black man killed by the police; and the neighborhood stores, clinics, dentist offices, food banks, mental

(Continued)

(Continued)

health services—everything was destroyed. Some of our Hispanic families had businesses—food trucks or little botanicas or beauty salons—that were also destroyed. Those were their jobs, their livelihood.

One video coffee chat with teachers I led after the murder of George Floyd got emotional. I was very vulnerable and talked about the racism and discrimination I've seen. I had prepared my agenda for that talk the night before, and I was nervous. The Floyd killing had opened a gate to be raw and talk about it, and I knew it was going to be a courageous and compassionate conversation. After we said our hellos, I was very honest and said, "I'm tired. I appreciate the Martin Luther King, Jr., and All Are Welcome Here posters; the Black Lives Matter T-shirts; and the sayings about "let's not just talk the talk, but walk the walk." I'm beyond that. I'm tired of that superficial level. The racism I experience is on the day-to-day level, how you say hi to me or not in the building, how you speak to me on the phone. I'm tired of people saying they're doing the work. OK, we already know that. Act on it. Be open. If you say or do something hurtful, be open so that I can say, "What you just said was a problem—can we talk about it?" We need to start calling out these microaggressions and talking about them in the moment. It has to be real between us, you and me individually. We need to know each other and respect and value each other for who we are. They were open to listening to me and started responding, and many thanked me for being vulnerable. They were so grateful. It was refreshing, and at the end we were all thanking each other. A lot of people must have e-mailed my principal, because he said he heard a lot of great things about that specific coffee talk, and that some teachers had been crying. Maybe some needed to cry. I cried too. It created a sense of hope (I. Rodriguez, personal communication, July 30, 2020).

We hope this book has raised your awareness about the underlying factors of systemic racism that marginalize people of color. We hope we have presented our model for becoming a racially conscious leader as a clear and practical pathway that leads to a quality education for all students. And we hope the voices of leaders in these pages inspire you to stay with your mission when resistance comes up, as it will.

We invite you to return to the mentor sections time and again to remind yourself that you are not alone in your passion for dismantling old systems and replacing them with new so that your school can be a place of joyful learning. Let their voices inspire you to be a leader who helps teachers and parents evolve from people of good intentions to true advocates who take action on behalf of children of color. As we discussed about Kendi's (2019) work in Chapter 5 and as Singleton (2015) writes, "It is not enough simply to become *non*-racist. Educators of all races should become *anti*-racists, which means to actively fight racism and its effects wherever they may exist" (p. 56). We believe that as you continue to evolve in your racial awareness and leadership, your impact will build a broader consciousness that will improve policy beyond your school and community. This is the road to an equitable educational system because, as Kendi (2019) explains, "individual behaviors can shape the success of individuals. But policies determine the success of groups. And it is racist power that creates the policies that cause racial inequities" (p. 94). We would add that it is *antiracist* power that replaces those policies with those designed to help everyone thrive. That power is in your hands.

Our respect, admiration, and confidence in your success go out to you. May the words of Ojibwe poet Heid E. Erdrich (2016) remind you that the idea of race was constructed to divide us, and our biased assumptions must go. Her truth telling brings us to a common center:

> You would think
> (divide described)
> I live like this
> One thing on one side
>
> Wrong
> Nothing like one side
> Or another side
> not there or there
>
> Here
> I live
> Here
>
> Here
> We live
> Here
>
> Where you live

References

Anderson, C. (2016). *White rage: The unspoken truth of our racial divide.* New York: Bloomsbury.

APM Research Lab. (2020, August 5). *The color of coronavirus: COVID-19 deaths by race and ethnicity in the U.S.* Retrieved from https://www.apmresearchlab.org/covid/deaths-by-race.

Carpenter, Z. (2020, May 4). What we know about the Covid-19 race gap. *The Nation.* Retrieved from https://www.thenation.com/article/society/covid-19-racial-disparities/.

Centers for Disease Control and Prevention. (2020, July 24). *Health equity considerations and racial and ethnic minority groups.* Retrieved from https://www.cdc.gov/coronavirus/2019-ncov/community/health-equity/race-ethnicity.html.

Centers for Disease Control and Prevention. (2020, August 7). *Hospitalization rates and characteristics of children aged <18 years hospitalized with laboratory-confirmed COVID-19—COVID-NET, 14 states, March 1–July 25, 2020.* Retrieved from https://www.cdc.gov/mmwr/volumes/69/wr/mm6932e3.htm?s.

Erdrich, H. E. (2016). Red, white, and blank. In S. Y. Shin (Ed.), *A good time for the truth: Race in Minnesota* (pp. 109–120). St. Paul: Minnesota Historical Society Press.

Friedline, T. (2020, June 4). How banks are exploiting the coronavirus crisis for profit. *The American Prospect.* Retrieved from https://prospect.org/coronavirus/how-banks-are-exploiting-the-crisis-for-profit/.

Gould, E., & Wilson, V. (2020, June 1). *Black workers face two of the most lethal preexisting conditions for coronavirus—racism and economic inequality.* Retrieved from https://www.epi.org/publication/black-workers-covid/.

Griffin, L. (2018, April). Empathetic support for refugees. *School Administrator.* Retrieved from http://my.aasa.org/AASA/Resources/SAMag/2018/Apr18/Profile.aspx.

Kendi, I. X. (2019). *How to be an antiracist.* New York: One World.

King, J. B., Jr. (2020, June 10). *Written testimony for the United States Senate Committee on Health, Education, Labor, and Pensions* [PDF file]. Retrieved from https://www.help.senate.gov/imo/media/doc/King12.pdf.

Lewis, J. [repjohnlewis]. (2018, June 27). *Do not get lost in a sea of despair. Be hopeful, be optimistic. Our struggle is not the struggle of a day, a week, a month, or a year, it is the struggle of a lifetime.* [Tweet]. Retrieved from https://twitter.com/repjohnlewis/status/1011991303599607808?lang=en.

McKernan, S-M., Ratcliffe, C., Steuerle, E., & Zhang, S. (2014, April). *Impact of the great recession and beyond: Disparities in wealth building by generation and race* [PDF file]. Retrieved from https://www.urban.org/sites/default/files/alfresco/publication-pdfs/413102-Impact-of-the-Great-Recession-and-Beyond.PDF.

Minnesota Report Card. (2020). *South Senior High School: Demographics.* Retrieved from https://rc.education.mn.gov/#demographics/orgId--30001362000__p--9.

Oppel, R. A., Jr., Gebeloff, K. K., Lai, K. K. R., Wright, W., & Smith, M. (2020, July 5). The fullest look yet at the racial inequity of coronavirus. *New York Times.* Retrieved from https://www.nytimes.com/interactive/2020/07/05/us/coronavirus-latinos-african-americans-cdc-data.html.

Patton, L. D., & Haynes, C. (2020). Dear white people: Reimagining whiteness in the struggle for racial equity. *Change: The Magazine of Higher Learning, 52*(2), 41–45. doi:10.1080/00091383.2020.1732775

SAMHSA (Substance Abuse and Mental Health Services Administration). (2017, July). *Greater impact: How disasters affect people of low socioeconomic status* [PDF file]. Retrieved from https://www.samhsa.gov/sites/default/files/dtac/srb-low-ses_2.pdf.

Singleton, G. E. (2015). *Courageous conversations about race: A field guide for achieving equity in schools* (2nd ed.). Thousand Oaks, CA: Corwin.

Trump, D. J. [realDonaldTrump]. (2020, July 30). *With Universal Mail-In Voting (not Absentee Voting, which is good), 2020 will be the most INACCURATE & FRAUDULENT Election in history. It will be a great embarrassment to the USA. Delay the Election until people can properly, securely and safely vote???* [Tweet]. Retrieved from https://twitter.com/realDonaldTrump/status/1288818160389558273.

Index